THE · MACDONALD · ENCYCLOPEDIA · OF

Cacti

THE · MACDONALD · ENCYCLOPEDIA · OF

Cacti

Mariella Pizzetti

Macdonald

A **Macdonald** BOOK

©1985 Arnoldo Mondadori Editore S.p.A., Milan
©1985 in the English translation
 Arnoldo Mondadori Editore S.p.A., Milan

Translated by Cynthia Munro

First published in Great Britain in 1985
by Macdonald & Co (Publishers) Ltd
London & Sydney

A member of BPCC plc

British Library Cataloguing in Publication Data

Pizzetti, Mariella
 The Macdonald encyclopedia of cacti.
 1. Cactus 2. House plants
 I. Title
 635.9'3347 SB438

 ISBN 0-356-10924-0

Printed and bound in Italy
by Officine Grafiche A. Mondadori Editore, Verona

Macdonald & Co (Publishers) Ltd
Maxwell House
74 Worship Street
London EC2A 2EN

CONTENTS

KEY TO SYMBOLS

Plant habit
(the most frequent form for each subgenus or subtribe is illustrated)

Tribe PERESKIEAE

Tribe OPUNTIEAE

Opuntia

Cylindropuntia

Tephrocactus

Tribe CACTEAE

Cereinae

Hylocereinae

Echinocereinae

Echinocactineae

Cactanae

Cactinae

Epiphyllinae

Rhipsalidinae

Minimum temperatures for adult plants in cultivation

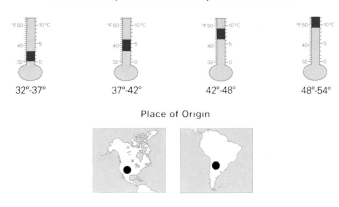

32°-37°   37°-42°   42°-48°   48°-54°

Place of Origin

NOTE

According to the International Code of Botanical Nomenclature, the scientific name of every plant must be accompanied by the name of the first author to have adopted it after 1753, the year in which Linnaeus' *Species plantarum* was published. This work established the binomial system of nomenclature.

The name or abbreviation which follows the bionomial (generic and specific name) is that of the author who classified the species. The name of the author who established the genus is used only if the genus is mentioned in isolation, or as a precise definition in scientific works.

Occasionally, a botanist attributes a name to a species which is then re-evaluated and transferred to a different genus. The original specific name is then retained and the original author's name appears in parentheses, followed by that of the author responsible for the reclassification. For example, Britton and Rose established the genus *Neomammillaria*, which they considered distinct from the *Mammillaria* described by Haworth, and included in it the species *lanata*. The genus *Neomammillaria* was subsequently abolished, because it was not considered sufficiently different, and the species *Neomammillaria lanata* Britton and Rose thus became *Mammillaria lanata* (Britton and Rose) Orcutt. The attributions may be given in compact form and in Latin—for example, "Britt. et Rose"—but in this book longer forms are generally used. Unless the name first attributed to a species is invalidated, all subsequent names do not supersede it and are merely considered synonyms.

Opposite: *the four main types of cacti. Top left,*
Pereskia aculeata, *var.* godseffiana; *top right,*
Opuntia diademata, *var.* inermis; *bottom left,*
Mammillaria gracilis; *bottom right,* Rhipsalis
micrantha.

THE CACTACEAE

It has often been said that there can be no half measures in regard to cacti: people either love them or hate them. This assertion would appear to be borne out by the fact that on the one hand, many people find them unattractive, or indeed repulsive, because of their prickles, while on the other hand, there are innumerable associations of cactus lovers throughout the world—for example, in New South Wales, Vienna, Zurich, Prague, Tokyo, Moscow and, naturally, Mexico City and El Centro, California.

The fascination that people feel for cacti is as multifaceted as the plants themselves and as mysterious as their origins, and it is a fascination that deepens as one's knowledge of the plants increases. Comprising over 2,000 species, Cactaceae is the largest of the many plant families—such as the euphorbias, crassulas, agaves, mesembryanthemums, milkweeds and lilies—that are known as succulents because they store water in their leaves, stems and roots. (In other words, to clarify a point that puzzles many people, all cacti are succulents, but not all succulents are cacti.)

The origins of the Cactaceae are thought to be very ancient in terms of the development of plant forms, although few succulent plants survive in fossilized form to tell us their history. The system of classification adopted by botanists for Cactaceae is based not only on the affinities between different genera but also on their presumed chronological development. It divides the cacti into four categories, as follows:

1. Plants that still produce leaves in spite of the special characteristics of the cactus family
2. Plants that produce leaves, but in most cases lose them very soon
3. Plants with rudimentary leaves similar to scales, or with no leaves at all
4. Plants with stems resembling leaves (*cladodes*), epiphytes or semi-epiphytes

This is a rational sequence based on the premise that succulent plants of families other than the Cactaceae lose their leaves because they have to adapt to dry climates, but it does not mean that cacti developed in precisely this way. Indeed they may well have been able to adapt contemporaneously to diverse climates. How and why the genus *Rhipsalis,* which belongs to a family native to the Americas, came to grow wild in equatorial Africa, Madagascar, the Mascarene Islands and Ceylon is a mystery, although it is likely that the plant was introduced into these areas by birds which carried its sticky seeds to the Old World.

All members of the Cactaceae are xerophytes in the broadest sense of the word: they are adapted for growth under dry conditions. In particular, they are designed to reduce moisture loss

to a minimum, and they are capable of storing water in their tissues.

In addition, all members of the family—no matter what their shape—have a characteristic that distinguishes them from all other plant families: they produce *areoles*. These round to oval structures ranging from 1/16 in. (1½ mm.) to more than 1/2 in. (13 mm.) across are found in widely varying positions on the cacti. They are composed of two perpendicular buds. From the upper bud come either the flowers and subsequent fruits or the new branches, which consist of segments—often called "joints," like the upper and lower joints of a chicken leg—that are knotted tightly together at the base. From the lower bud come the spines. These may resemble a cluster of small, wicked daggers (sometimes with barbed ends); or the dagger-like spines may be surrounded by tiny bristles or prickles and/or curly wool or hair. One of the peculiarities of the cacti is that the spines—like the thorns on roses—are not connected to the tissues below them; consequently no real harm is done to a plant when a spine is torn off. By contrast, when a spine is removed from a succulent such as *Euphorbia*, the tissue beneath it is damaged.

Cacti have numerous other distinctive features, but none of them is common to the entire family. They are simply features that enable us to distinguish one cactus genus from another. For example, roots may be quite superficial but very extensive,

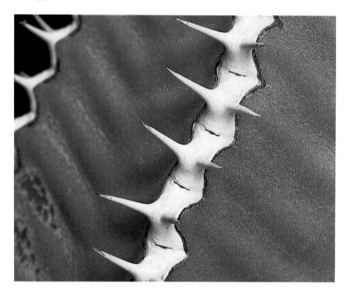

or they may be taproots, in some cases swollen and shaped like carrots, serving as a reserve for water and nutrients. Large taproots are particularly characteristic of small cacti growing in extremely dry areas. In some species the taproot resembles a dahlia's "foot," being subdivided so that some parts may continue to function even if others dry up or are damaged.

The stems of cacti with persistent leaves are woody, since the leaves are the mechanism through which the plants transpire (give off moisture). By contrast, in cacti without leaves, transpiration as well as photosynthesis is a function of the stems, and these are especially adapted to the job in several ways. For one thing, they are generally compact cylinders, semicylinders or globes; therefore the surface area from which moisture can be transpired is reduced. In the second place, the stem is covered with a thick, waxy skin through which moisture cannot pass. Even the stomata are designed to slow moisture loss. Finally, transpiration is limited by the spines, bristles and small hairs, which, if fairly dense, insulate the epidermis and thus protect it from excessive cold or overexposure to ultraviolet rays. This protection mechanism is especially marked on the upper part of the stem or at its apex, where the tissues are more delicate and the flowers usually grow. This area is spectacular in the columnar cacti with heads of extremely dense bristles and hairs known as the *cephalium*. A particularly showy example is the *Melocactus*. It develops a special struc-

ture that appears to be superimposed upon the apex of the stem and is thickly covered with colored hairs and bristles from among which the flower buds appear.

The characteristic roundness of stems and joints, no matter what their length, ensures that no one part is at the mercy of the sun's rays for more than a short time in the course of a day, and that only a minimal part is permanently exposed to the north. In a great many species the base of the stem appears to lignify with the passage of time, but it does not become wood. The spongy tissues harden, but the water vessels continue to pass through them. The vessels are protected by an outer layer properly described as suberose, since it is far more like cork than true bark.

Sometimes stem tissues grow together to form an irregular shape; and joints may produce twin forms along the whole or most of their length, occasionally becoming distorted, opening out like fans, or bending over as they grow. This phenomenon, known as fasciation, results from various physical or bacteriological causes. It is not hereditary; affected plants or their offspring may indeed regress. It occurs in other succulents and gives rise to so-called "monstrosities" that are highly prized by cactus collectors. Monstrous shapes are generally grafted onto other plants, since—except for unusually strong plants such as *Cereus*—they are supported only precariously by their roots and may revert to normal.

Leaves are persistent only in the first category of cacti, consisting solely of the genus *Pereskia*, which is considered a transitional form between normal plants and xerophytes. The stem bears normal, often very prickly, areoles. The lower part produces leaves, petiolated to a greater or lesser degree, and new shoots spring from their axils.

The second category, composing the tribe Opuntieae, includes one genus with leaves that are more or less persistent. The leaves of the other genera are usually small, fall very soon, and perform no functions, the latter having been taken over by the stem. In all the genera of this tribe the areoles have groups of minute barbed bristles (*glochids*) that can be very troublesome and painful because they become detached at the slightest touch and penetrate the skin. Glochids are not found in any other members of the Cactaceae.

The cacti of the other two categories have rudimentary leaves reduced to often minute scales. Alternatively, leaves are absent altogether, in which case there are enlarged leaf bases that are fused together in various arrangements to form what are known as *ribs* or *tubercles*. The areoles grow on the ribs, often at the apex, though in some genera—*Mammillaria* in particular—both flowers and joints spring from an axillary areole at the base (or axil) of the tubercle, while the areole at the apex has no vegetative function. In other genera, the two areoles are still connected: although they appear to be separate, the one is

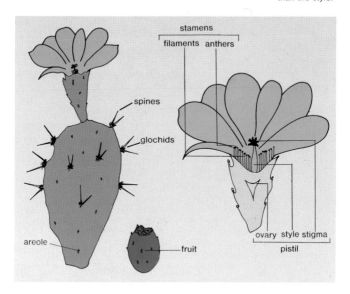

Diagram showing the structure of an Opuntia. *The flowers are actinomorphic (or regular), the pistil consists of a stellate stigma and a long style that terminates at the ovary, and the fruit, which grows inside the floral tube, develops from the ovary. The filaments of the stamens, with their pollen-laden anthers, are sh rter than the style.*

in fact an extension of the other, connected by a very fine groove. When this is the case, new joints may also appear at the apex of the tubercle.

Cactus flowers are generally solitary, and there is no clear distinction between calyx and corolla in the perianth: there is a gradual transition from sepaloid to petaloid segments that are spiral-shaped and are often fused at the base or united to form a tube of varying shape and length. The segments (petals) may be oval, lanceolate, obtuse, acuminate, dentate or even laciniate; they may be white, yellow, red or violet, while the external sepals may be greenish or brownish. These flowers are mostly regular, and the perianth is inserted above the ovary, which is generally round or oval (in some species it becomes elongated at maturity) and often bears areoles, scales, spines or hairs. The stamens, which are always numerous, have long filaments. The pistil may be even longer, and the stigma is often stellate and sometimes colored. Some genera (e.g., *Opuntia*) have sensitive stamens: when touched by an insect or by a finger, they close over the top of the pistil, straightening up again a minute or two later. This experiment can generally be made only in bright sunlight when the flower is open, since the flowers of most day-flowering genera remain closed whenever sun is not shining directly upon them—they close even when the sky clouds over, reopening when the clouds have passed by. The fruit of almost all cacti consists of a berry containing several or a great many seeds. In *Opuntia,* fruits are fairly large, but they are small and often tiny in other genera. The fruit of some genera becomes elongated and remains umbilicate, with a slight depression at its apex at the point where the perianth joined the ovary. In other cases this point was so small that all that remains of it is a small hole to which the residue of the dried corolla clings for a long time. Fruits are indehiscent in many cases. When they are more or less dehiscent, the seeds fall prey to ants, which to a certain extent help to disseminate them.

NATURAL HABITATS AND DISTRIBUTION OF THE CACTUS

The greatest problem presented by the cultivation of any type of plant is the need for raising it under conditions similar to those of its native habitat. In point of fact, most plants have an almost incredible capacity for adaptation, but this flexibility inevitably brings about a change for the worse in their structure and appearance. This is true in the case of all succulents, including cacti. An increase or decrease in light, the wrong amount of moisture, or a dormant period that is too short or too long will, at best, result in feeble growth, lack of color, loss of the defense systems peculiar to every species, and an absence of flowers. At worst, the root system will be damaged, the tissues will rot, and the plant will eventually die.

A large number of disappointments and the death of many plants are due more to ignorance about geography or climate than to a lack of horticultural knowledge. For this reason, the descriptions of cacti given in this book include brief notes on their natural habitats. However, since it is impossible to describe the peculiarities of each plant's habitat in minute detail, and since cacti are very adaptable, we give a brief overview of their environmental distribution below. It is hoped that this will be a useful adjunct to the details given in each entry.

With one exception of no practical importance, all members of the Cactaceae family are native to the continents of North and South America. In this vast area there is a huge variety of habitats, from the tropical to the polar. Even the physical geography of the mountain chains differs markedly. Winds and ocean currents bring violent hurricanes to the essentially dry, mild climate of North America. Freezing air rolls off the high peaks of the Andes into the tropical forests of South America.

One of the chief adaptational achievements of the cactus is its tolerance to periods of drought. This tolerance is only relative, however, since it invariably depends upon the amount of water held in the substratum and, above all, on how long it takes for this to become stagnant. Strange as it may seem, neither the floods that occasionally devastate Texas and Colorado nor the hurricanes that strike Florida cause as much damage to cacti as one might imagine. This is mainly because cacti tend to grow on well-drained high ground, and also because such violent storms occur infrequently. Conversely, the dryness of the

The fruit of Cereus is a dehiscent berry containing a large number of small black seeds in spongy tissue that remains fairly moist until the seeds are completely ripe. It then dries up and allows the seeds to fall. These are dispersed by land insects.

air in Arizona would in quite a short time prove fatal to *Epiphyllum* cacti, which grow in warm, damp, wooded areas.
On a purely practical, rather than botanical, basis, let us subdivide the members of the Cactaceae into four broad groups, according to habitat. The variants that occur in each group are ignored.

1. Plants from a desert or near-desert habitat
2. Plants from a mountainous habitat
3. Plants from steppes and grasslands
4. Plants from tropical or subtropical forests

These categories are not always applicable. For example, the many species and varieties of the genus *Opuntia* are so widely distributed as to make it appear ubiquitous. The flat-branched *Opuntia polyacantha* grows in the Canadian provinces of Alberta and British Columbia at a latitude of more than 50° N, while *Opuntia australis,* which has more or less oval or globular joints, and many other similar species grow in Patagonia (in order to survive there, all are of low and prostrate habit). Other species of *Opuntia* are to be found along the coasts of Florida and the Carolinas, in the Antilles, in the Galapagos Islands, in all the desert regions and in the Andes. Thus this genus, which is the largest of the Cactaceae, is able, through a variety of forms, to live in three out of four of the above habitats.

In desert regions the sun's rays strike the ground with full force, giving off hardly any reflection (top); at night, however, there is no vegetation to prevent the heat from dispersing rapidly, and as the ground cools down, a small amount of moisture is formed through condensation.

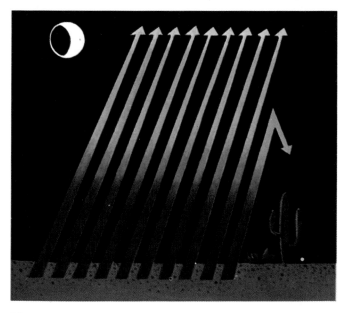

Desert or near-desert regions in which periods of complete aridity often alternate with torrential rain are found largely in the southwestern United States (although they extend southward into Mexico). This huge expanse of country reaches from Montana and Utah in the north to the Mexican border and from California in the west to beyond the Rocky Mountains, across the whole of the Texas plateau. Climatic conditions vary widely. The area of true desert is relatively small: it lies mainly to the west of the mountains, stretching eastward beyond the Great Salt Lake, along the Colorado River and the Rio Grande. Desert cacti are found in great abundance in Arizona. Less than 60 miles (100 kilometers) from the Mexican border is a desert center for the study and preservation of desert plants, set up under the auspices of the Carnegie Foundation. The name of a small town to the south of Tucson, Sahuarita, is significant in that sahuaro, or saguaro, is the local Indian name for *Carnegiea gigantea*. In this area, bounded by the Gila Desert to the east and the San Francisco and Colorado plateaus to the north, there exists a unique forest of *Carnegiea*—giant cacti that may reach a height of 50 ft. (15 m.) or more. Their relatively superficial roots may spread over an area more than 65 ft. (20 m.) wide. All the cacti of this and similar regions like intense sunlight and absolutely dry soil during their dormant periods, though they need abundant water during their vegetative period.

Although they grow on plateaus and high ground, none of the cacti in the United States can truly be described as plants with a mountainous habitat, since they always occur in a sheltered position. The slopes of the Rocky Mountains are well forested, mainly by conifers, and the Coast Range is the home of the fabulous *Sequoia*. Since the variation between daytime and nighttime temperatures in desert regions is very great, a certain amount of humidity results from the cooling down of the soil. This is particularly true in the case of plateaus, and it is this phenomenon that allows the survival and determines the characteristics of the cacti and other succulents of the huge central plateau of Mexico. This rises to a height of 6,500 ft. (2,000 m.) and is swept by dry winds from the northeast. In summer it is extremely hot and sun-scorched, while in winter snow occasionally falls. The eastern and western ranges of the Sierra Madre which border it have peaks rising to 11,500 ft. (3,500 m.) but do not form a continuous chain: there is an opening onto the coastal plain around the Gulf of Mexico through which winds sweep into the hinterland. The far-flung volcanic lakes, the network of often torrential rivers, and the seasonal rains are not sufficient to mitigate the extreme conditions to which these plants, growing on calcareous and stony soil, are subjected. The difference in temperature between the extremely hot days and the cold nights has either strengthened the protective issues of all the succulents or produced new defense mechanisms. Thus we find that *Sedum* and *Echeveria* have a brightly colored surface wax which thickens and becomes blue-green or reddish, and that certain cacti have developed extremely

The distribution of the principal genera of the Cactaceae is shown on these two pages.

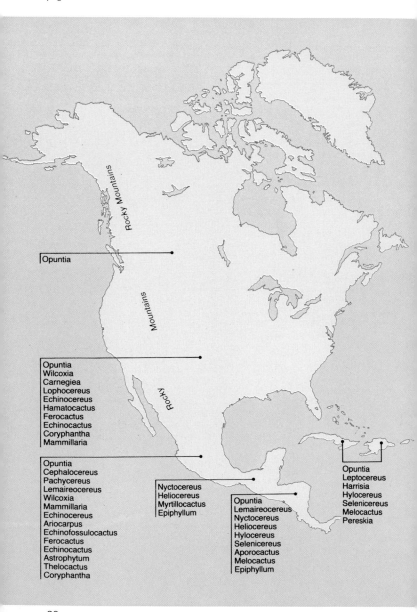

Rocky Mountains

Mountains

Rocky

Opuntia

Opuntia
Wilcoxia
Carnegiea
Lophocereus
Echinocereus
Hamatocactus
Ferocactus
Echinocactus
Coryphantha
Mammillaria

Opuntia
Cephalocereus
Pachycereus
Lemaireocereus
Wilcoxia
Mammillaria
Echinocereus
Ariocarpus
Echinofossulocactus
Ferocactus
Echinocactus
Astrophytum
Thelocactus
Coryphantha

Nyctocereus
Heliocereus
Myrtillocactus
Epiphyllum

Opuntia
Lemaireocereus
Nyctocereus
Heliocereus
Hylocereus
Selenicereus
Aporocactus
Melocactus
Epiphyllum

Opuntia
Leptocereus
Harrisia
Hylocereus
Selenicereus
Melocactus
Pereskia

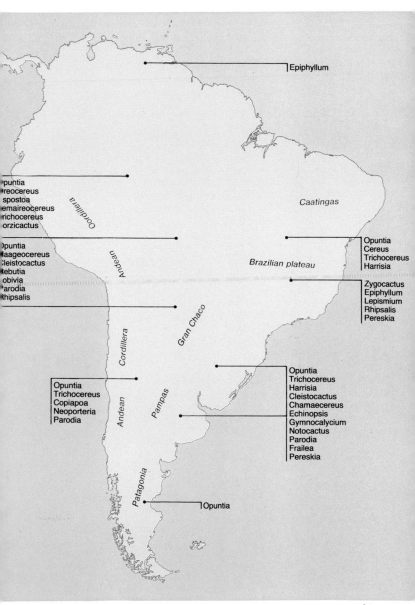

Epiphyllum

Opuntia
Oreocereus
Espostoa
Neomaireocereus
Trichocereus
Borzicactus

Caatingas

Cordillera

Opuntia
Haageocereus
Cleistocactus
Rebutia
Lobivia
Parodia
Rhipsalis

Andean

Opuntia
Cereus
Trichocereus
Harrisia

Brazilian plateau

Zygocactus
Epiphyllum
Lepismium
Rhipsalis
Pereskia

Gran Chaco

Cordillera

Opuntia
Trichocereus
Harrisia
Cleistocactus
Chamaecereus
Echinopsis
Gymnocalycium
Notocactus
Parodia
Frailea
Pereskia

Opuntia
Trichocereus
Copiapoa
Neoporteria
Parodia

Andean

Pampas

Patagonia

Opuntia

21

hard and bright-colored spines while their epidermis turns bronze-colored.

On the Mexican plateau and particularly in the states of Hidalgo and San Luis Potosí, an impressive number of cacti, including the strangest and least-known genera, are to be found. These are rarely cultivated in some countries because the climate in which they have developed has apparently made them extremely slow-growing and has also discouraged production of the shoots necessary for propagation. What's more, it is impossible to take cuttings from many of them because they are small and globular. They tend to have taproots swollen out of all proportion to their aboveground bodies.

Because of these propagation problems and because the plants are extremely difficult to find in the first place, they are the gems of any cactus collection. Among the most interesting are the flat and horny *Ariocarpus,* which buries itself so completely that it is hard to distinguish from the surrounding soil; the distinctive *Leuchtenbergia,* which has adapted to the environment by dividing its surface into long tubercles, similar to the leaves of the agave, so that all the moisture forming during the night collects in the center; *Obregonia,* which also has leaflike tubercles, though they are less conspicuous; and *Pelecyphora aztechium,* whose bizarre raised tubercles may be so shaped to ensure that all moisture runs gradually into the soil.

South of the Tropic of Cancer, where there is either periodic or constant rainfall, lies the equatorial forest. This type of vegetation dominates the whole of Central America, skirting the northern end of the Andean cordillera to both the east and west, extending into Guyana and covering the enormous area of the Amazon Basin. Here, as on all the islands of the West Indies, epiphytic and semi-epiphytic cacti are to be found. They include the splendid *Epiphyllum* with perfumed flowers, and the bizarre members of the Rhipsalidinae, which hang from the branches of tall trees where they are attached to tiny amounts of humus. They absorb moisture from their surroundings through fine, hairlike roots and often form a fringe around the large leaves of epiphytic ferns or the stiff leaves of the Bromeliaceae. Although the epiphytic cacti are semidormant during periods of scant rainfall, the atmosphere is always warm and humid enough to prevent their drying up. Their flowers may not be as showy as those of the orchids living beside them, but aerial shrubberies formed by their tiny fleshy stems are intricate and delightful.

In addition to these specialized forms, classic globular or cylindrical cacti grow in the flat coastal regions of the West Indies. Although these do not appear to differ from desert cacti, they actually enjoy radically different conditions of growth: a minimum and fairly constant temperature of 65–68° F. (18–20° C.); perfectly drained soil that is light and slightly salty——suitable for a root system that is relatively poor and delicate (since there is nothing for it to contend with)——and an atmosphere that, even in times of scarce rainfall, remains humid.

Some genera grow in both North and South America, although the species differ. For example, the *Opuntia* cacti of South America tend to be cylindrical or globular rather than flat, as they generally are in North America.

In South America particularly we find cacti associated with mountainous areas, steppes and grasslands. On the slopes of the Andes, for instance, grow the large *Cereus* cacti, such as *Espostoa* and *Oreocereus,* that are covered with wool or bristles as a protection against the cold. Also growing here are the *Trichocereus* species with fairly short stems that split into branches at the base in order to resist the wind. In the mountains of Bolivia and northern Argentina, cacti grow at an altitude of 11,900 ft. (3,630 m.) down to the almost steppelike plains and prairies. A great many cacti well known in their cultivated form—*Rebutia, Lobivia, Parodia, Cleistocactus* and *Haageocereus*—originate in this area. Some species of *Lobivia* have been found at altitudes of more than 9,850 ft. (3,000 m.). Here they flourish in strong sunlight and are unaccustomed to any kind of shade. By contrast, genera such as *Echinopsis,* which also grow on the prairies of central Argentina, prefer a certain amount of shade in summer and therefore seek shelter under a layer of dry grass.

The mountains of southern Brazil, Paraguay and Uruguay are the home of the widely cultivated *Cereus,* the flowering *Chamaecereus,* and *Gymnocalycium.* The very common *Schlumbergera* is one of the epiphytes that grow sheltered from the north wind in the coastal forests of the Rio de Janeiro hinterland. The habitat of *Gymnocalycium* is transitional between mountain and forest; the plants generally prefer a certain amount of shade and much richer soil than desert cacti.

One of the great problems in trying to cultivate Andean—and particularly Peruvian—cacti involves the duplication of the exact environmental conditions under which the plants grow naturally. To achieve success, you must first determine exactly where the plants come from. Then you must remember that while the peaks of the Andes are exposed to intense direct sunlight, the lower slopes are often shaded by clouds that shut out the direct rays of the sun but produce a strong diffused light, and the valley floors receive even less sunlight. Finally, you must find a window in which these light conditions can be closely approximated. In the United States and Europe, the summer sun often is too strong or, more important, shines for too many hours a day; consequently, plants that are not well protected by wool or hair may be severely burned when exposed to it.

THE DISCOVERY AND HISTORY OF CACTI

It has sometimes been claimed that Christopher Columbus brought the first cactus to Europe, but the earliest European record of it actually dates from 1635. This was the year that the first volume of *Historia de las Indias Occidentales* by Gonzalo Hernández de Oviedo y Valdés appeared with illustrations of what we would now call a *Cereus* and an *Opuntia*. The *Opuntia*, so closely associated with Mexico, figures in much older history. According to one legend, the Aztecs founded their capital, Tenochtitlán, in 1325, on the basis of a priest's dream that a cactus growing out of a rock became a tree so luxuriant that an eagle settled upon it. This legend was recounted in detail by Fra Diego Duran in his *Historia de las Indias de la Nueva España* (1581), but the fulfilling of the prophecy had been depicted as early as 1541 in the *Codex Mendoza,* compiled by the Aztecs on the orders of the Spaniards. The first colored illustrations of cacti are also of a *Cereus* and an *Opuntia*. They appear in what is known as the *Codex Badianus,* written by a learned Indian, Martín de la Cruz, in 1552.

The best accounts of native cultures, particularly those in Mexico, were written by the missionaries. Since their task was to convert the natives, they also had to learn their language (Nahuatl), get to know their religion and customs and understand something of their earlier civilizations. The best-known missionary was a Franciscan friar named Bernardino de Sahagún, who went to Mexico in 1529. His great work *Historia Universal de Nueva España* brought together all available information about the country and its inhabitants. He collected his material in an unusual manner. He would put questions to a number of natives who knew no Spanish. They would write their replies in the ideographic signs they used. Fra Bernardino would then submit the replies to some of his fellow scholars at the College of Santa Cruz, who interpreted the signs and translated them into Nahuatl. The results of these interviews were then used to form the friar's history, which was also written in the language of the country.

Fra Bernardino learned that the natives used a certain plant to induce a hallucinatory state during religious ceremonies. Since he probably knew that among all ancient or primitive peoples the chief source of hallucinogens was the mushroom, he named this hallucinogenic plant *teonanacatl,* or divine mushroom, partly because that is what the Aztec hieroglyph resembled. Today we know that the plant was the cactus *Lophophora williamsii,* better known by the local names of peyote, mescal, mezcal and peyotl. It is possible that other cacti were used in a similar way; *Ariocarpus, Pelecyphora* and *Obregonia,* for example, are all small enough to resemble a mushroom, and all contain at least one hallucinogenic alkaloid.

It is interesting that although the use of peyote has been widespread since the early eighteenth century, it is officially prohibited in the United States, even to American Indian tribes. However, a legal exception has had to be made in the case of the Native American Church, a Christian sect including about 40,000 Navajos as members, because its constitution declares that believers have the right to use peyote as a sacrament during religious services.

Page from the Codex Mendoza *showing the district of Tenochtitlán, the future
capital, and the ten tribes that came together to build it. The pueblos remain
outside it. According to mythology, the eagle poised on an* Opuntia *indicated the
place where Mexico City now stands. This cactus is still the nation's symbol and
appears on its flag.*

25

A *Melocactus* was one of the first of the Cactaceae to become known in Europe. This is not surprising, since for a long time the Antilles were the most accessible and Europeanized part of the New World, the flora of which was virtually unknown.

Although information about the discovery of cacti is less reliable and precise than that regarding other plants, a number of specimens must have arrived in Europe during the second half of the sixteenth century. These provided the basis for the descriptions contained in the herbals that were then proliferating. Oviedo, besides writing his *History*, collected a great many plants in his garden on the island of Haiti; and since he made regular visits to Spain, he probably brought with him specimens of the plants. We do know that during this period *Opuntia ficus-indica* arrived from the New World, as did *Melocactus communis* and some others. The *Melocactus* was described and illustrated by Matthias de l'Obel in 1576 under the name *Echinomelocactus*. There are also occasional references to the efforts made to keep these cacti alive in an uncongenial climate.

In 1597 one of the most famous of all herbals was published in London: *The Herball or Generall Historie of Plants*, by John Gerald. This contained illustrations of two *Cereus* ("The Torch or Thorne Euphorbium" and "The Thorne Reede of Peru"); a *Melocactus* ("The Hedgehogge Thistle"); and an *Opuntia* ("The Indian Fig Tree").

In the seventeenth century, in botanical gardens all over Europe, the study of plants became greatly intensified, and plants and seeds were imported in considerable numbers. During the period, several cacti arrived and survived comparatively well because heated buildings known as orangeries were being used to grow citrus fruit. Some of these cacti were classified, although they were later renamed by post-Linnaean botanists. In 1623, Gaspard Bauhin mentioned *Opuntia ficus-indica* and a *Cereus peruvianus spinosus fructu rubro* in his *Pinax Theatri Botanici;* and in 1688 John Ray, in his *Historia Plantarum, II,* mentioned an *Echinomelocactus lanuginosum tubercolis spinosis* that was obviously a *Mammillaria.* In 1696, Plunket described and illustrated an *Epiphyllum* as *Phyllanthos americana sinuosis folis longis,* and in the same year, Abraham Munting of Groningen published a herbal, entitled *Naauwkeurige Beschryving der Aardgewassen* ("A Precise Description of the World's Plants"), in which there is an illustration of a stylized, but flowering and fruit-bearing, *Opuntia major augustifolia.*

In 1718, Richard Bradley, the first professor of botany at Cambridge University, published his *History of Succulent Plants,* and two years later he followed with an article on the cultivation of succulents. In the first edition of Philip Miller's *Gardener's Dictionary,* published in 1731, twelve *Cereus* and eleven *Opuntia* each are listed. The following year, Johann Jakob Dillen, better known as Dillenius, wrote the two-volume *Hortus Elthamensis.* In it he illustrated an *Epiphyllum, Pereskia, Opuntia* and *Nopalea cochenillifera* that were being grown in James Sherard's garden at Eltham, England.

In 1753, Linnaeus published his *Species Plantarum*—the work that laid the foundations of botanical nomenclature. In this he grouped together all the members of the family then known by the name cactus—a term derived from the Greek *kaktos,* which Theophrastus and Theocritus had used to describe an unidentified prickly plant that was probably a thistle. Linnaeus coined the word from the ending of *Echinomelocactos,* and used the other names which had already become established to indicate the species. Soon after this, however, in a later edition of his *Gardener's Dictionary,* Miller pronounced this grouping inadequate and established four genera, placing alongside *Cactus* the three old names of *Opuntia, Cereus* and *Pereskia.*

The etymology of the familiar name *Opuntia* is somewhat complicated. It derives from Opus, the capital of Locris, in ancient Greece. Around the city there apparently grew a great many fig trees bearing very sweet fruits from which the latex (*opos*) used as rennet was extracted. Thus *opuntios,* the adjective meaning "of Opus," came to be associated with a plant producing figlike fruit. It is generally accepted that Miller took the name from Joseph Pitton de Tournefort, who identified four types of *Opuntia,* but there were other precedents: as early as 1656 (the year of Tournefort's birth) a *Ficus indicus minor, Opuntia* was mentioned in a catalog of the plants growing in John Tradescant's garden in Chelsea.

The name *Cereus* came into use in somewhat similar fashion. Miller gave the credit for it to Paul Hermann, the director of the

Botanical Gardens at Leyden during the second half of the seventeenth century. However, the name had been used earlier by Jacob Theodore Tabernaemontanus in his herbal entitled *Kraecherbuch*. The second part of this, published posthumously in 1625, contains an illustration of a *Cereus peruvianus*.

Miller took the third "new name," *Pereskia,* from that used by the French naturalist Charles Plumier to designate a single species. Plumier spent a long time in the Caribbean and was the author of *Nova Plantarum Americanorum Genera*. Linnaeus also adopted the name *Pereskia,* but in accordance with his single-genus scheme, it became *Cactus pereskia*. (Actually *Pereskia* is an incorrect name, because the plant was named after Nicholas Claude Fabry de Peiresc, another French naturalist; but all attempts to change the spelling have been overruled by the International Code of Botanical Nomenclature.)

Miller's four genera were accepted during the second half of the eighteenth century and must have been considered adequate to cover the twenty-two species that were cultivated in Kew in 1789 and listed by William Aiton in the first edition of his *Hortus Kewensis*. Antoine Laurent de Jussieu's *Genera Plantarum Secundum Ordines Naturalis Disposita* (1789) represents the first attempt to classify plants in natural orders. It was also the first time a family of Cacti was recognized, although the family did not assume its present-day proportions until

1799 with the publication of *Tableau du Règne Végétal,* by Etienne P. Ventenat. In this the family was called Cactoides. The great Geneva botanist Augustin Pyrame de Candolle was only twenty-one when the first part of his *Plantarum Historia Succulentarum,* illustrated by Pierre-Joseph Redoute, was published in 1799. He continued to work on the book until 1829, but before it came to fruition, Andrian H. Haworth revolutionized the cactus family again. In his *Synopsis Plantarum Succulentarum* of 1812, he kept Miller's three additional genera but completely abolished Linnaeus' *Cactus,* and established other genera—of greatest importance, *Mammillaria.* Yet the abolition of the term "cactus," except as the basis for the family name and as a component of various generic names, was not really a defeat for Linnaeus, because it is now accepted as the common name for all plants belonging to the family Cactaceae.

In the nineteenth century, there was a great increase in the number of expeditions and botanical discoveries made, and in the study of herbaria and living specimens in collections. The journeys undertaken by Friedrich Alexander von Humboldt and described in the mighty thirty-volume work *Voyage aux regions equinoxiales du Nouveau Continent, fait en 1799–1804* were of fundamental importance. Other botanists who made invaluable contributions included the Prince of Salm-Dyck, Link, Otto, Martius, Lemaire, Riccobono, Engelmann and Karl Schumann. Many of them attempted to introduce new systems of plant classification and family orders, but the overall effect of this tumult of research was the proliferation of genera and species rather than a clarification of the subject as a whole.

The sorting out of this confusion of names—many of which were invalid, or were merely discarded as synonyms—was begun in 1904 by two dedicated Americans: Nathaniel Lord Britton, director of the New York Botanical Gardens, and Joseph Nelson Rose, assistant curator of the United States National Museum Herbarium of the Smithsonian Institution. With the powerful backing of the Carnegie Institution, founded by the great steel magnate Andrew Carnegie, Britton and Rose traveled the length and breadth of the American continents, went to Europe to see the European collections of cacti, consulted herbals and archives, and obtained the collaboration of famous botanists, collectors and private individuals. Between 1919 and 1923 their four-volume *Cactaceae* was finally published. In this they divided the family into tribes, subtribes, and occasionally series; they established many new genera and eliminated others. This division is still followed by many today, although new discoveries have been added and some modifications have been made.

Numerous botanists, most of them German, have specialized in the study of succulent plants in general and cacti in particular since before World War II. The most famous was Curt Backeberg (1894–1966), who revolutionized the classification system that had been followed until then. His new system retains the three main groups but promotes them to the rank of subfamilies, and divides them into tribes, subtribes, groups and subgroups. Plants are placed in these categories not only on the basis of botanical affinity, but also on the basis of a geographic-environmental concept. One result of this concept has been the creation of numerous very restricted genera, several of which are monotypic. Many of Backeberg's genera were never accepted; others persist merely as synonyms. The most interesting aspect of his system is that he heads his list of *Cereus*-group cacti with the epiphyte genera, starting with the *Rhipsalis,* followed by the Hylocereinae and the Cacteae (the latter are divided into Austrocereeae from South America, and Boreocereeae from North America), and ending with the *Mammillaria.* Other authors have also considered the epiphyte genera to be descendants of the Hylocereinae with structural modifications brought about by their habitat. In view of the mystery surrounding their origins, this hypothesis cannot be disproved.

Many members of the family Cactaceae, like the members of other plant families, have been given common names as well as formal botanical names. Virtually all of these, however, are residents of the United States. Only a tiny handful of South and Central American cacti have common names.

In the United States the general practice has been to give the same common surname to one cactus genus. For example, the

Rhipsalis cacti were known as early as 1788, but they are not commonly found in cultivation. Although they have small, not very showy flowers, they deserve to become more widespread, because they are among members of the Cactaceae suitable for cultivation as houseplants.

Opuntia cacti that have acquired common names (many have not) are generally known as prickly pears, or prickly pear cacti. This group includes the beaver tail prickly pear, the fragile prickly pear, the porcupine prickly pear, the yellow spine prickly pear, and many others.

The surnames of other large groups include the barrel cacti (genus *Ferocactus*), beehive cacti (genus *Coryphantha*), hedgehog cacti (genus *Echinocereus*), and pincushion cacti (genus *Mammillaria*). Members of genus *Cylindropuntia* are generally known as chollas—bush pencil cholla, jumping cholla, teddy bear cholla, etc.

In the individual plant entries that follow, common names are given for those species that have them.

CACTI IN USE

No species of the Cactaceae family can possibly be said to be economically important in the usual sense of the term, but many of them are put to use in some way in the areas in which they grow. For example, in areas where there are no trees and there is therefore no wood, dried *Cereus* stems are used as less efficient substitutes for wooden building planks and logs, while in grassless regions the flat branches of *Opuntia*, stripped of their glochids, are used as forage. Moreover, very young branches of *Opuntia*, whose prickles can easily be scraped off, are eaten fried in Mexico and boiled in Texas. They are known as *nopalitos, nopal* being a common name applied to several different species. To ward off scurvy, seventeenth- and eighteenth-century sailors ate boiled branches; they remained fresh for a long time, because of their succulence, and provided a substitute for perishable green vegetables.

Most people are acquainted with the prickly pear. *Opuntia ficus-indica* grows in many warm countries and has become naturalized in several Mediterranean countries, where its fruit is grown for export. This is not the only cactus to produce edible fruit, although prickly pears are undoubtedly the sweetest and most delicious. Other species that are widely cultivated for their fruit are *Opuntia tuna, Opuntia streptacantha* and *Opuntia cardona.*

The Mexicans commonly eat the fruit of various native cereus cacti—*Hylocereus undatus,* for example—or the bluish berries of *Myrtillocactus geometrizans,* which are sold in Mexican markets under the name *garambullos.* The fruit of the big saguaro, *Carnegiea gigantea,* is also considered excellent— quite good enough, at any rate, to compensate for the difficulty of picking it at a height of 30 ft. (10 m.) or more.

Some species of *Echinocereus* are known by the common name "strawberry cactus," since their fruit is not only fleshy but also edible. Although the fruit is prickly, the spines become soft when it ripens, and are easily removed.

In view of its formidable array of spines, it is extraordinary that *Echinocactus* should be put to any use; yet beneath its prickly epidermis there lies a watery pulp, vaguely reminiscent of watermelon, from which a preserve known as *dulces de viznaga* is made. *Viznaga* is commonly used to describe several species, not just *Echinocactus visnaga,* whose specific name is derived from popular usage.

Probably the most extensive use to which cacti are put is that of providing protective enclosures. Several species of *Cereus* are used for this purpose because they put up a particularly impenetrable thicket of branches. Also popular in hedges are the *Pachycereus* and *Stenocereus* species that grow with such an upright and regular habit that they are called organ-pipe or organ cactus. *Opuntia,* too, is often used as hedging. Indeed, a long flowerbox filled with prickly cacti and placed on top of a wall might well prove a more efficacious—and certainly a more aesthetic—deterrent to trespassers than the iron spikes or barbed wire commonly used.

GENERAL RULES OF CULTIVATION

From the standpoint of the gardener who wants to grow them, cacti are best divided into two main groups—those from desert and mountain habitats, and those from tropical and subtropical forests. Several general rules regarding cultivation are applicable to these two categories, but significant individual variations must be taken into account.

Top: *Many* Echinocactus *species have juicy pulp from which sweets and candied fruit are made.*
Below: *The prickly pear. The fruits are never poisonous. Some are very sweet.*

Temperature and Climate

One of the most commonly held but erroneous popular beliefs is that cacti are houseplants. The truth is that few succulent plants are suitable for cultivation indoors, because of the difficulty of duplicating the special growing conditions they demand.

Today most houses have central heating, and they are therefore too warm for a cactus, which needs a complete rest and good airing in winter. Excessive heat during the daytime is accompanied by another drawback: although the indoor temperature drops at night, it does not do so to the same extent as in the cactus's natural environment. Even more important, the indoor air is always dry, and no nocturnal humidity is produced to compensate for a plant's lack of moisture. Cacti should be watered, therefore, even if only now and again. It should be noted that if the supply of light and air is inadequate, watering will promote an unnatural growth cycle that results in the production of delicate and weakly spined tissues.

In temperate climates the most favorable conditions for cactus cultivation are to be found in a greenhouse. This should be cold, the temperature ranging from a minimum of 36–50° F. (2–10° C.) to a maximum of 47–54° F. (8–12° C.), depending on the various species. However, if a few factors are taken into consideration, cultivation indoors can also be feasible. Modern houses with large window area are best suited to the growth of all kinds of plants, cacti included. Apartments with covered balconies are ideal because the balconies can be glassed in to form conservatories. Since it is on window panes that moisture condenses during the night, if a cactus is placed on a windowsill indoors, it will enjoy the sunshine flooding through the glass on bright days and a relatively cool atmosphere at night. In addition, it should be able to obtain sufficient moisture to keep its tissues turgid, making winter watering unnecessary. Radiators are often placed beneath windowsills, but this need not affect the plants if a shelf with an air space below it is placed above the radiator. The plants should be set on this in trays containing a layer of gravel that is quite dry. The gravel can be slightly moistened from time to time if any wrinkling from excessive heat is noticed. This arrangement is particularly suitable for young plants, which are usually rather delicate and need a slightly warmer atmosphere than old plants.

For cultivating cacti outdoors in a garden or on a terrace it is advisable to put up a shelter. The most suitable type depends on the local climate. In warm areas a simple roof of glass or rigid plastic often suffices to protect plants from frost, rain or—worst of all—hail. Where the temperature regularly falls to below freezing for long periods, a greenhouse should be erected for adult plants that cannot conveniently be brought indoors. A collapsible greenhouse is perfectly adequate. Do-it-yourself enthusiasts may wish to build their own, and in areas not subject to strong winds or torrential rain, a wooden framework covered with heavy-duty polyethylene will do. This should

Many cacti can be grown on a sunny windowsill, particularly if the atmosphere is not very hot in winter. This permits them to enjoy their necessary rest period—provided they are given the right amount of water.

be constructed so that the southern end can be raised to ventilate the greenhouse in good weather. On really cold nights, matting anchored by hooks in the roof should be thrown over the house to prevent daytime heat from escaping.

Most of the greenhouses on the market are easily assembled. In colder climates, those with glass panes can be heated by electricity, but heating is not advisable in plastic-covered greenhouses since the plastic may be stretched or damaged if direct heat is unequally dispersed. In the case of glass greenhouses, the need for well-planned periods of ventilation is greater because the plants are vulnerable to attack by parasites, and the constant humidity may give rise to green algae on the panes.

In summer, cacti should be outside——in sunshine, shade, or semishade, according to the species. It is difficult to say exactly how long they should be left out, since local seasonal variations in the weather must be taken into account. There is usually a period when the temperature ranges between 54° and 65° F. (12° and 18° C.), and the possibility of a sudden drop is unlikely. At these temperatures most cacti begin to show the first signs of growth, but this sometimes slows down or ceases during the summer as a result of two climatic differences. In their countries of origin, the extreme daytime heat is tempered by nighttime cold, and the number of daylight hours in the tropics is much smaller than in temperate zones, hence many cultivated cacti suffer from too many hours of sunshine. If cacti are subjected to thirteen to fifteen hours of sunshine per day at summer temperatures of over 86° F. (30° C.) in the shade and minimum nighttime temperatures of over 68° F. (20° C.), they enter a semidormant state in which they still require regular watering. In hot weather such as this, therefore, it is advisable to remove even those species that normally like a sunny position from the midday sun. In Britain and the cooler parts of Europe, however, few cacti can be grown successfully outdoors in the summer. Although they may not die, a long, dull wet spell will damage them. To guard against this, most growers keep the great majority of their plants in the greenhouse, putting only the overflow outside.

Light and Air

Almost all species of the Cactaceae require as much air as possible, and most of them require exposure to the sun. During the winter months, however, no matter how well they have been looked after, their tissues become weakened and their defenses destroyed; so unless they are transferred outdoors in stages, their epidermis may suffer burns, which, though they eventually heal, will leave the plant permanently blemished. By the same token, plants that are kept behind glass should be shaded by a thin curtain from very hot, bright sunshine, since the sun's rays are magnified by the glass. These precautions apply especially to young plants, which are much more sensitive to sunlight than adult plants. (The truth of this statement may seem questionable when you consider how easily cactus seeds germinate and grow in strong sunshine, but it must be remembered that in their natural environment fledgling plants are normally shaded by other plants, rocks, etc.)

However, epiphytic or semi-epiphytic cacti that originally grew in the forest need to spend more of their lives in shade or semishade. Some *Epiphyllum* hybrids can tolerate a little sunshine because they have been crossed with *Helicereus*. But they are exceptions. Generally, a position of semishade in very bright surroundings results in a greater abundance of more beautiful flowers.

Soil

It is absolutely essential that all members of the cactus family be grown in soil that is porous and perfectly drained. If it is not and the soil becomes waterlogged, the roots will rot and the plant will die. Many people believe that cacti can be kept completely dry or almost so, and that this is a solution to the problem; but dry, hard soil prevents oxygen from reaching the roots, and asphyxiation results. This is why even succulent plants wither. It is true that in their natural habitat many species live on hard, rocky terrain; but one must bear in mind how far their roots reach out, growing around obstacles and down into the earth until they find a place where they can spread. Such spreading is not possible in a flowerpot.

Sand must be added to the soil in which all cacti are grown to ensure that it is highly porous. In addition, the soil must always be free of any sort of decomposing organic matter, although fully decomposed matter is essential. Desert or mountain cacti require soil that is very rich in mineral salts; epiphytes and semi-epiphytes grown mainly for their flowers—*Epiphyllum, Hylocereus* and *Selenicereus,* for instance—need a soil with more humus, such as completely decomposed leaf mold and a little well-rotted horse manure or similar fertilizer. *Rhipsalis* and similar genera grown in pots require mainly leaf mold and peat. Delicate or very young plants benefit from the addition of some crushed charcoal as well as sand. This will neutralize any fermentation of residual matter. (Both ordinary charcoal chips and the so-called activated charcoal sold for aquarium filters should be washed in a colander or through gauze before use.) At the end of this discussion we list four types of basic soil for pot-grown cacti. With experience, you can vary them to suit particular needs. Every keen grower tends to have his own secret formula.

Various materials can be added to the growing medium. Tiny pellets of expanded clay or polystyrene can be used instead of grit. Builder's sharp sand used for making mortar has the advantage of containing pebbles of various sizes. If the sand is shaken a little at a time, the largest gravel can be removed and what is left will be a mixture of two of the requisite materials. All-purpose potting soil should be avoided, as it is peaty, holds moisture, and easily forms lumps. It may be used in place of leaf mold if leaf mold is hard to find; but the proportion used should be smaller.

Fertilizer other than horse manure, which is not always available, can be used, although because of their lack of leaves cacti do not need much nitrogen. The three numbers given on fertilizer packages refer to the percentages of nitrogen, phosphorus and potassium—in that order—in the fertilizer. All fertilizer used for cacti should have a much lower percentage of nitrogen than of the other two elements, since phosphorus and potassium help to increase a plant's growth and flowering potential. However, fertilizers should be used as little as possible; if they are absolutely necessary, it is best to add to the soil a granular fertilizer that dissolves slowly.

Contradictory advice is often given regarding the suitability of acid or alkaline soil. Many species live on chalky (limy) soil; therefore it is advisable to add a few flakes of plaster or shells ground almost as fine as powder to the soil in order to strengthen the tough, colored spines. If too much is given, hypercalcification of the spines and a thickening of the tissues may ensue. Although some growers believe that many cacti prefer slightly acid conditions, it is undoubtedly true that highly acid soil is harmful to all genera except *Rhipsalis.* In the least serious cases, the plants appear perfectly healthy, but rather unnaturally florid. While this may make them attractive commercially, it can create problems for inexperienced growers, who should strive for the strongest plants possible.

1. 2 parts seasoned, slightly fibrous garden loam free of unrotted organic matter; 1 part coarse river or lake sand; 1 part very fine grit; a little granular fertilizer.

This compost is suitable for *Opuntia, Cereus* and similar genera, *Echinopsis* and *Mammillaria*. For *Selenicereus* and *Aporocactus*, 1 part well-rotted leaf mold should be added.

2. Equal parts of garden loam, leaf mold and sand; ½ part grit; a little granular fertilizer.

This is suitable for *Echinocereus*. For *Rebutia* and *Lobivia* the leaf mold may be reduced to ½ part, the other ½ part being made up with peat.

3. Soil that is predominantly inorganic: 3 parts sand; 2 parts garden loam; 1 part leaf mold; 1 part grit.

This is suitable for *Echinocactus* and similar genera. *Echinofossulocactus, Astrophytum* and *Gymnocalycium* may need the loam reduced to 1 part and the leaf mold increased to 2 parts.

4. Equal parts of loam, leaf mold and sand, with a little fertilizer consisting almost entirely of phosphates.

This is suitable for *Epiphyllum* and *Schlumbergera*. For *Rhipsalis*, fibrous peat should be substituted for the loam.

Watering
Many people believe that cacti should be watered a thimbleful at a time—and usually those same people complain that in their homes no plant lives for very long. This is hardly surprising.

It cannot be emphasized too strongly that the majority of cacti need a rest period during the winter. During this period they may be left for as long as a month without water, particularly if they are kept at a fairly low temperature. But it is cruel not to water them during their growing period; their need for moisture must not be ignored just because they don't have leaves that droop.

As with other aspects of cactus cultivation, it is impossible to give precise rules about watering because there are too many variables. Consider a specific example that illustrates the important considerations: a desert cactus grown in a clay flowerpot of suitable size. In winter it is kept on an indoor windowsill at a temperature of 64–68° F. (18–20° C.). In summer it is put outside in the sun. In January this plant would need to be watered once, or at the most twice, and its stem sprayed three or four times. In February it should be watered two or three times, and in March and April four times—a little supplementary spraying also being given. In May the plant can begin to go outside, either in semishade or for no more than a few hours in the sun; four to five waterings should be sufficient if the weather is not unusually hot. When the plant is finally placed in full sun, the frequency of watering should be increased: from the end of June until September it may be watered daily. Then, as the weather becomes cooler, this program should be reversed, so that by December the plant is being watered only a couple of times, and sprayed now and then.

As regards the amount of water to be given, a thimbleful is certainly too little. The water should be sufficient to soak all the soil in the pot, and any excess should drain away freely. It is often better to water each plant in two stages, stopping as soon as water starts to seep out of the bottom of the pot and repeating the operation rather more frugally ten minutes later. If the soil in the pot has become too dry, it is quite possible that no water will reach the center, merely running away down the sides of the pot. To avoid this, the infrequent waterings necessary in winter should be carried out by immersing the pot in a bowl filled almost to the brim with water, leaving it there for half an hour, and allowing it to drain well before putting it back in its usual place.

In the summer when plants are left outside, an occasional rain-shower does no harm; on the contrary, it is a tonic for cacti accustomed to weathering cyclones. A protracted period of rain, however, is bad for the plants, and they should be placed under some kind of shelter.

Unexpected summer downpours are sometimes followed by brilliant sunshine. Obviously nothing can be done to prevent this from happening, and actually cacti do not appear to suffer from it. Nevertheless, it is not advisable to emulate nature in this way: cacti should not be watered when the flowerpots are hot from standing in the sun. Not many growers are likely to water their plants before dawn, although this is beneficial. The best time to water them is after sunset, or at least after the pot has cooled down from standing in the sun. This procedure has the advantage of keeping the plant's soil cool for the whole night.

Although technically the water should be free from chlorine and alkaline salts, ordinary tap water considered safe for human consumption seems to suit cacti perfectly well in the United States. However, in Britain ordinary tap water is too rich in chlorine and alkaline salts to be suitable, and rainwater should be used instead. It is important that water for spraying plants should resemble distilled water as closely as possible. Use the thawed frost from a refrigerator freezing compartment, the water collected in a dehumidifier, or tap water that has been boiled for half an hour and decanted slowly to separate it from its deposits of lime. Ordinary water leaves ugly whitish marks on the plant's stem and blocks the stomata. The effort involved in purifying water is worthwhile, since one saucepanful, bottled, should last the whole winter.

The epiphytes and semi-epiphytes of the Epiphyllinae and Rhipsalidinae subtribes should be given only a short rest after their flowering period. Thereafter they should be watered very seldom, but sprayed frequently to keep the stems from wrinkling. If *Epiphyllum* is kept at a low temperature throughout the winter, its rest period will prove more beneficial.

Below: *The Andean* Matucana *cactus needs frequent watering in summer, but its soil should be well drained. Like all cacti from the same habitat, it should also be shaded from the midday summer sun.*
Opposite: *A group of* Mammillaria. *All the species of this huge genus should be grown in pots, even if they offset, since hardly any will survive the rigors of the outdoor world except in their native habitats.*

Repotting

In the cactus's natural state, the roots may spread for several yards (meters), or penetrate the earth deeply. But cacti are very amenable plants, and when cultivated, manage to attain a respectable size with a much reduced root system. The only consequence is a slowing down of the growth rate.

Repotting cacti is hardly one of the most enjoyable gardening activities, particularly when the cactus in question is a spine-covered globe or, worse still, an *Opuntia.* However, it is possible to make the repotting quite painless. With ordinary plants, the usual method is to bang the rim of the pot on a hard surface and allow the root ball to fall into one's hand. In the case of cacti, the flowerpot should be laid on its side on a hard surface, and the bottom tapped gently but firmly as the pot is rotated. This should detach the root ball from the sides of the pots. (This happens more easily in plastic pots, to which roots do not stick, than in clay pots.) If the roots still seem to be adhering to the pot, stand it on its base and pass a knife blade around the inside between the soil and the pot wall so as to cut any clinging root ends. With old specimens of globular cacti, such as *Echinopsis* and the like, it is sometimes impossible to carry out either of these operations because the stems are wider than the pot rim. The only way to avoid damaging both tissues and spines in these cases is to smash the flowerpot.

Once the soil has been loosened, the rim of the pot, lying on its

side, should be tapped somewhat harder. This will usually free the whole root ball when the pot is given a gentle shake. If it does not slide out of the pot, push a small stick up through the drainage hole to release it. Now hold the root ball between the fingers and knock off a little of the soil on the sides with the stick. If the roots have formed a thick matted outer layer, cut it off with a knife or pair of scissors, because these are withered roots that will prevent the growth of new roots, no matter how much new earth is provided for them.

The new flowerpot should be only a little larger than the old one. Lay a stone or crock over the drainage hole, and pour in a drainage layer of gravel, expanded clay or potsherds to a depth suitable to the size of the pot. In very small pots the layer should be very thin indeed; in large pots it can be about 1/2 in. (13 mm.) thick. Plastic pots have several holes and should be filled with gravel only. This allows more water to drain away than the other materials, and that is important, since plastic pots retain more moisture than clay ones.

The gravel should be covered with a layer of fresh soil, and the plant should then be carefully placed in the pot. Use a small stick to position it in the center and hold it upright while the pot is filled with more fresh soil. Shake it from time to time. When the soil is within about 1/3 in. (1 cm.) of the top, press it down gently—with a finger if there is room between the soil and the cactus spines, otherwise with the stick. The neck of the plant

Left: *When repotting cacti, add the soil with a teaspoon, since a larger implement rarely fits between the spines at the base of the plant and the pot.*
Right: *Large flowerpots should be given an adequate drainage layer to prevent waterlogged soil that will cause root rot.*

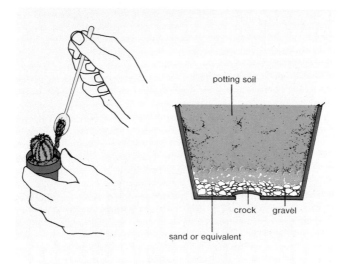

potting soil

crock   gravel

sand or equivalent

must never be buried; if too little soil has been placed beneath the roots and the neck of the plant is therefore too far down in the pot, the repotting operation will have to be repeated. However, if the neck is only very slightly too deep, it can be covered with a very thin layer of fine gravel. This will allow the passage of air and avoid rot.

This operation takes far less time to perform than it takes to describe; even so, it's fortunate that most cacti are repotted only once every two or three years because of their slow growth rate. However, in the case of young "Tom Thumb" plants bought in tiny pots, repotting is essential. A brief description of how these plants are propagated explains why. Seedlings that have germinated in a higgledy-piggledy fashion in a seed pan are pricked out into another pan containing very porous, coarse soil in which they have room to grow to reasonable size. Alternatively, young shoots or cuttings from joints are planted out in seed pans. When either kind of plantlet has developed a sufficiently strong root system, it is removed from the seed pan to a tiny pot containing a small amount of soil. This is a simple operation that does not damage the plantlets. However, no plant can live long in such cramped conditions, so the sooner "Tom Thumbs" are transferred to pots at least twice the size of those they were sold in, the better for their development.

If the soil used for repotting is completely dry, it should be lightly watered after the cactus has been set in place, but if it is damp, do not water under any circumstances. However, plant and soil should both be sprayed once a day for the first two or three days, and the plant should then be watered to the extent appropriate for the season of the year. In addition, especially in summer, the pot should be kept in the shade for a week and then exposed to the sun very gradually.

Propagation

The commonest, quickest and most convenient way to propagate most cacti is by cuttings. Indeed, in the case of especially floriferous and attractive hybrids, cuttings are the only means of propagation that guarantees new plants that are identical to their parents. Cacti are not often raised from seed because (1) no one can be sure the plants will come true and (2) it is difficult to collect seed from many species because only the adult plants bear fruit and they don't do it reliably in most climates. Seeding is generally done only in the case of plants that don't have branches or shoots from which cuttings can be made (unfortunately, this includes most of the rare cacti). On the other hand, even branchless and shootless species can sometimes be grown from cuttings by using the apex of the stem as a cutting.

But generally, upright or lateral branches or basal shoots (the branches that grow from the neck of the main stem or that part of the stem that is beneath the soil) are used for cuttings. These must be removed with care: the stem must not be damaged. It's also important to think about the appearance of the parent plant. For instance, old specimens that grow particularly large sometimes put out lateral branches that should not be cut off because this would leave the plant disfigured and in danger of dying.

To make a cutting, use a very sharp knife or, if necessary on big plants, a fine-toothed saw. Do not use pruning shears, since they are likely to crush the tissues. All cuts should be made at a node. When a cutting is taken from an *Epiphyllum,* it is advisable to make a diagonal or V-shaped cut to remove the basal portions of its fleshy side projections, thus leaving the node intact. These projections are so succulent that they are likely to rot, whereas if they are removed, the new plant will produce a proliferation of new shoots after it has put down roots.

Once a cutting has been made, let it dry in the shade until the wound has formed a callus. This may take as much as three weeks. Don't try to hurry the process, for unless the wound is completely dried and healed, rot is likely to set in.

The type of soil in which cuttings are planted should be the same as that used for mature plants of the same species. Delicate species should be planted in pure coarse sand that is washed free of salts. In all cases, the soil or sand should be almost dry. Never push a cutting deep into the soil. If it is so tall that it is likely to flop over, support it with a stake. Globular shoots should just be laid in a shallow depression to avoid

Cuttings of branches are very easy to take, particularly from Opuntia and Cereus. The cutting should not be planted deeply, since the base may rot; and in all except very hot weather it should be kept completely dry for quite a long time.

burying their lower areoles and spines. For the first few days the new plant should be kept in the shade and sprayed very lightly. It should then be watered extremely sparingly, even during the summer, until it has definitely put down roots.

The best time of the year for taking cuttings is in late spring and summer. However, it can be done at any time if the cutting is allowed to dry long enough in a warm, well-aired place and if it is kept almost dry at a temperature of not less than 64° F. (18° C.) after repotting.

As noted above, cacti are rarely grown from seed except by commercial growers who want a lot of plants with which to fill orders. Many Europeans, however, do grow cacti from seed. The following describes the process.

Cactus seed retains its ability to germinate for more than two years, but germination takes place much more quickly if the seed is fresh. While some species may put out seed leaves after hardly more than a week, some take a month and others as much as a year. The seeds of *Opuntia* have such a hard coating that it is a good idea to soak them in hot water for two or three days before sowing.

Seeding is usually best done between April and October. But since the chief requirements are a temperature of about 70° F. (21° C.) and intense light, sowing can take place at any time of the year if these two conditions are met. With a lower temperature, germination takes longer, and in some cases may not occur at all.

Cacti can be grown from seed in flowerpots, the surface of the soil being sectioned off for different species. (a) Three-week-old Echinocactus texensis *plantlet. (b)* Ferocactus wislizeni *plantlet at two months old. (c)* Coryphantha radians *aged three months; at this age most species produce their first spines. (d)* Astrophytum *plantlet.*

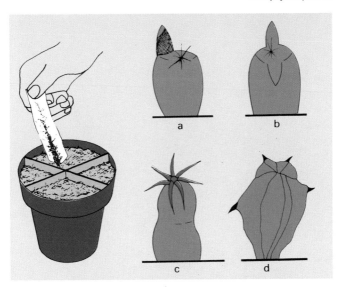

Seed should be sown preferably in shallow clay pans half filled with a drainage layer of gravel or clay shards. This is covered to within 1/2–3/4 in. (1–2 cm.) of the rim of the pan with a mixture of very coarse sand and well-rotted leaf mold in equal parts. Experts often recommend mixing tiny pellets of expanded clay and a little loam with the sand. Experiments can also be made with tufa dust and other substances, but this requires some experience on the part of the grower. The soil in the pan should be wetted, lightly pressed down, and leveled off with a piece of wood or a spatula. Scatter the seeds over it as evenly as possible, press down and cover with fine sand. If the seeds are tiny, merely sprinkle the sand over them; if they are large, it should reach to a depth of about 1/8 in. (3 mm.). It is easier to scatter very small seeds evenly if they are first mixed with sand on a sheet of paper; the paper should then be folded, and the mixture strewed uniformly over the soil surface. Water the seeds by immersing the pan in a basin of water until the soil has become saturated.

Many people recommend covering the seed pan with a sheet of glass or plastic, taking care to air it now and again in order to prevent excessive condensation. A cover of this type is particularly appropriate when seeds are sown outdoors, because even if they are kept in the shade, they are likely to dry out. Indoors a cover of heavy paper or cardboard is more suitable. This permits a small amount of moisture to condense for germination while absorbing the excess.

46

When the seed leaves appear, it is advisable to syringe them gently with a fungicide solution, and to repeat the operation several times, since they are very susceptible to mold.

Seedlings should not be potted until they measure at least 3/8 to 3/4 in. (1 to 2 cm.) in diameter, or, in the case of cylindrical cacti, until they reach a height of 1 1/4 to 1 1/2 in. (3 to 4 cm.). If they become too crowded, they can be pricked out into other seed pans containing the same type of soil. Set them in straight rows at a reasonable distance from one another.

Moving Plants from the Wild

There is, of course, one other tempting way to acquire new kinds of cacti or to increase your supply. That is to dig them up from the wild and move them into either the garden or flower-pots. But whereas this was once generally accepted practice, it is now frowned upon.

Stealing from nature is inadvisable if not actually illegal on two counts: (1) The thief, unless very knowledgeable about cacti, may make off with a rare species that cannot easily be replaced. (2) The desert areas in which cacti abound have so little vegetative cover that the loss of just a few plants may result in serious erosion and vast loss of greenery.

And to make matters worse, the thief too often is unable to keep the plants he pilfers growing.

To prevent such problems, the Southwestern states have enacted laws against the unauthorized removal of cacti from the countryside. These require that the would-be plant hunter check with the appropriate authority to determine whether the plant he wants is or is not legally collectible. If it is on the prohibited or endangered lists, special permission to acquire it must be secured in writing. Failure to do this can result in a steep fine or imprisonment.

Grafting

Grafting of cacti was originally done only in the case of certain species with weak root systems or of species whose natural habitat was difficult to simulate in cultivation. Today, grafting has become fashionable, and many plants now offered for sale have been grafted, even though their own root systems are capable of supporting them.

The basis for this trend is probably the fact that young plants raised from seed grow very much more rapidly if they are grafted onto other stock as soon as possible. In one year they then grow to the size that a nongrafted plant reaches in four or five years. The time factor is obviously important to the commercial grower, but it does not compensate for the fact that grafted cacti are hideous. And they are then sometimes further disfigured by sticking tiny, brightly colored artificial flowers into them.

It is recommended that a grower wishing to try the technique of grafting should do so only on plants that really need to be grafted, or whose habit lends itself to such an operation. In addition, the graft should usually be made as low down as possible, if only for aesthetic reasons.

The general rule is that the scion should always be grafted onto a stock stronger than itself. A weak species grafted onto a vigorous species grows much faster than it would otherwise, but the root system of the stock becomes weaker. If the scion is stronger than the stock, sooner or later the stock withers and the whole plant dies.

Epiphytic cacti lend themselves well to grafting because of their pendant habit and their minimal root systems; and they flower much more abundantly as a result. All epiphytes can be grafted onto rooted cuttings of *Hylocereus undatus.* In the case of *Schlumbergera,* the fleshy side portions of the lower joint of the scion should be removed, as when taking a cutting. The resulting wedge should then be inserted into a cleft made in the stock in the upper part of the edge of a rib. Three scions may thus be grafted onto *Hylocereus,* creating a more pleasing effect than if only one scion is grafted. The secret of getting a graft to "take" successfully lies in accurate cutting: the wedge-shaped base of the scion must fit the cleft in the stock snugly, and it should be possible to push it really far in without forcing it. The scions can be held in place by a very fine spine from another cactus, which is then removed after eight to ten days. This should be enough time for the wound to heal if the plant is kept at about 77° F. (25° C.) in a very dry atmosphere. Needles and pins should not be used, since they might rust. Most of the grafted specimens of globular and cylindrical species have been grafted onto rooted cuttings of *Hylocereus undatus.* However, *Cereus, Espostoa, Echinocactus, Lobivia* and *Melocactus* prefer *Trichocereus*—particularly *Trichocereus spachianus*—as a stock.

Whatever stock is used, it is essential that the two surfaces to be joined together be of equal diameter. Perfectly smooth, horizontal cuts should be made on both the stock and the scion. The two are then gently pressed together and rubbed against each other to prevent any air bubbles from being trapped between them. They are then held in place by an elastic band stretched under the flowerpot and over the top of the scion, which should preferably be protected by a piece of cloth. One or two other elastic bands are arranged crisscross, depending on the diameter of the scion. String can be used, of course, but it is very difficult to gauge the correct pressure when tying the knot. The elastic bands should keep the two stems in close contact but should not be too tight. The wound will take a month to heal if the plant is held at an optimum temperature in a dry atmosphere. It should be kept entirely in the shade, watered only sparingly, and never sprayed, since moisture might cause the wound to rot.

OUTDOOR CULTIVATION, AND THE GREAT CACTUS COL-
LECTIONS

Wherever the climate is mild enough and the temperature
rarely falls below freezing, many species of cactus can be successfully grown out of doors. In the United States, the great
Southwest is obviously ideal growing country. But plants
should also do well in Climate Zones 10, 9, and the warmer
parts of 8 in other areas. In Europe the shores of the Mediterranean—in Greece, southern Italy, the Italian and French Ri-
vieras, southern and southeastern Spain—are particularly
favored localities. Some species of *Opuntia* (*Opuntia phae-
cantha, Opuntia rafinesquei* and others) are hardy in continen-
tal Europe, and some types of cactus native to the Chilean and
Peruvian Andes are able to survive in the relatively mild climate
of southern England, provided they are well sheltered from
cold winds and are kept dry during the winter.
Besides a suitable climate, the chief requirement for growing
cacti outdoors is that they be planted in perfectly drained soil.
A rugged, rocky terrain is usually preferable. However, steep
slopes should be leveled off into narrow terraces; otherwise
heavy rains, falling vertically, may wash away the soil and un-
cover the base of the plants, leaving their necks trapped in
pockets of damp.
Shelters, whether natural or artificial, should be positioned so

that they protect the plants from cold prevailing winds, whether from the north, northeast or northwest. Winter winds that bring heavy rainfall should be especially guarded against, since this is the time that cacti must be kept dry. Rainfall is often lighter in coastal regions than it is inland, which is one reason why succulents often thrive by the sea.

The most famous gardens and collections in which cacti are grown tend also to cultivate succulents from other families; but all give pride of place to the most spectacular species of the Cactaceae: large columnar *Cereus,* globes bristling with spines, many-branched *Opuntia,* bizarre creeping varieties, and small specimens that sometimes resemble ancient sculptures in miniature.

Good to excellent cactus collections are on display in the United States in the following places:

The Huntington Botanical Gardens in San Marino, California, has the world's largest collection of succulent plants grown outdoors. Covering an area of more than ten acres, it contains approximately 30,000 flourishing specimens. Cacti live alongside aloes, agaves and yuccas, and great masses of *Euphorbia* vie for attention with huge groups of *Echinocactus.*

The Boyce Thompson Arboretum at Superior, Arizona, is interested in all kinds of plants that are adapted to arid regions; but inevitably, a large part of its display is given over to the cactus family.

On previous page: *The Desert Botanical Garden at Phoenix, Arizona.*
Below: *Although such phenomena are rare, in its natural state even* Carnegiea gigantea *sometimes displays fasciation. Perhaps because such fasciation is often only partial, the effect is exceptionally spectacular. In the case of this specimen some kind of damage to its apex probably gave rise to such unusual growth forms.*

This is also true of the Desert Botanical Garden at Tucson, Arizona. One of the particularly interesting things about this garden is the Home Demonstration Center run by *Sunset* magazine. Here you can get a better idea of how cacti are grown and can be used in the home garden.

Another small but fine collection of cacti is to be found in the Phoenix (Arizona) Botanic Gardens run by the city. And an outstanding natural exhibit called the Cholla Cactus Garden is a feature of Joshua Tree National Monument, north of Interstate 10 in California.

Cactus collections in Europe are in some ways superior to those in the United States. This is not surprising when one considers that in Europe the cacti are something of a novelty, whereas they are well known in the Americas.

On the Italian Riviera close to the French border are the La Mortola gardens, which feature, among other things, some eighty species of *Opuntia*. About 30 miles (50 km.) to the west is the Jardin Exotique, which is given over entirely to succulent plants dominated by spectacular columnar and globular cacti. The latter are of such exceptional size that even though the whole area is sheltered by a rugged terrain, they are supported by rings to keep them from blowing over or snapping in the wind.

Not far away at St. Jean–Cap Ferrat is the magnificent park known as Les Cèdres. Here, in addition to the large plants growing in the open, is a whole series of greenhouses contain-

A particularly attractive corner of the Jardin Exotique of Monte Carlo, with flowering aloes growing alongside columnar cacti. Because of its exceptionally sheltered position, this famous garden provides one of the best environments in Europe for the growing of succulents.

ing what is perhaps one of the biggest collections of succulents in the world. This is constantly being augmented by the addition of rare specimens.

Finally at Balnes, on the Spanish coast north of Barcelona, is F. Rivière de Caralt's beautiful outdoor collection of *Opuntia*.

DISEASES AND PARASITES

The worst enemies of cacti are the fungal diseases that cause the stems and roots to decay in conditions of excessive humidity. Various types of mold and rot are likely to attack any part of the plant. If the roots are affected, there is very little one can do, since the disease has often attacked the inside of the stem first. On the other hand, if rot sets in around the neck of any other external part of the plant, there are steps—often successful—that can be taken to save the plant. First, it should be removed from its pot, washed and cleaned carefully with absorbent tissues to remove all decomposed material. All dead roots, as well as any part of the neck that is flaccid and obviously diseased, should be cut off with a sharp knife or scissors. All parts of the plant that were cut or scraped during this treatment should be dusted with sulfur or, preferably, an antifungal powder to promote healing. Finally, the plant is repotted in pure sand, like a cutting, and kept dry at a temperature of at least 64–70° F. (18–21° C.).

Since prevention is always better than cure, care should be

taken to limit the amount of water given to the bare minimum, particularly in damp weather, and to move plants to a warmer spot during very cold weather or when they have been soaked by rain. It should be remembered that cacti, like all succulents, have an almost incredible capacity for recovery after long periods of drought; roots that seem withered and stems that are wrinkled from excessive water loss will start to grow again and will regain their plumpness after being watered a few times and placed in reasonably warm surroundings.

Fortunately there are few insect parasites which prey upon cacti. Chief among them are scale insects, which could be called the cactus's specific parasite; they are likely to appear at any moment on any part of the plant. Scale insects belong to the enormous superfamily *Coccoidea*. Some attack a single species, while others show no such marked preference. *Opuntia dillenii,* for example, is prey to *Cactoblastics cactorum* to such an extent that for once a parasite has proved itself useful: this cactus, introduced to southern Madagascar, had become so intrusive that the islanders had despaired of ever getting rid of it, but this was achieved thanks to the insect.

In contrast, one type of scale insect, *Dactylopius coccus,* has been bred since pre-Columbian times on various species of *Opuntia*—notably that with the apposite name *Nopalea coccinellifera*—for the red coloring produced in quantity by the glands of the females before they lay their eggs. About 60,000 insects are needed to produce 1 lb. (1/2 kg.) of red dye. When the Spaniards conquered Mexico, they found the breeding of these insects already firmly established, but failed to understand how the cochineal was produced. They supposed that it was of vegetable origin, until in 1703 it was established with the aid of a microscope that it was produced by insects. From Mexico the extraction of cochineal spread to Algeria, South Africa and India and even to southern Spain and the Canary Islands, where it constituted one of the chief economic resources for a long time, right up until the advent of synthetic coloring. As soon as any type of scale insect appears on a cultivated cactus it is wise to paint the plant (using a soft brush that will not damage the delicate spines) with a solution of rubbing alcohol and water permeated with nicotine (a little tobacco wrapped in gauze so that it does not have to be filtered out should be left to soak in the solution). The alcohol will dissolve the waxy covering protecting the insect eggs, and the nicotine will kill the larvae. In more serious cases of infestation, the plant is syringed with white oil after the flowerpot is laid on its side to prevent the oil from reaching the roots.

In nurseries and large plantations the soil may become infested with nematodes. If this happens, dig up the plants, cut off their roots, and replant them in good soil. Disinfect the infested soil and burn the cut-off roots. The same treatment is used for cacti grown in pots.

Although Opuntia *cacti are very strong in other respects, they easily fall prey to various species of scale insect—so much so that they were bred as host to* Dactylopius coccus, *the scale insect that produces cochineal. Other species, however, may also appear on* Cereus *and on a few of the globular cacti.*

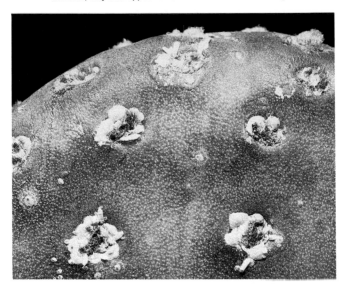

CLASSIFICATION OF THE CACTACEAE FAMILY

TRIBE *Pereskieae*
Plants with woody stems, erect or sarmentose; leaves persistent or semideciduous, sometimes rather fleshy. Areoles spiny and more or less woolly at the leaf axils. Flowers pendulous, solitary or in clusters; fruit fleshy. Two genera only: *Pereskia* and *Maihuenia.*

TRIBE *Opuntieae*
Usually very fleshy, branched plants, with consecutive branches that may be either rounded or flattened, studded with areoles, with or without spines but always bearing glochids. Leaves flat or cylindrical and generally caducous apart from a few exceptions with more or less persistent leaves. Spines usually straight and slender, sometimes hooked or with a protective sheath. Flowers, borne singly on the areoles, are sessile; the corolla is formed from numerous sepals and colored petals. The fruit is a berry with numerous seeds and is often edible.
——————— Principal genus: *Opuntia.* Largest of the family, comprising more than 300 species. Since its morphology differs widely according to the different environments in which the members of the genus grow, a division into subgenera is necessary. The subgenera are divided in turn into series. There is

some disagreement among authorities regarding the number of subgenera. According to some there are six, but since two are often difficult to distinguish from two others, they may be reduced to four:

——————— *Subgenus Consolea:* Initially considered a separate genus, the plants, which grow to a height of 33 ft. (10 m.), are all native to the West Indies. The main stem is cylindrical. The branches, consisting of more or less oval segments, grow from lateral areoles, giving the plant, particularly when it is young, the appearance of a many-armed cross. Flowers have a nectary at the base of the pistil.

——————— *Subgenus Opuntia:* A huge subgenus comprising from seventeen to twenty-nine series, depending on the authority. We shall include in it *Brasiliopuntia,* consisting of a few South American species, which has now been reestablished as a separate genus. Plants may be tall and erect, prostrate or semiprostrate. All have segments that are more or less flat, round, oval or elongated, and covered all over with areoles. Spines either completely absent, or one to four on each areole; glochids generally very numerous and dense. Main stem when present becomes cylindrical as the plant ages.

———————*Subgenus Cylindropuntia:* Segments (joints) rounded, cylindrical or elongated; main stem tall and erect or short and prostrate.

——————— *Subgenus Tephrocactus:* First established as a genus by Lemaire; its name is derived from the Greek *tephra,* meaning ashes, because the plant is usually grayish in color. It is a subgenus whose members are all of South American origin. Main stem fairly conspicuous, with lateral branches consisting of one or more segments generally grouped together, globular or slightly cylindrical. We include the subgenus *Clavatopuntia* Fric from North America, which has club-shaped segments (i.e., wider at the apex), because many species assume cylindrical shapes, so that, apart from a few small botanical details, it is difficult to distinguish one from another.

TRIBE *Cacteae*

Since this is the largest of the tribes, comprising three-quarters of the family's species, it has been divided into subtribes. The plants may be more or less fleshy, and either terrestrial or epiphytic; the stem may be simple or branched, the branches consisting of one or more segments that are globular, cylindrical or flattened, or have side projections that give the appearance of leaves. Most of the plants have more or less prominent ribs or tubercles. Leaves are totally absent, replaced by scales on the tube of the perianth, which is well defined and contains the ovary. Apart from the epiphytes and one or two other weakly armed genera, the plants of this tribe usually have spines varying greatly in size, structure and color, but they are never enclosed in a sheath, and the areoles never have glochids. The flowers, sessile and varying in color and size, may

bloom by day or by night and may grow in different positions, although they are almost always solitary. The fruit is usually a fleshy berry containing many small seeds.

Subtribe Cereinae
Mostly erect, sometimes semiprostrate, ramifying plants with a gigantic columnar main stem, either solitary or tillering from the base. The branches consist of many segments. They, too, are ramified, and most of their segments have pronounced ribs with very spiny areoles. The white or colored flowers may be diurnal or nocturnal, and are often strongly scented, budding almost horizontally from the upper part of the stem. The flower-bearing areoles are often different from the others. The fruit is a smooth or spiny, fleshy berry, and in some cases is edible.
Principal genera: *Cereus, Cephalocereus, Oreocereus, Pachycereus, Heliocereus, Trichocereus, Cleistocactus, Espostoa.*

Subtribe Hylocereinae
The name comes from the Greek *yle*, meaning a wood or forest. These plants have sarmentose stems, are able to cling to a support by means of aerial roots and are epiphitic or semi-epiphitic in their natural state. They are native to wooded regions of central and equatorial America. The stems tend to be slender and are made up of numerous segments from the base of which aerial roots grow. The stems are generally triangular or

winged, with small spines borne on the areoles that grow in depressions between the raised parts. Flowers are large, nocturnal and almost always white although occasionally pink, with reddish or greenish sepals. Some are so beautiful and sweet-scented as to have acquired the popular name "Queen (or Princess) of the Night." The tube of the perianth is scaly, and so is the large spiny or spineless fruit. There are nine genera in the subtribe.
Principal genera: *Hylocereus, Selenicereus, Aporocactus.*

Subtribe Echinocereinae
This and the following subtribe were both named after the porcupine (*echinos* in Greek), because their usually globular stems are exceedingly prickly. The plants are low-growing, with globular, oval or elongated stems; they are terrestrial, and normally have one main stem that puts forth shoots from its base in sufficient numbers to form a large cluster. The stems have raised ribs, or ribs consisting of tubercles arranged vertically, bearing the areoles, which are more or less woolly and have spines. The colorful flowers are always solitary, and usually spring from the lateral areoles. The fruit is fleshy, usually dehiscent, with black seeds. The subtribe comprises seven genera, all South American except *Echinocereus.*
Principal genera: *Echinocereus, Echinopsis, Lobivia.*

59

Opposite, above: *The small flowers that grow from the youngest areoles of* Echinocactus *around the center of the plant.*
Below: Melocactus *flowers are small, often remaining half hidden among the bristles of the raised cephalium, which is the real ornamentation of the plant.*

Subtribe Echinocactinae

These plants have a globular or short cylindrical stem that is often solitary, sometimes branched, and always has pronounced ribs that are formed, as the plant ages, from the fusion of the tubercles, which are separate when it is young. The stem sometimes grows to a considerable size, and older plants may produce lateral shoot-like segments—particularly if the main stem is damaged. The flowers are small and not very showy; they are always solitary, and spring from new areoles either at the apex or in the center of the stem. The fruit is fleshy, sometimes edible, and almost always dehiscent. There are about thirty-six genera, which include some of the strangest and least cultivated cacti. These are of unusual shape, difficult to propagate, and extremely slow-growing.

Principal genera: *Echinocactus, Ferocactus, Gymnocalycium, Neoporteria, Parodia, Stenocactus, Echinofossulocactus.*

Subtribe Cactanae

The stem of these plants is globular or a swollen cylinder. It is solitary, but may branch through basal shoots; the strong ribs are mostly made up of vertical rows, which have fused into almost continuous lines broken only by slight protuberances bearing the always spiny areoles. The plants develop a very distinct cephalium, which is very woolly and sometimes bristly, upon which small flowers appear.

There are only two genera, *Melocactus* and *Discocactus,* both of which are found in cultivated form. The first-named is a very attractive genus correctly called *Melocactus.* (It was at one time simply *Cactus.*) The genus comprises about thirty species, all native to the tropical regions of Central and South America and the West Indies.

Subtribe Cactinae

From the grower's point of view, this is the most important subdivision of the Cacteae tribe, because it includes the *Mammillaria.* Although this genus comprises fewer species than *Opuntia,* there is such a wealth of varieties and hybrids as to make identification sometimes almost impossible.

All these plants are low-growing, with a globular stem that can become slightly cylindrical in adult plants, and rows of tubercles or raised parts arranged in spirals. Spines grow from the apex of the areoles, which continue along the upper side of the tubercle where the flowers grow. Alternatively, the areoles divide, giving rise to a woolly formation at the base of the tubercle that produces the flower. The flowers are always solitary and very variable in size; they never actually appear at the same time as the spines. The fruit is a green or red indehiscent berry.

Principal genera: *Mammillaria, Coryphantha, Thelocactus, Escobaria.*

Most Mammillaria *cacti have small but numerous flowers which appear at the axil of existing tubercles, forming a crown around the apex of the stem.*

Subtribe Epiphyllinae

The last two subtribes cover a type of Cactaceae that is quite different from those described above. Native to tropical forests, they are almost all epiphytes, although they are also able to grow on the ground if the soil is rich in humus and well drained. In their natural state, some plants grow in cracks in rocks, but none is able to survive in strong sunlight, since they flourish in the shade in a hot, damp atmosphere.

The plants are made up of many consecutive branched segments, each with a fine, rigid central nerve, which is often raised, with fleshy side projections. This gives the segment a flat, leaflike appearance (but the basal segments are cylindrical). From the branches, aerial roots often sprout; they serve only to absorb moisture from the atmosphere, and are very rarely able to provide support or to take root. The colorful flowers are sometimes zygomorphic (irregular)——in some cases conspicuously so, in other cases only to a slight degree. The segments may be joined together at the base by a protuberance on which the flowers appear at different levels. They are particularly large and beautiful in *Epiphyllum, Phyllocactus, Zygocactus, Schlumbergera.*

Subtribe Rhipsalidinae

The eight genera belonging to this subtribe are, at first sight, difficult to recognize as members of the Cactaceae. They are

The flowers of the Rhipsalidinae *subtribe are regular; those of* Rhipsalidopsis *are pink or red, and are particularly large for the subtribe. They appear in springtime.*

all epiphytes, growing in the trees of tropical forests in the small quantities of humus that accumulate at the base of branches or in hollows in the trunks. They absorb moisture from the air through numerous hairlike aerial roots that quickly wither if the atmosphere becomes dry. The highly branched stems bear minute, spineless areoles from which the segments divide. The segments are either alternate or whorled, and may be cylindrical, angular or flat. The flowers are small and generally solitary, lasting for several days and remaining open at night. The fruit lasts for some time and consists of small juicy berries, white, red or violet in color, and often translucent or pearly.

Principal genera: *Rhipsalis, Hatiora, Lepismium.*

1 ACANTHOCALYCIUM KLIMPELIANUM
(Weidl. and Werdermann) Backeberg
Tribe Cacteae — subtribe Echinocereinae

Etymology The name comes from the Greek *akantha*, spine, and *calyx*, chalice: scales on the tube and ovary are spiny.

Place of Origin The Sierras de Córdoba in central Argentina, near the town of Córdoba.

Description This species was in *Lobivia*, then *Echinopsis*, before Backeberg moved it to its present genus. Its stem is globular, depressed or flattened at the apex, dark green and about 4 in. (10 cm.) in diameter. Adult plants have about nineteen straight or tuberculate ribs. Areoles are elliptical and covered with a yellowish-brown felt; later they become almost glabrous. Six to eight radial spines, sometimes more, grow from the areoles. They are unequal, straight or slightly curved, thick, conical and rigid. There are usually two or three central spines, though sometimes only one. The lowest spine is longer, sometimes more than 1 ½ in. (4 cm.), and points downward. They are all brown at first, then become light brown and eventually grayish. Flowers are 1 ¼ to 1 ½ in. (3 to 4 cm.) long. The base of the tube has a small woolly ring peculiar to the genus as a whole. Perianth segments are white.

Cultivation The plant needs strong sunlight, but will not tolerate intense cold. It is propagated by seed or cuttings.

---

2 ACANTHOCALYCIUM THIONANTHUM
(Spegazzini) Backeberg
Tribe Cacteae — subtribe Echinocereinae

Place of Origin The mountain slopes near Cachi in the province of Salta in northwestern Argentina.

Description This spherical plant in time becomes slightly cylindrical, branching through basal shoots and growing to a height of 4¾ in. (12 cm.) or more, and a diameter of 2⅓ to 4 in. (6 to 10 cm.). There are about 14 ribs. The areoles appear at the apex of tubercles and at first are covered with yellowish-brown felt.

The lower part of the areole is elongated while the upper part curves around the sides of the rib, more or less in the shape of a small shield. As the tubercles widen in the course of growth, the areoles become elliptical and almost glabrous. There may be ten radial spines and one to four central spines; they are all more or less of the same length—about 3/5 in. (1.5 cm.)—and are brown at first, becoming gray or whitish-yellow. The flowers are about 2 in. (5 cm.) long, and have a very hairy tube, and the segments of the perianth are sulfur- or lemon-yellow. The species appears to have variants, since recently some very similar, unnamed plants with a different number of spines and some radial spines intersecting have been found.

Cultivation Preferably propagated by cuttings.

3 APOROCACTUS FLAGELLIFORMIS (Linnaeus) Lemaire.

Tribe Cacteae — subtribe Hylocereinae
Common name: Rat-tail cactus

Etymology The name derives from the Greek word *aporos*, meaning impenetrable: the plant has a dense tangle of creeping stems. The genus was established by Lemaire in 1860; Linnaeus' *Cactus flagelliformis* is the type of the genus.

Place of Origin The state of Hidalgo in Mexico—though when introduced into Europe at the end of the sixteenth century it was thought to be South American. Described by Sloane in 1696 as *Cereus minima serpens americana*.

Description This extremely popular flowering plant has cylindrical decumbent or creeping stems, up to 6½ ft. (2 m.) long, though only 3/4 in. (2 cm.) in diameter. There are 10 to 14 ribs. They are not very pronounced and only very slightly tuberculate, with areoles placed close together. The 10 to 15 radial spines are slender, 1/4 in. (5 mm.) long, reddish when young and yellowish or brown later on. The three to four central spines are brown with yellow tips. The flowers, which bloom diurnally, appear along the whole length of the stem and are about 3 in. (7 to 8 cm.) long; they persist for four to six days or more, are light crimson in color, and blossom in late spring.

Cultivation This is an epiphytic plant that grows well in hanging pots, from which it droops. It needs a rest period, strong sunshine and plentiful watering in summer. It is propagated by cuttings during the summer months.

4 AREQUIPA RETTIGII (Quehl) Oehme

variety **ERECTOCYLINDRICA** (Rauh and Backeberg) Krainz
Tribe Cacteae — subtribe Echinocactinae

Etymology This plant was named after Arequipa in southern Peru, because it was found in the vicinity of the town.

Place of Origin Peru.

Description This species initially has an almost spherical stem that becomes cylindrical and nearly prostrate; it has 10 to 20 short, close-set ribs with areoles 1/4 in. (5 mm.) apart. These are gray and felted on the younger parts. The 20 to 30 slender, transparent radial spines are 2/5 in. (1 cm.) long. Central spines, as many as ten on older plants, are stronger and longer, reaching up to 1¼ in. (3 cm.) long. The scarlet, hairy flowers arising near the stem apex are 2½ in. (6 cm.) or more long and have a long, slender tube; their irregular perianth is slightly oblique. *Erectocylindrica* was thought by Backeberg to be a separate species, but it's now considered a variety; it has many affinities with other forms of the species. Young plants are candle-shaped and grow to 20 in. (50 cm.). The stem has 15 to 17 ribs, and the ¼ in. (5 mm.) areoles are yellowish-gray at first. The 12 to 14 slender subulate radial spines are white but become gray. The 1½ in. (4 cm.) long central spines are light-colored with dark tips. Red flowers are 2¾ in. (7 cm.) long.

Cultivation Sandy, stony soil. Propagation is by cuttings.

5 ARIOCARPUS FURFURACEUS (Watson) Thompson
Tribe Cacteae — subtribe Echinocactinae

Etymology The name derives from *Sorbus aria,* the white-beam tree, and *karpos,* fruit; this cactus has fruit similar to the whitebeam's. The genus was created by Scheidweiler in 1838, replaced by Lemaire's *Anhalonium* and reestablished by Schumann in 1898.

Place of Origin The state of Coahuila in northern Mexico.

Description Like all other members of the genus, this species has a large taproot and a stem almost invisible because ribs have been replaced by long deltoid tubercles arranged spirally to form a flattened rosette. Tubercles are usually light gray, sometimes a very glaucous light green. They're compressed and have sharp points; the upper surface is horny with minute whitish or rust-colored scales. At the apex of every tubercle is a small felted areole that becomes almost glabrous later. White wool grows at the base of the tubercles and is most conspicuous near the plant's apex. In natural surroundings the plant is often sunk into the ground; its morphology is a camouflage. Flowers spring from the axil of the tubercles near the center of the plant, and 1½ to 2 in. (4 to 5 cm.) across; the white or pink segments of the perianth are large.

Cultivation This is a rare cactus in cultivation, since propagation is by seed and growth is extremely slow.

6 ARIOCARPUS KOTSCHOUBEYANUS (Lemaire) Schumann
Tribe Cacteae — subtribe Echinocactinae

Place of Origin The states of Zacatecas, Querétaro, Nuevo León and San Luis Potosí in central and north-central Mexico.

Description The German botanist Wilhelm Karwinsky von Karvin collected the first specimen of this plant and sent it to Europe in 1840. It is recorded that he paid $200 for it. The root is very thick and fleshy, cylindrical, and far longer than the stem, which is only 2 in. (5 cm.) high. In its natural habitat the plant is more than half buried, its apical part being level with the ground. The stem is made up of triangular grayish-green tubercles that are felted at the base. A very woolly median groove runs across the flat top of the tubercles. These are arranged spirally, overlapping closely, and measure less than 2/5 in. (1 cm.) in thickness at the base. They are completely rigid, with a horny epidermis. The flowers spring from the center of the axil of the youngest tubercles, are surrounded by a tuft of hair and measure about 1¼ in. (3 cm.) in diameter. The perianth has a few brownish external segments while the inner ones are pink or crimson. Old plants may branch.

Cultivation Of very slow growth, this plant needs a great deal of sunshine and ample space for its roots. It will tolerate a certain amount of cold if it is kept dry, though mild heat is preferred. It may be propagated from the shoots of old plants.

7 ARIOCARPUS TRIGONUS (Weber) Schumann
Tribe Cacteae — subtribe Echinocactinae

Place of Origin   Nuevo León state in northeast Mexico.

Description   The novice might not recognize this small plant as a member of the Cactaceae. Its apex, rising from a long tap-root that resembles a large carrot (typical of the genus), is completely covered by tubercles shaped like acute triangles. The inner surface of these is flattened; the outer is keeled. They are gray-green or olive-green, erect and numerous; have horny, angular edges; measure from 1⅓ to 2 in. (3.5 to 5 cm.) in length and 4/5 in. (2 cm.) wide at the base. An areole is situated near the apex. The base of the tubercles is densely woolly, and near the center gives rise to often numerous yellow flowers measuring about 2 in. (5 cm.) in diameter. The diameter of the whole plant, excluding the flowers, is 4 in. (10 cm.) or more—especially in the variety *elongatus*, which has longer tubercles. The fruit is a smooth, globular berry covered with long down; its seeds are preserved for a long time after the berry has dried up because they're protected by the down.

Cultivation   All *Ariocarpus* are rare in cultivation and are therefore much sought after by collectors. Their rarity is mainly because they are very difficult to propagate by means of cuttings, even when they produce any, and are among the slowest-growing of all cacti. Since they're susceptible to rot, they should be watered very seldom and grown in porous soil.

8 ARROJADOA AUREISPINA Buining and Bred.
Tribe Cacteae — subtribe Cereinae

Etymology   This plant was named in honor of Dr. Miguel Arrojado, who explored the arid and semiarid regions of Brazil. The genus *Arrojadoa* was established by Britton and Rose, but for some time was considered part of *Cephalocereus*. Following the discovery of new species, however, it was reinstated as a genus, and this status is now generally accepted.

Place of Origin   The state of Bahia in Brazil.

Description   This species, discovered by Horst and Buining in 1966, belongs to a candle-shaped, slender and often creeping genus of cactus. Its stem may reach a length of over 3 ft. (1 m.) and a diameter of about 2 in. (5 cm.), and it may branch from the base. The blunt ribs are relatively far apart, and the areoles bear a dozen short, slender radial spines, while the eight or nine central spines are 2/5 in. (1 cm.) or more in length. The stem bears a cephalium of bristles from which the pink flowers emerge, and which gives rise to new growth. This produces a new cephalium during the following season. When they wither, the flowers remain attached to the fruit, which is light red and about the size of a cherry.

Cultivation   These plants prosper in semishade. They may be propagated by cuttings in warm surroundings.

9 ARROJADOA RHODANTHA (Gürke) Britton and Rose
Tribe Cacteae — subtribe Cereinae

Place of Origin Eastern Brazil; near São Raimundo Nonato in the state of Piauí.

Description This plant has a candle-shaped stem that may reach a length of 3 to 6½ ft. (1 to 2 m.), and a diameter of 3/4 to 2 in. (2 to 5 cm.). It is erect at first, but becomes prostrate or sarmentose. It usually branches from the base, though it sometimes produces short cylindrical segments. The 10 to 12 ribs tend to be flat, with downy, brownish areoles about 1/2 in. (1 cm.) apart. The 20 to 50 needlelike radial spines are brown, becoming whitish with age. The five or six central spines differ only slightly in that they are stronger, longer and dark brown at first. A cephalium grows at the apex of both the stem and the branches. This consists of a brownish woolly tuft about 1/2 in. (1 to 2 cm.) long and several reddish-brown bristles up to 1¼ in. (3 cm.) long. The reddish-violet flowers are almost tubular, about 1¼ to 1½ in. (3 to 4 cm.) long. They grow singly on the upper areoles of the stem, but since they often all come out at once, they appear to grow in a group. The fruit is small, round or oblong, and purple.

Cultivation Like all the other species of this genus, these cacti need semishade and a soil that is rich in humus, yet sandy and gravelly. They are propagated by cuttings.

10 ASTROPHYTUM ASTERIAS (Zuccarini) Lemaire
Tribe Cacteae — subtribe Echinocactinae
Common name: Sea-urchin cactus

Etymology The name comes from Greek words *astron* (star) and *phyton* (plant): the ribs of most species are star-shaped.

Place of Origin The Rio Grande Valley in Texas, and the states of Tamaulipas and Nuevo León in Mexico.

Description This species' stem is spherical, though much flattened. It may grow to 4 in. (10 cm.) in diameter and half as high, though when cultivated it's usually smaller. The plant is completely spineless and gray-green. It has eight almost flat ribs divided by deep, narrow grooves. Areoles are large, prominent, round, white and felty. They grow like points of a star about 1/5 in. (5 mm.) apart along the center of the ribs. The areoles are surrounded by dots, curving downward, formed by minute white scales. The dots grow denser toward the edges of the ribs and apex. Apical flowers are 1¼ in. (3 cm.) long, with a diameter of 2½ in. (6.5 cm.); segments are yellow with red centers. The plant is sometimes crossed with *Astrophytum myriostigma*. The hybrid has intermediate characteristics and an epidermis covered by silvery scales.

Cultivation The plant can be propagated only by seed: it doesn't offset and cuttings can't be taken because of its shape. It's very slow-growing, thus it's the rarest species of the genus. It needs high temperature in winter, strong sun in summer.

11 ASTROPHYTUM CAPRICORNE (Dietrich) Britton and Rose
Tribe Cacteae — subtribe Echinocactinae

Place of Origin Neighborhood of La Rinconada in Nuevo León, northern Mexico, very near the border with New Mexico.
Description The stem, globular at first, elongates to become as tall as 8 in. (20 cm.). Its green epidermis is more or less covered by minuscule white scales, giving some plants a grayish look. It has eight or nine very prominent sharp ribs, with large areoles growing ¾ to 1¼ in. (1.5 to 3 cm.) apart. Covered in brownish down, each areole has up to ten irregular spines about 2¾ in. (7 cm.) long. They are brown or black, curved and very flexible, flat and not very sharp. As the plant grows older, some may drop off, leaving the basal part inermous. Flowers grow from areoles at or near the apex, and the reddish color of the extension changes gradually to the yellow of the interior with red or orange spots at the base. The flowers last for three or four days; plants bloom several times during the summer. The fruit is shaped like an olive and is reddish, woolly and slightly spiny, as are all fruit of this species. There are three varieties: *crassispinum*, which is larger with stronger, dark gray spines; *niveum*, whose stem is completely covered with white scales; and *minus*, which is smaller and spiny.
Cultivation Propagated by seed. The plant needs full sun and winter rest period at a temperature just above freezing.

12 ASTROPHYTUM MYRIOSTIGMA Lemaire
Tribe Cacteae — subtribe Echinocactinae

Place of Origin The plateau of north-central Mexico.
Description This genus, established by Lemaire in 1839, comprises only a few species that for a long time were known as *Echinocactus*. *A. myriostigma* is one of the most widely cultivated and has many varieties. It can have between three and eight sharp, prominent ribs; it usually has five. The typical species has a globular stem that is depressed at the apex and cylindrical when adult. It is green, but is densely covered with tiny white scales that give it a whitish-gray appearance. Areoles grow very close to each other on the rib, but in some varieties they are very small and farther apart; they are completely spineless and generally covered with brownish woolly hairs. The yellow flowers are about 2½ in. (6 cm.) in diameter. The variety *quadricostatum* has only four ribs, and another variety, at one time considered a subspecies, called *Astrophytum myriostigma potosinum*, native to San Luis Potosí, has a gray-green or completely green stem with no scales. It is known horticulturally as *Astrophytum myriostigma nudum*.
Cultivation Since the plant does not produce shoots, propagation should be by seed, but if the top part of the old plant is removed, new shoots will appear from the cut. The plant tolerates cold as long as it is not persistent; it requires strong sunshine and very well-drained soil.

13 ASTROPHYTUM ORNATUM (de Candolle) Weber ex Britton and Rose
Tribe Cacteae — subtribe Echinocactinae

Place of Origin The states of Hidalgo and Querétaro on the Mexican central plateau.

Description This is the tallest species of the genus: the plants, which are spherical to start with, become columnar with age, and in their natural surroundings the oldest among them may reach a height of 6½ ft. (2 m.) and a diameter of 1 ft. (30 cm.), though in cultivation they are unlikely to grow to a greater height than 10 to 12 in. (25 to 30 cm.), even these measurements suggesting a plant of exceptional size. Backeberg tells of a plant that would seem to have been nearly 10 ft. (3 m.) high. The stem has eight sharp-pointed ribs, straight or slightly spiral, and more or less covered with silvery scales arranged in curving bands. The areoles, which are fairly far apart, have 5 to 11 spines that are straight and sharp, colored yellow or brown, and vary in length; the longest measure 1¼ in. (3 cm.). The flowers have a diameter of about 3 in. (8 cm.) and are pale yellow. The fruit is less fleshy than that of the other species, and splits open when ripe; generally, however, it contains only a few seeds. There is a variety called *glabrescens* that has a dark green epidermis showing very few scales or none at all. Conversely, there is another variety called *mirbelii* that has scales of such density as to cover the stem entirely, and golden yellow spines.

The lower photograph opposite shows an *Astrophytum* hybrid. A great deal of crossbreeding has been carried out between *Astrophytum asterias* and *Astrophytum myriostigma*, and the hybrids are then sometimes crossed with *Astrophytum ornatum*, the intention being to produce plants with a less uniform, more attractive distribution of tiny silvery scales and a taller stem. In addition, these hybrids grow faster and are capable of producing shoots after pollarding; the apical part may be used as a cutting. Such hybrids often turn out to be completely inermous. Their characteristics tend to be intermediate between those of the two original species.

Cultivation This species, like the others of the genus, is propagated by seed, but its growth is faster, and the plant is stronger and tougher. However, it needs soil that is porous and well drained, and it should be placed in a sunny position.

14 AUSTROCEPHALOCEREUS DYBOWSKII
(Gosselin) Backeberg
Tribe Cacteae — subtribe Cereinae

Etymology This is a species similar to *Cephalocereus,* which originates in the southern hemisphere: they're Brazilian.
Place of Origin The arid hills in the hinterland of the state of Bahia in northeastern Brazil.
Description Until a short time ago this species was classified as *Cephalocereus* and it is still known as such. It was described as early as 1908. Branching thickly from its base, the plant produces colonies of stems rising to a height of 13 ft. (4 m.). They have a diameter of about 3¼ in. (8 cm.), are all erect and are covered with a soft down up to 3¼ in. (8 cm.) long. Each stem may have 20 slender, not very prominent ribs, bearing close-set areoles. The numerous short radial spines are hidden by the hairs, while the two or three central spines, yellowish or brown in color, are more dense and abundant and appear whiter on the upper part of the stems, particularly along the side (normally that facing west) which bears the floriferous areoles. They also bear the cephalium, which in old plants can reach 2 ft. (60 cm.) down from the apex. The flowers are 1 ½ in. (4 cm.) long, white and campanulate, with segments inside the short perianth. The fruit is pink, spherical and smooth.
Cultivation This plant needs shelter in winter and strong sunlight in summer. It is easy to propagate by cuttings.

---

15 AZTEKIUM RITTERI (Boedecker) Boedecker
Tribe Cacteae — subtribe Echinocactinae

Etymology This genus, created by Boedeker in 1929, comprises one single species and is named after the Aztecs.
Place of Origin The state of Nuevo León in northeastern Mexico.
Description This small plant has a short taproot and a spherical, depressed stem measuring about 2 in. (5 cm.) in diameter and is grayish-green with a felted apex. Older plants branch from the base. It has 9 to11 rounded ribs, protruding about 2/5 in. (1 cm.) and characterized by more or less irregular horizontal corrugations. They bear close-set areoles covered in short white hairs with one to three weak spines about 1/8 in. (3 to 4 mm.) in length. Between the main ribs are much narrower, irregularly tuberculate subsidiary ribs. They start a little below the apex and increase in number toward the base. The horizontal corrugations form a fan shape and are reminiscent of the design of certain Aztec sculptures. This, rather than the plant's place of origin (which was not at the center of the Aztec empire), accounts for the name given to the plant. The apical flowers are about 2/5 in. (1 cm.) wide, and have white segments; the outer perianth parts have pink edges.
Cultivation Sandy soil and full sunshine; the plant will not tolerate cold. Grafted specimens remain green, and are less attractive.

16 BORZICACTUS HUMBOLDTII (Humboldt, Bonpland and Kunth) Britton and Rose
Tribe Cacteae — subtribe Cereinae

Etymology   In 1909 Vincenzo Riccobono named this genus after Antonio Borzí, founder of the botanical gardens at Messina and Palermo in Sicily.

Place of Origin   From southern Ecuador to northern Peru.

Description   This species is still sometimes called *Seticereus*, a genus no longer accepted. The plant is semiprostrate, ascending later, with a dark green stem about 28 in. (70 cm.) long and 1 ¼ to 2 in. (3 to 5 cm.) in diameter. The 10 to 12 ribs are more or less tuberculate, with transverse depressions between the small areoles, which are about 1/2 in. (1 to 1.5 cm.) apart and covered with yellowish down. There are numerous slender radial spines, and about six central spines that may be over 1/2 in. (1 cm.) long. All spines are chestnut-brown or sometimes reddish, and are rigid and straight. The spines on the cephalium are the same color but are more flexible, and grow along with straight or curly silky-looking whitish bristles. Flowers are pink to crimson and about 2¾ in. (7 cm.) long with a long scaly tube the same color that has short whitish hairs. The segments of the perianth are lanceolate.

Cultivation   Although adult plants flower very freely, this cactus is not often cultivated; it is more suitable for growing out of doors than in pots. Propagation is by cuttings or seed.

17 BORZICACTUS MADISONIORUM Hutchison
Tribe Cacteae — subtribe Cereinae

Place of Origin   Paul Hutchison discovered this plant in the Rio Maranon canyon in northern Peru, and classified it in 1963.

Description   The grayish-green stem is initially spherical, becoming more or less elongated. Very young plants have no ribs, but these gradually become apparent as the plant grows until there are 7 to 12, with slightly raised tubercles bearing the areoles. Spines are sometimes absent; otherwise there are from one to five, all markedly curved and brown on the young areoles, becoming whitish with age. The flowers have a long, slighty funnel-shaped tube bearing brownish hairs. They are 3 to 4 in. (8 to 10 cm.) long and are about 2 in. (5 cm.) in diameter. The segments of the perianth are red. The downy fruit is spherical, measuring 3/4 in. (2 cm.), and has glossy brown seeds. Backeberg placed this plant in his genus *Submatucana*, and in some collections it is still classified under this name.

Cultivation   Although it can grow perfectly well on its own roots, this plant is often grafted in order to speed up its development and flowering. Propagation is by seed.

18 BORZICACTUS SAMAIPATANUS Cárdenas
Tribe Cacteae — subtribe Cereinae

Place of Origin The Cochabamba cordillera in Bolivia, near Samaipata, south of Santa Cruz, at an altitude of 6,000 ft. (1,900 m.).

Description This recently discovered species led the Bolivian botanist Martin Cárdenas to create the genus *Bolivicereus*. It was then transferred to the genus that is now considered correct by Myron Kimnach, specialist in cacti at the Huntington Botanical Gardens. The stem is erect, branching from the base, and very slender—it sometimes reaches a height of nearly 5 ft. (1½ m.) with a diameter of only 1½ in. (4 cm.). It has 14 to 16 ribs, with brownish areoles growing at intervals of 1/4 in. (5 mm.) and alternating with those on adjacent ribs, thus creating an impression of both vertical and transverse depressions. Spines may vary in length from 1/6 in. (4 mm.) in the case of the slender radial spines to 1¼ in. (3 cm.) in the case of the strong, slanting central spines. They are yellowish with red tips when young and turn grayish later. The flowers are borne laterally and grow almost horizontally; their color varies from light crimson to dark purple. Their scaly tube is hairy, particularly at the base. The fruit is woolly and spherical. The variety known as *multiflorus* has fewer spines and numerous flowers.

Cultivation Propagation is by seed or by cuttings taken from the stem and placed on moist sand. The plant tolerates cold as long as it is kept dry.

---

19 BORZICACTUS SAMNENSIS Ritter
Tribe Cacteae — subtribe Cereinae

Place of Origin The western slopes of the western cordillera in Peru. The species was discovered near Samne in the small department of La Libertad.

Description The plant was described and classified by Ritter in 1964. It is of shrublike habit. The stem, only 2 to 2¾ in. (5 to 7 cm.) in diameter, may reach 20 ft. (6 m.) in height. It may be erect or prostrate. There are six to nine tuberculate ribs. The spines, which are more numerous on old stems, are yellowish or reddish-brown at first, later becoming whitish. There is one central spine reaching as much as 3¼ in. (8 cm.) in length, and sometimes one to three shorter spines as well. The flowers have a tube bearing black down, and their purplish-violet edge is about 1/2 in. (1 cm.) in diameter. The oval, yellowish fruit is about 1½ in. (3.5 cm.) long.

Cultivation This species is not really suitable for cultivation because young specimens are not very attractive and older specimens are cumbersome and untidy. The plant tolerates cold, but needs strong sunshine, a clearly defined rest period and particularly well-drained soil. Propagation is by cuttings.

20 BORZICACTUS SEPIUM (Humboldt, Bonpland and Kunth) Britton and Rose
Tribe Cacteae — subtribe Cereinae

Place of Origin Slopes of Andean valleys in Ecuador, from Riobamba to the foothills of the extinct volcano Chimborazo.
Description This species, described in 1823 by Humboldt, Bonpland and Kunth as *Cactus sepium,* is now thought to be the same as the plant propagated by seed at La Mortola which Riccobono named *Borzicactus ventimigliae;* the latter is now merely a synonym. The stem, initially prostrate and later erect, is nearly 5 ft. (1.4 m.) tall and 1½ in. (4 cm.) in diameter. It puts forth shoots from its base, but rarely branches higher up. V-shaped depressions in the 8 to 11 ribs subdivide the ribs into transversely alternating tubercles, each of which bears a slightly oval, felted areole. There are eight to ten slender, brownish, radial spines, 1/4 to 1/2 in. (1/2 to 1 cm.) in length. The central spines are longer, measuring more than 3/4 in. (2 cm.) but are not easily distinguishable; there is usually one, or occasionally two. The spines around the apex are reddish-brown. The flowers are borne laterally, bloom during the day and are 1½ in. (4 cm.) long. The tube is scaly and woolly at the axil of the scales. The outer segments of the perianth are red and the inner ones pink. Overall the flower is slightly irregular.
Cultivation The plant grows rapidly and flowers when young. It requires sunshine in summer. Propagation is by cuttings.

21 BROWNINGIA ALTISSIMA (Friedrich Ritter) Buxbaum
Tribe Cacteae — subtribe Cereinae

Etymology Britton and Rose named the plant after W. E. Browning, director of the British Institute in Santiago.
Place of Origin Along the Río Marañón, near Buenavista in the western cordillera of northern Peru.
Description The plant is arborescent, its thick trunk reaching a height of 16½ ft. (5 m.) in dry regions, doubling this height in more humid areas. Branches are erect and can branch in turn. The seven to eight ribs are broad at the base and have tubercles with raised edges. These are interspersed with wedge-shaped depressions where white, felted areoles appear on the younger parts; the felt later becomes brown and then grayish. The sides of the ribs on new branches retain fan-shaped glaucous stripes for some time. They develop as the plant grows, disappearing as the epidermis thickens. Areoles are initially spineless but later produce five to six flexible radial spines of about 1/2 in. (1 cm.). These grow into a more or less radial arrangement with a central spine that points downward. Flowers are 2 to 2½ in. (5 to 6 cm.) long, with a tube covered by large scales. Perianth segments are greenish-white. Flowers curve outward and are lightly scented.
Cultivation In cultivation this plant remains at its youthful stage permanently. Flowering is nocturnal, but unlikely to take place in cultivation. Propagation is by seed or cuttings.

22 **BROWNINGIA HERTLINGIANA** (Backeberg)
Buxbaum
Tribe Cacteae — subtribe Cereinae

Place of Origin The valley of the Rio Mantaro in Peru, between the western and eastern cordilleras northeast of Lima.
Description Since the plant's stem is bright blue Backeberg took this species as the type of his now-synonymous genus *Azureocereus*. The branching stem reaches a height of 26 ft. (8 m.) and a diameter of 12 in. (30 cm.). It has about 18 ribs, swollen around the areoles, becoming tuberculate later, with wedge-shaped depressions between the tubercles. Areoles on the new joints have about four radial spines and one to three longer central spines, which may reach a length of 3 in. (8 cm.). Spines are either yellow with brown tips or yellow at their base only. On older parts of the plant there may be up to 30 spines, all of the same length, and more flexible than those growing from the apical areoles. On the transitional parts of the plant, the number of spines is variable. The flowers, which bloom nocturnally, have a more or less curved tube, 2 in. (5 cm.) in diameter, which is purplish-brown and scaly. The segments of the perianth are white and slightly slanting.
Cultivation This species is rarely found in cultivation (the famous collections excepted), yet even the smaller specimens are attractive because of their unusual color. Propagation is by cuttings from joints. Seed is difficult to obtain.

23 **BROWNINGIA RIOSANIENSIS** (Backeberg)
Buxbaum
Tribe Cacteae — subtribe Cereinae

Place of Origin The Rio Sana valley (its eponym) in Peru, from the slopes of the western cordillera to the Pacific.
Description In its natural habitat the plant has a thick, branching trunk, up to 13 ft. (4 m.) high; in cultivation it's much smaller. Slender branches are 3¼ in. (8 cm.) in diameter and are bluish-green with about six tuberculate ribs. Tubercles, more noticeable on the younger parts, are not prominent; they are wide at the base, and divided by a transversal groove, a widened V-shape pointing towards the base. It has six converging protuberances at the apex which, though not conspicuous, give a prismatic shape to the tubercles. Areoles covered with white down grow at each tubercle's apex and have six to eight irregular spines; the radial ones are difficult to distinguish from the central spines. The thick conical spine at the top, which grows on the youngest part of the segment (actually the upper spine) is 2 in. (5 cm.) long, is yellowish with a crimson base and often has a black tip. It later turns whitish, like the other spines, which are either thick and long or, more often, slender and short. Flowers bloom nocturnally and have a scaly, hairy tube and white perianth segments.
Cultivation It's hard to find specimens. It does not tolerate cold. Propagation is by seed or perhaps by cuttings.

24 CARNEGIEA GIGANTEA (Engelmann) Britton and Rose
Tribe Cacteae — subtribe Cereinae
Common name: Saguaro, giant cactus

Etymology This species, named *Cereus giganteus* by Engelmann in 1848, was renamed by Britton and Rose in 1908 in honor of Andrew Carnegie, the industrialist and philanthropist.

Place of Origin Arizona, southeastern California and the state of Sonora in Mexico. The precise locality of the type of the species is the Gila Desert in Arizona, crossed by the Gila River. Near Tucson the Saguaro National Monument, comprising over 78,000 acres was set up in 1933 exclusively for the plant, whose flower is the state flower of Arizona.

Description This species, the only one of its genus, is one of the largest and slowest-growing cacti known. It sometimes reaches a height of 60 ft. (18 m.) and a diameter of 25 in. (65 cm.). A 16½ ft. (5 m.) plant weighs about 1500 lb. (750 kg.) because of the tremendous volume of water it contains (near the apex it is 98 percent water). Because the plant grows at a snail's pace, it may take a century to reach treelike proportions. The oldest specimens are thought to have lived for over two centuries. Because the saguaro is hardy to 25° F. (−4° C.) it survives farther north than any other big cacti.

The plant has 12 to 24 blunt ribs, with brown areoles growing about 3/4 in. (2 cm.) apart. There are 12 or more radially arranged spines, and three to six central spines measuring up to 2¾ in. (7 mm.). All the spines are brown, becoming grayish later. Near the apex the areoles are set close together and covered with brown felt. The flowers appear on the upper part of the stem and branches of adult specimens. They are white and about 4¾ in. (12 cm.) in both length and width, with a green, scaly tube and short, spreading petals. The fruit is red, inside and out, dehiscent, and edible. It was a staple item of diet for the Papago Indians, who also fermented the juice and used it in celebrating their new year, which is in late June.

The great stem of the saguaro is strengthened and held upright by a concealed cylinder of woody poles. The branches, which may not appear until a plant is 15 to 30 years old, are put forth from the main stem at a height of about 7 ft. (2 m.) aboveground. There are eight or more of these, and as they slowly grow they rather closely parallel the main stem and help to balance the plant against wind and earth movement. The branches in turn put out smaller branches. The sizable holes that are seen in the branches and trunk are made by nesting woodpeckers and flickers.

Cultivation Growth is so slow that two years after seed has been sown the plant will have reached a height of only 3¼ in. (8 cm.) and it takes 30 years for the plant to reach a height of 3 ft. (1 m.).

25 CASTELLANOSIA CAINEANA Cárdenas
Tribe Cacteae — subtribe Cereinae

Etymology   The Bolivian botanist Martin Cárdenas named this plant in honor of Alberto Castellanos, an Argentinian specialist in South American cacti.

Place of Origin   Eastern Bolivia, at an altitude of 2,300 ft. to 5,300 ft. (700 to 1600 m.)

Description   At present the genus comprises only this species. A large, erect, branched shrub, it grows to nearly 20 ft. (6 m.) tall and has very long branches that are grayish-green and more or less flexible. The main stem has nine rounded ribs up to 1½ in. (3.5 cm.) wide. Younger branches have more ribs with white, round, felted and slightly pitted areoles. There are 15 radial spines 2/5 to 1½ in. (1 to 4 cm.) long, and three or four central spines that may reach a length of 2¾ in. (7 cm.); they are all stiff, ranging from brown to gray in color. The young part of the branches where flowers appear have modified spines that are spinescent bristles, 2/5 to 1½ in. (1 to 4 cm.) long, growing from the areoles in tufts. They are straight, point upward and may be white, gray or brown. Flowers are 1¼ to 2 in. (3 to 5 cm.) long, purplish and bloom at night, although they open during the following day. The yellowish-green fruit is 1¼ in. (3 cm.) long and appears to be poisonous, which is extremely rare among members of the Cactaceae.

Cultivation   Not a very attractive plant, it is rarely cultivated. Propagation is by cuttings.

26 CEPHALOCEREUS MAXONII Rose
Tribe Cacteae — subtribe Cereinae

Etymology   The name comes from the Greek word *kephale* (head): the cephalium of this genus is large and woolly.

Place of Origin   Near El Rancho and Salamá in the mountains of central Guatemala.

Description   The species is named after William R. Maxon, who found the first specimens in about 1905. It is almost shrublike, growing to a height of nearly 10 ft. (3 m.). The main stem, similar to a short trunk, is pale green and glaucous, measures about 5 in. (12 cm.) in diameter, and produces branches that slant upward. It has six to eight ribs with sharp edges. Areoles are very hairy on the young parts of a plant, are rather small, and have about ten slender, radial spines, which are short and yellowish-brown, growing darker with age, and one central spine, which may reach a length of 1½ in. (4 cm.), though it is often shorter. The apex is hidden under a pseudo-cephalium consisting of a mass of long white hairs that spread downward along the ribs of the flower-bearing stems for about 12 in. (30 cm.) and are so dense that they conceal the spines. The reddish-purple flowers are 1½ in. (4 cm.) long. The fruit is spherical, slightly flattened, and 1½ in. (3.5 cm.) in diameter.

Cultivation   The plant requires heat in winter, strong sunshine, a porous, gravelly soil, and a fairly humid atmosphere. Propagation is by cuttings.

27 CEPHALOCEREUS PALMERI Rose
Tribe Cacteae — subtribe Cereinae

Place of Origin The coastal plain of Tamaulipas state in eastern Mexico, particularly between Matamoros and Tampico.

Description The stem is erect and columnar, 13 to 20 ft. (4 to 6 m.) high, with many branches. Segments have a diameter of 2 to 3 in. (5 to 8 cm.). New growth is glaucous and pruinose. It has seven to nine wide, prominent ribs, rounded at the edge, along which large, circular, woolly areoles grow. Areoles bear long, grayish-white hairs that are particularly dense at the apex and on the flowering parts. The thick down and the hairs, from 1½ to 2 in. (4 to 5 cm.) long, form a pseudocephalium that extends down the ribs from the apex in a tangled mass, concealing the spines and forming spherical swellings on the flower-bearing areoles. Each areole bears 8 to 12 slender radial spines 1/2 in. (1 cm.) long, and a single central spine that is much thicker and more than twice as long. All spines are yellow on young plants, brown on adults, and gray on the oldest parts. Funnel-shaped flowers have a hairy tube and are purplish-red, although there is a variety with pink flowers.

Cultivation Since plantlets raised from seed grow very slowly, have very little wool on their areoles, and are uncharacteristic of the species, propagation by cuttings is preferable. The plant needs heat during the winter and shade in very hot climates. Watering should be done in moderation.

28 CEPHALOCEREUS SENILIS (Haworth) Pfeiffer
Tribe Cacteae — subtribe Cereinae

Place of Origin The states of Hidalgo, Vera Cruz and Guanajuato in central Mexico.

Description The name and description of this species date from 1824, when Haworth described it as *Cactus senilis;* in 1828 de Candolle renamed it *Cereus senilis.* In its natural state its columnar stem may reach a height of 30 to 50 ft. (10 to 15 m.) and 16 in. (40 cm.) in diameter, but its slow growth makes it eminently suitable for cultivation as a pot plant. Very occasionally the pale green stem branches from the base, but it is more often solitary. Young plants have 10 to 15 ribs; specimens 3 ft. (1 m.) or more high have double this number. The areoles are set very close together, and have one to five yellowish spines and 20 to 30 white bristles that are as fine as hairs. As the plant grows, the lower part of the stem sheds bristles and becomes bare, apart from the spines, while the upper part is thickly covered with white hairs. Plants about to flower develop a very hairy swelling to one side of the apex. This pseudocephalium bears night-blooming flowers with cream-colored inner petals and reddish outer petals. The fruit is red with yellowish hairs.

Cultivation Adult plants tolerate cold well. Propagation by seed produces specimens 4 in. (10 cm.) high after about four years.

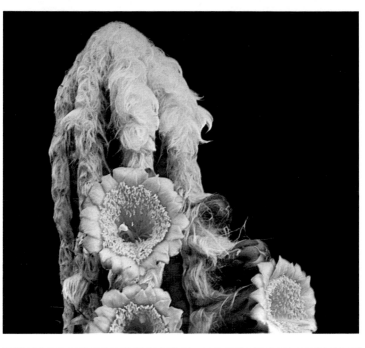

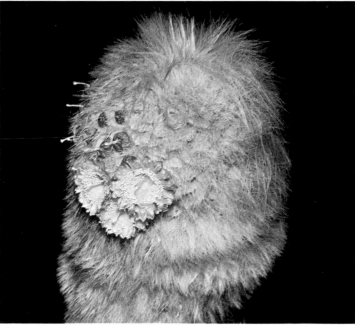

29 CEPHALOCLEISTOCACTUS SCHATTA-TIANUS Backeberg
Tribe Cacteae — subtribe Cereinae

Etymology Friedrich Ritter established this genus, taking its name from *kephale,* meaning head, and *kleistos,* closed, because the plant is very similar to *Cleistocactus,* even in that the flower petals do not open. However, it differs in having greater development of spines and bristles on the flowering parts. Initially it flowers laterally and later over the whole of the upper part of the stem.

Place of Origin Bolivia.

Description The plant, whether erect or decumbent, forms thick colonies of stems that grow to a length of 2 ft. (60 cm.) and a diameter of 2 in. (5 cm.). There are about 16 slender, not very pronounced, slightly tuberculate ribs. The areoles borne on the ribs are round, felted, yellowish at first and white later. They have more than 30 spines, varying from pale yellow to whitish. The radials are indistinguishable from the central spines; they are all fairly short except for one or two that may be more than 1/2 in. (1 cm.) long. The cephalium consists of brownish-yellow bristles of increasing length, which initially grow on one side, but then spread all around the stem. The tubular flowers are 1½ in. (4 cm.) long and have a red tube and pale yellow perianth segments that almost never open.

Cultivation This plant is quite easy to grow, but becomes cumbersome when adult. Propagation is through cuttings.

30 CEREUS AETHIOPS Haworth
Tribe Cacteae — subtribe Cereinae

Etymology The name comes from the Latin *cereus* (wax).

Place of Origin From Mendoza along the Rio Negro in Argentina, on the slopes of the Andean cordillera.

Description This shrublike species is sometimes still called *Cereus coerulescens,* its old name. Its erect bluish stem reaches a height of 6½ ft. (2 m.) and a diameter of 1¼ to 1½ in. (3 to 4 cm.). The plant is initially solitary but branches with age. Branches are 12 in. (30 cm.) or more long, sometimes tapering towards their apex. There are eight not very prominent, slightly tuberculate ribs. Each of the slight protuberances has a large black areole with 9 to 12 radial spines and four central spines. Radial spines are black at top and white at bottom and 1/4 to 1/2 in. (5 to 10 mm.) long. Central spines are black, thicker and about twice as long. The 8 in. (20 cm.) long flowers are funnel-shaped; the receptacle has a few scales. The outside of the perianth is greenish with a pink or reddish border; the inside is white or pink. The oval fruit is dehiscent, brownish when ripe, and 3¼ in. (8 cm.) long, and has black seeds. There are two varieties: *landbeckii* has white radial spines; *melanacantha* often has purplish-red spines and the stronger, longer central spines are a glossy black.

Cultivation The plant tolerates cold well as long as it is dry. Propagation is by seed or cuttings.

31   CEREUS JAMACARU de Candolle
Tribe Cacteae — subtribe Cereinae

Place of Origin   From Brazil's coast to the inland desert.
Description   This arborescent plant is widespread throughout Brazil and cultivated as far away as the West Indies. It's commonly called *mandacaru* and its species name is probably a corruption of this. In its natural state it grows taller than 30 ft. (10 m.). Its short, woody trunk measures 14 in. (35 cm.) or more in diameter. Branches growing from this ramify in turn to form a large, tall, erect crown. The young plant is light blue almost all over, but with age it turns green and eventually becomes corklike at the base. It usually has seven or eight ribs, sometimes as many as ten. These are initially slender and protrude about 1 ¼ in. (3 cm.). Their edges are indented where yellow or brownish areoles grow. The ribs later become wider, with more rounded edges and depressions set farther apart. The number of spines is variable: there are usually 15 to 20, of which seven to nine are short radial spines. Central spines may be up to 5 in. (12 cm.) or more long and much thicker and stiffer. All the spines are yellowish-brown when young, turning gray later. The 10 in. (25 cm.) flowers are borne laterally and bloom nocturnally. The outer segments of the perianth are greenish; the inner segments are white. The fruit is large and red.
Cultivation   Propagation is normally by cuttings.

---

32   CEREUS URUGUAYANUS Kiesl.
Syn. *Cereus peruvianus*
Tribe Cacteae — subtribe Cereinae
Common name: Hedge cactus

Place of Origin   Uncertain. It's found on the coasts of southern Brazil and northern Argentina.
Description   The stem is erect, columnar, up to 50 ft. (15 m.) tall and 7¾ in. (20 cm.) in diameter. It is dark green and ramifying; young parts are glaucous. Young plants have four ribs; adults have five to nine with slight projections, with round brown areoles, five to ten radial spines and one stiff central spine up to 1 ¼ in. (3 cm.) long. Blooming, 6 in. (15 cm.) long flowers face outward, growing from areoles on the upper part of the stem or branches; they have a long, scaly, brownish tube. Upper scales and outer petals are reddish-brown, particularly at the apex; inner petals are white. The spherical, 2½ in. (6.5 cm.) long fruit is orange or light yellow; seeds are black. Monstrous forms are common and often preferred in small specimens. The *monstrosus* variety is large and slender, with irregular ribbing; the *monstrosus minor* variety is small and very cristate, particularly at the apex.
Cultivation   It needs strong sun and sandy, well-drained soil. It tolerates freezing temperatures if kept dry. Adults can survive in the open in a mild climate if sheltered. Propagation is by cuttings or seeds, though seeds give slow results.

33 CHAMAECEREUS SILVESTRII (Spegazzini)
Britton and Rose
Tribe Cacteae — subtribe Echinocereinae

Etymology The name derives from the Greek *chamai*, meaning on the ground, and *cereus*, wax candle, and refers to the prostrate habit of the plant. The specific name was established by Spegazzini in memory of his friend Dr. Filippo Silvestri.

Place of Origin The Andean foothills in the provinces of Tucumán and Salta in northern Argentina.

Description The genus is monotypic, comprising this species only. The dwarf, prostrate plants are candle-shaped and put forth numerous shoots. The short stems are 2½ to 6 in. (6 to 15 cm.) long and have a diameter of 1/2 to 1 in. (1 to 2.5 cm.). The six to nine flat ribs bear close-set areoles with spines similar to bristles. A profusion of funnel-shaped scarlet flowers appears in May, June and July. The flowers are about 2 in. (5 cm.) long and have a scaly, hairy tube, and the segments of their perianth open wide. The cultivar *Crassicaulis Cristata* has shoots that show considerable fasciation and larger flowers. It has been crossbred with *Lobivia densispina*, resulting in plants with stronger stems and flowers in various colors.

Cultivation The plant is self-sterile, but may easily be propagated by offsets. It is subject to attack by red spider mites, which can be combated with special acaricides. Strong sun and much watering during the growing period are essential.

---

34 CLEISTOCACTUS STRAUSII (Heese) Backeberg
Tribe Cacteae — subtribe Cereinae

Etymology The name derives from the Greek word *kleistos*, (closed): the perianth hardly opens at all.

Place of Origin At altitudes above 5,500 ft. (1,700 m.) in the district of Tarija, Bolivia, near northern Argentina.

Description This species has a light green stem 2 to 3¼ in. (5 to 8 cm.) in diameter and up to 10 ft. (3 m.). It may have numerous basal shoots, but rarely branches above unless the apex has been cut. It has 25 slender, flat ribs, bearing close-set, alternating areoles. Their 30 to 40 white radial spines intermingle and almost conceal the stem, particularly at the apex where they are denser and more bristly. It usually has four pale yellow central spines, about 3/4 in. (2 cm.) long. The flowers are borne horizontally on the upper part of the stem. They consist of a red tube covered with hairs and scales. Segments of the perianth are short and stay almost closed. Filaments of the stamens, the long style and stellate stigmas protrude from the tube. The fruit is spherical, red and woolly. The variety *fricii* is often found in cultivation. Its bristly radial spines are 2 in. (5 cm.) long; its central spines white.

Cultivation The plant needs mild heat and strong sunshine, but is easy to grow. Flowers appear only on adult specimens. Propagation can be by seed or cuttings.

35 CLEISTOCACTUS WENDLANDIORUM
Backeberg
Tribe Cacteae — subtribe Cereinae

Place of Origin This species was discovered quite recently in Bolivia, but its exact distribution is not known.

Description The plant has a slender erect stem only 1 ¼ to 1 ½ in. (3 to 4 cm.) in diameter that ramifies from the base. It has about 22 very flat ribs that protrude only very slightly. These bear fairly large, roughly oblong areoles with about 40 very fine, short, bristly spines, pale yellow at first but becoming grayish-white later. The central spines are hardly distinguishable from the radials, since they are the same color, merely growing a little more densely. The flowers are about 2 in. (5 cm.) long and have a slightly curved, light orange tube. The outer segment of the perianth may vary from crimson to bright orange, while the inner ones are a darker shade of the same colors. The filaments are joined at their base, forming a sort of membrane enclosing the nectary. The overall shape of the flower is almost cylindrical.

Cultivation This species is still only rarely found in cultivation, although it should not be difficult to grow. In winter the temperature should not be allowed to fall to near freezing point; the plant should be set in a warm, sunny position during the growing period and watered frequently when in flower. Propagation is by cuttings.

---

36 COCHEMIEA POSELGERI (Hildmann) Britton and Rose
Tribe Cacteae — subtribe Cactinae

Etymology The name is taken from that of an American Indian tribe that used to live on the peninsula of Baja California.

Place of Origin The southern part of Baja California, Mexico.

Description This species was included by H. Hildmann in the genus *Mammillaria* until the botanist Walton separated the genus *Chocemiea* from it. The blue-green or gray-green stem sometimes reaches a length of 6 ½ ft. (2 m.) and has a diameter of about 1 ½ in. (4 cm.). It is erect at first, later becomes prostrate or drooping. The plant branches abundantly, putting forth numerous stems from a central root. The stems have conical tubercles bearing white woolly tufts, sometimes bristles, and at their apex the areoles. The new aeroles are very woolly and have seven to nine stiff radial spines, yellow at first and later grayish, measuring 1/2 in. (1.5 cm.) long. The flowers spring from the axil of the tubercles near the apex. They are about 1 ¼ in. (3 cm.) long, a glossy scarlet and both the stamens and style protrude. The fruit is globular, measuring about 1/4 in. (6 to 8 mm.) in diameter.

Cultivation These plants grow well and rather rapidly. Flowers appear only on old stems. The plant needs strong sunshine and a marked rest period. Propagation is by cuttings.

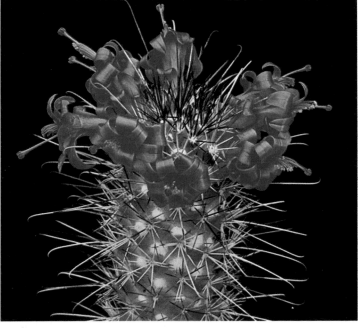

37 COCHEMIEA SETISPINA (Coulter) Walton
Tribe Cacteae — subtribe Cactinae

Place of Origin   The granite slopes of the hinterland in central Baja California, Mexico.

Description   It is easy to mistake this species for a *Mammillaria*. *Mammillaria setispina* was, in fact, the name given to the plant by Engelmann in 1897 before Walton put it in its correct genus. The plant produces large clusters of stems that are globular at first, later becoming elongated and growing to a height of 12 in. (30 cm.) with a diameter of 1 ½ in. (4 cm.). They have short, conical tubercles that are woolly at their base and have a round, white areole at the apex. The youngest part of the areole is felted, becoming almost glabrous later. There are 9 to 12 slender, white radial spines with a brownish tip, about 3/4 in. (2 cm.) long. They are straight or slightly curved and radially arranged. The one to four central spines are the same color but longer; the upper one may exceed 2 in. (5 cm.) and is hooked. Flowers grow from the side axils near the apex, and generally appear only on old stems. Nearly 2 ¼ in. (6 cm.) long, they have a conspicuous funnel-shaped tube and an irregular perianth whose segments are shaded from crimson to scarlet. The fruit is club-shaped, dark red, and almost 3/4 in. (2 cm.) long.

Cultivation   It's easy to grow this plant in strong sun. It needs a strict rest period in winter at a little above freezing. The soil must be very well drained. Propagated from shoots.

38 COPIAPOA CHANARALENSIS Ritter
Tribe Cacteae — subtribe Echinocactinae

Etymology   Britton and Rose established this genus, naming it after the city of Copiapó, which is the capital of the Atacamá province in Chile, because all the species of the genus are native to the coastal area of northern and central Chile.

Place of Origin   The coastal village of Chañaral near the southern border of the province of Atacamá, Chile. The species is named after the village and the small island facing it.

Description   This species was discovered only recently, and may prove to be merely a local variety of one of the numerous species. Its olive-green stem is thick and spherical and has about 18 slightly tuberculate ribs. In younger plants, at least, the apex is covered with thick white wool. The spines are brown with dark tips. They gradually become lighter and eventually are grayish. The plant develops areoles and younger spines in the course of its growth.

Cultivation   Although it has not been verified, since the plant grows at a latitude of 29°, close to sea level, it probably does not tolerate cold. It is rarely found in cultivation, except in large collections. Propagation is by seed.

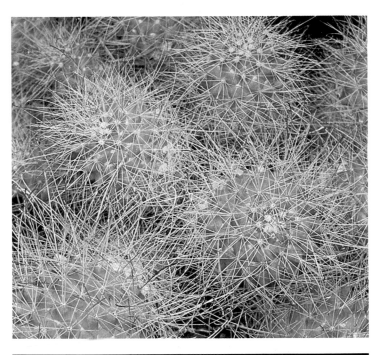

39 COPIAPOA CINEREA (Philippi) Britton and Rose
Tribe Cacteae — subtribe Echinocactinae

Place of Origin From Taltal and Paposo to Caleta Cobre on the coast of northern Chile, in the province of Antofagasta.
Description The plant is initially spherical, becoming columnar later. In its natural state it grows to a height of 3¼ ft. (1 m.), and puts forth basal shoots. Its chalky-white stem has about 20 ribs, divided by deep transverse incisions between the wide, depressed tubercles. The slightly woolly areoles are sunk into the tubercles. At the apex the white tomentum is very dense and in young plants the tubercles are wider, with an almost hexagonal base. The number of spines is variable: there may be only one, or in some varieties as many as seven radial and one or two central spines. In the typical species these are black, but in the variety *columna-alba*, whose solitary columnar stem is about 30 in. (75 cm.), they are yellowish-brown to begin with, becoming black later, and the down on the apical areoles is yellowish-white at first, only later turning gray. The funnel-shaped flowers are about 1¼ in. (3 cm.) long and have a pale yellow tube with reddish scales at the tip. The perianth segments are yellow inside and orange on the outside. The fruit is spherical or oval, dehiscent. In the plant's natural habitat dissemination of seed is carried out by ants.
Cultivation Propagation is generally by seed, but the plants may not come true because there are so many natural hybrids.

---

40 COPIAPOA CINEREA (Philippi) Britton and Rose
variety **DEALBATA** (Ritter) Backeberg
Tribe Cacteae — subtribe Echinocactinae

Place of Origin The coastal region of Chile at a latitude of 30° S.
Description This is one of the most common varieties of *Copiapoa cinerea* (some authors having actually treated it as a species of its own). It forms hemispherical clusters of stems, each of which has a diameter of 2½ to 5 in. (6 to 12 cm.) and an apex covered with whitish-gray felt. There are 21 to 23 tuberculate ribs with sunken, elongated areoles more than 1/4 in. (5 mm.) long and covered with gray felt. They normally bear only one erect, rigid spine, 3/4 to 2 in. (2 to 5 cm.) long, but sometimes there are also one to three smaller spines. The flowers are funnel-shaped, measure about 1½ in. (3.5 cm.) in both length and width, and have pale yellow perianth segments. The spherical fruit is greenish-white shaded with red. Seeds are black. Although the color of the epidermis in this variety is the same chalky white as that of the typical species, the shape of the areoles and the solitary spine make it easily recognizable even when young.
Cultivation Mild heat is required in winter, bright sunshine in summer, and very porous soil. Propagation is by seed or, if available, a secondary stem.

41 COPIAPOA COQUIMBANA (Rümpler) Britton and Rose
Tribe Cacteae — subtribe Echinocactinae

Place of Origin The hills around the coastal towns of Coquimbo and La Serena in the province of Coquimbo, Chile.
Description This is one of the old species, described in 1885 by Rümpler as *Echinocactus coquimbanus* and later transferred to the genus *Copiapoa* by Britton and Rose. It has a spherical stem that branches profusely, forming a cluster almost 3 ft. (1 m.) across. Branches are about 4 in. (10 cm.) in diameter. Roots are fibrous, unlike other species which have taproots. Stems have a pale green epidermis and are woolly at the apex, particularly at flowering time. There are 10 to 17 tuberculate ribs with a rounded, raised edge and a wide base: apical areoles are about 3/4 in. (2 cm.) apart. It has eight to ten fairly slender, slightly curved radial spines, and one or two thicker central spines. Spines are black, becoming gray with age. The campanulate flowers are 1 ¼ in. (3 cm.) long and grow from the center of the white wool at the apex. Outer segments of the perianth are linear and greenish; inner segments are wide, blunt and yellow. A recently discovered variety has larger tubercles, fewer and thicker spines and wider flowers.
Cultivation It needs mild heat in winter, scant water but some humidity. Propagation by seed or stem planted as a cutting.

42 COPIAPOA KRAINZIANA Ritter
Tribe Cacteae — subtribe Echinocactinae

Place of Origin The coastal mountains above Taltal, in the province of Antofagasta in northern Chile.
Description This species was also discovered by Ritter and described by him in 1963. (These *Copiapoa* species are still rare, since it takes over twenty years to study a cactus, obtain seed or shoots, and produce it in quantity for the market. Although North America has been well explored by botanists, South America, particularly the mountainous Andean region, has been studied only recently; many surprises still await explorers.) The plant has a gray-green stem about 5 in. (12 cm.) in diameter, and produces branches that form a cluster over 3 ft. (1 m.) wide. It has 13 or 14 slightly scalloped, raised ribs, protruding by 1/2 in. (1.5 cm.); areoles are particularly concentrated toward the apex, where the gray felt is very dense. There are 10 to 12 radial spines 1/2 to 3/4 in. (1 to 2 cm.) long, and 14 to 20 central spines, 3/4 to 1 ¼ in. (2 to 3 cm.) long. All the spines are slender, cylindrical and sharp, white at first and gray later; most are curved. The yellow flowers are 1 ½ in. (3.5 cm.) long. The fruit is yellow or red.
Cultivation It is difficult to obtain old plants that have already tillered, so propagation is mainly by seed.

43 CORYPHANTHA ANDREAE (Purpus and Boedecker)

Tribe Cacteae — subtribe Cactinae

Etymology The name was derived from the Greek word *koryphe,* meaning summit, and *anthos,* flower, because the flowers grow from the apex of the plant.

Place of Origin Mountains near Perote, Vera Cruz, from 8,000 to 13,000 ft. (2,500 to 4,000 m.) in central Mexico.

Description The plant has a spherical stem that becomes slightly cylindrical. It has a diameter of 3½ in. (9 cm.) and a depressed, woolly apex. Tubercles are arranged in a small number of spirals. They are thick, rounded, succulent, protrude by about 3/4 in. (2 cm.) and have a diameter of 1 in. (2.5 cm.). They have a deep, felted groove extending from the elliptical areoles along the upper part of the tubercles. When young, their base is also very felty. On older parts the felt disappears, leaving the tubercles glabrous. In adult plants there may be ten ½ in. (1 cm.) long radial spines, yellowish-gray with a brown tip, conical, radially arranged and often curved inwards. The five to seven thicker and sharper spines are the same color as the radial spines but curved back toward the tubercle. The lower spine points downward and may be as long as 1 in. (2.5 cm.). Flowers are large, with a diameter of 2 to 2½ in. (5 to 6 cm.) when their linear segments are wide open.

Cultivation This plant is easy to grow. It tolerates occasional low temperatures. Limit the sunlight to which it is exposed during the summer. Propagation is generally by seed.

---

44 CORYPHANTHA CLAVATA (Scheidweiler) Backeberg

Tribe Cacteae — subtribe Cactinae

Place of Origin The state of Hidalgo, and adjacent areas in the states of Querétaro and Mexico, central Mexico.

Description The name of this species has been changed many times, and its allocation to a particular genus is still very uncertain. Though described as a *Mammillaria* in 1838, it differs in some of its characteristics. Britton and Rose included it among the *Neolloydia;* Backeberg then moved it to *Coryphantha.* Its genus is still undecided. The adult stem is about 8 in. (20 cm.) high with a diameter of 2¾ in. (7 cm.); at this stage it puts forth basal shoots. The tubercles are conical, have a woolly base and protrude by 3/4 in. (2 cm.); above them is a narrow groove with one or two red glands. Tubercles are arranged spirally and slant slightly with age. Apical areoles are felted and woolly in the center of the plant, becoming almost glabrous later. Those at the base fall off, leaving bare tubercles. It has six to nine brownish radial spines about 1/3 to 1/2 in. (8 mm. to 1.5 cm.) in length. There is usually one central spine that is longer and yellowish or brown. The flowers are 2 in. (5 cm.) long. The outer segments of the perianth are light brown with a reddish median line, and the inner segments are creamy white or yellow. The root is a whitish taproot.

Cultivation Propagation is generally by seed.

45 CORYPHANTHA ERECTA (Lemaire)
Tribe Cacteae — subtribe Cactinae

Place of Origin The state of Hidalgo in Mexico.
Description Lemaire moved the plants to this genus from *Mammillaria* in 1868; unlike the *Mammillaria*, their flowers are borne at the apex of the stem and a shallow groove runs along the upper part of the tubercle from the areole to its base. *Coryphantha erecta* has a yellowish-green cylindrical stem rounded at its apex; it puts forth many shoots that form large clusters. Individual stems are first erect and later prostrate, up to 12 in. (30 cm.) long and 2½ to 3 in. (6 to 8 cm.) in diameter. Tubercles are conical, spirally arranged, somewhat slanting, blunt and 1/3 in. (8 mm.) long. Their large base is woolly, with a gland that is initially yellow, then turns brown. Areoles are woolly when young, particularly at the apex where they form a white crown. They have 8 to 14 radial spines 1/2 in. (1 cm.) long, growing either horizontally or obliquely and changing from light yellow to deep yellow or brown. Two to four central spines may be 3/4 in. (2 cm.) long; the lowest one is curved. Yellow or light yellow flowers are 2 to 2¾ in. (5 to 7 cm.) wide.
Cultivation In cultivation the plant does not grow as tall as in its natural habitat and is unlikely to put forth shoots. It is therefore propagated by seed. Growth is slow the first two or three years unless the plant is grafted onto a different stock. Rest in winter and sun throughout the year are essential.

46 CORYPHANTHA PALMERI Britton and Rose
Tribe Cacteae — subtribe Cactinae

Place of Origin The states of Durango, Zacatecas and Coahuila in northern central Mexico. The plant was discovered in 1904 along the rocky ridges of the Sierra Magdalena, near Durango, by Edward Palmer.
Description The pale green, spherical stem of this plant becomes elongated with time and may put forth branches. It has a maximum diameter of around 3¼ in. (8 to 10 cm.). Conical, close-set tubercles protrude about 3/4 in. (2 cm.) and are arranged in 13 spirals, which are sometimes not very regular. The apex of each tubercle bears an areole that is very woolly when young, almost bare later. It has 11 to 14 fairly thick, radial spines, yellowish with black tips. They are radially arranged almost at right angles to a central spine that is conical, thick, brown, hooked at its apex, and 1/2 to 3/4 in. (1 to 2 cm.) long. The flowers are 1¼ in. (3 cm.) long, and vary from pale yellow to off-white. Outer oblong segments of the perianth have a brown median stripe; inner segments are pointed.
Cultivation Propagation is by seed and by shoots if an old plant that has tillered is available. The soil must be very sandy and gravelly, and should be watered only when completely dry.

47 CORYPHANTHA RADIANS (de Candolle) Britton and Rose
Tribe Cacteae — subtribe Cactinae

Place of Origin   The state of Hidalgo and adjacent states in central Mexico.

Description   This is generally thought to be the species classified in 1828 by de Candolle as *Mammillaria radians,* but this is unclear partly because of various name changes over the years. It has a spherical or oval stem 2 to 2¾ in. (5 to 7 cm.) in diameter, with a blunt, depressed apex covered with wool and spines. Tubercles are spirally arranged, large, conical-oval, somewhat slanting, widened laterally and compressed in height. They bear areoles that are elliptical and felted when young, and are extended on top by a narrow groove; on new growth this groove may also show some felt. The species is very variable. It normally has only radial spines — as many as 20 or less than 16; the average is 16 to 18. These are curved, pectinate, and straw-colored with brown tips, which grow splayed out. Occasionally there is also one erect central spine, thicker and longer than the others. The spines are usually about 1/2 in. (1 cm.) long, but they may be longer on older plants. Flowers are very big, with a diameter of 2½ to 2¾ in. (6 to 7 cm.). The linear segments are lemon-yellow, sometimes red at the base.

Cultivation   This plant does best in slight shade and very porous soil. It tolerates fairly low temperatures as long as it is kept dry. Propagation is by seed.

48 CORYPHANTHA REDUNCUSPINA Boedecker
Tribe Cacteae — subtribe Cactinae

Place of Origin   The coast of Tamaulipas in northern Mexico.

Description   The light green or yellowish stem is spherical at first, then becomes oblong. It is about 4 in. (10 cm.) in diameter. It is covered with erect conical-oval tubercles that protrude by 1/2 in. (1 cm.) and are arranged in spirals. Their base is felted at first, becoming glabrous later, as do the areoles, whose center is woolly with splayed out, nonerect spines. It has 15 to 20 stiff radial spines that are radially arranged and intersecting. They are 5/8 in. (1.2 cm.) long and whitish or straw-colored, often with a brown tip. There are two or three thick central spines up to 1 in. (2.5 cm.) long, curved toward the base, and brownish-black when they first appear, gradually becoming pale yellow. Flowers grow from the axils of the youngest tubercles, are 1½ to 2 in. (4 to 5 cm.) in diameter and have yellow perianth segments. The species name comes from the Latin *reduncus* (hooked or curved), and refers to its central spines. The species could be mistaken for *Coryphantha recurvata* (George Engelmann) Britton and Rose, although the latter produces more offsets and has more numerous, markedly hooked radial spines that cover the stem, and its central spines are almost 3/4 in. (2 cm.) in length.

Cultivation   This species needs shade and mild heat in winter. Propagation is by seed or by shoots if available.

49 DISCOCACTUS ARANEISPINUS Buining
Tribe Cacteae — subtribe Cactanae

Etymology The genus was established by Pfeiffer in 1837. The name comes from the Greek *diskos* (disc), because of the round and markedly flattened shape of this plant. Both *Disco-cactus* and *Melocactus* have an apical cephalium, but in the former this is smaller, shorter and has many bristles. The genus grows only in Brazil, Paraguay and Bolivia.
Place of Origin The state of Bahia in eastern Brazil.
Description This recently introduced species was described by Buining in 1977. Its stem is a flattened globe, from 4 to 5 in. (10 to 12 cm.) in diameter, which puts forth shoots from its base as it gets older. The cephalium stands up about 1¼ in. (3 cm.) above the stem and has a diameter of 1¾ in. (4.5 cm.); its whole surface is covered with white or grayish wool. On an adult plant there are 21 ribs, each bearing only six to seven oval areoles that are initially covered with creamy yellow felt; they become glabrous later. The more or less slender spines are all radial; there are 15, about 1¼ in. (3 cm.) long. Light-col-ored on the younger parts of the plant, they become grayish later. They overlap a great deal and curve laterally, with their tips pointing inward. The effect is suggestive of spiders' legs, hence the plant's specific name (*aranea* means spider in Latin). The small white flowers bloom nocturnally, as is the case throughout the genus. The red berries are roughly cylindrical.
Cultivation Propagation is by seed. The plant is often grafted onto other stock.

50 DOLICHOTHELE BAUMII (Boedecker) Werder-mann and Buxbaum
Tribe Cacteae — subtribe Cactinae

Etymology The name comes from the Greek *dolikos* (long), and *thele* (nipple or breast); it refers to the tubercles.
Place of Origin The state of Tamaulipas, Mexico.
Description The plant has an oval stem about 3 in. (8 cm.) high and 2½ in. (6 cm.) in diameter, which branches, putting forth basal shoots. The ½ in. (1 cm.) tubercles are not as long as those of other species. They are woolly at their base when young; as they grow older their axil becomes glabrous. At the apex of the areoles are 30 to 35 white, extremely slender radial spines of different lengths, the longest being from 1/2 to 5/8 in. (1 to 1.5 cm.). The five or six central spines are white com-bined with a light brown or cream color. They are stiffer, straighter and are nearly 3/4 in. (1.8 cm.) long. Flowers are strongly scented, funnel-shaped and are 1¼ in. (3 cm.) in both length and width. Outer segments of the perianth are greenish-white; the inner ones are sulfur-yellow and pointed at their apex. The fruit is gray-green, oval, and 1/2 in. (1.5 cm.) long. As the plant gets older it may put forth lateral branches as well as basal shoots. The species, once included with the *Mammil-laria,* is still often classified as such.
Cultivation Propagation by seed or shoots. Growth is rapid.

51 DOLICHOTHELE LONGIMAMMA (de Candolle)
Britton and Rose
Tribe Cacteae — subtribe Cactinae

Place of Origin   The state of Hidalgo in central Mexico.
Description   In 1828 de Candolle gave the name of this species to a *Mammillaria* with long tubercles, but it was later transferred to this new genus by Britton and Rose. Two distinct
types of plant exist within the genus: those with large flowers,
and those with small flowers. This species belongs to the first
type. The stem is short and globular at first, becoming elongated with age to about 4 in. (10 cm.). It consists of a central
nucleus and of elongated fairly soft conical tubercles measuring 3/4 to 2¾ in. (2 to 7 cm.), radiating outward. Each tubercle
has a more or less woolly base, although sometimes it is bare,
and an apical areole bearing about 10 slender, white or
cream-colored radial spines, measuring up to 3/4 in. (2 cm.) in
length. The one to three central spines are straight, shorter,
and yellowish with a dark tip. As the plant grows older it puts
forth a great many tillers and also ramifies from higher up the
stem, forming large clusters. The flowers are funnel-shaped,
2½ in. (6 cm.) long, greenish-yellow outside and yellow inside.
The variety *gigantothele* has longer tubercles, and *globosa* is
more spherical. There are also horticultural forms, one of which
is cristate.
Cultivation   The very large root needs a deep flowerpot.
Propagation is by seed or basal shoots.

52 DOLICHOTHELE SPHAERICA (Dietrich) Britton
and Rose
Tribe Cacteae — subtribe Cactinae

Place of Origin   Southern Texas and Nuevo León and Tamaulipas in Mexico, especially near the Rio Grande and the sea.
Description   This species, discovered on the Laguna Madre
near Corpus Christi on the Texas coast, was described as a
Mammillaria by Albert Dietrich in 1853. It is low-growing, with a
large, fleshy root, forming dense clusters as much as 20 in. (50
cm.) across. Each globular stem is 1½ to 2 in. (4 to 5 cm.)
wide. The conical-cylindrical tubercles are soft and are from
1/2 to 5/8 in. (1 to 1.5 cm.) long. They slant upward and are
close-set, with a slightly woolly base and round, apical areoles
bearing 12 to 15 pale yellow radial spines with a darker base.
They are about 1/2 in. (1 cm.) long and are radially arranged.
The single central spine is straight, slightly thicker and only
1/6 in. (4 mm.) long. Flowers appear near the apex, but not
from the axil of the youngest tubercles. They are funnel-shaped
and 2½ to 2¾ in. (6 to 7 cm.) in diameter, with many yellow
perianth segments which open wide. The fruit is oblong, 5/8 in.
(1.5 cm.) long, a greenish-white suffused with crimson, and
scented — an exception to the rest of the tribe.
Cultivation   The plant needs mild heat and some spraying
during its winter rest period. Propagation can be by seed, but
results can be more quickly achieved through basal shoots.

53 DOLICHOTHELE UBERIFORMIS (Zuccarini)
Britton and Rose
Tribe Cacteae — subtribe Cactinae

Place of Origin The state of Hidalgo in central Mexico.
Description The plant's stem is a depressed sphere, 2¾ in. (7 cm.) high with a diameter of 4 in. (10 cm.), which puts forth tillers in the form of basal shoots. The tubercles are conical-cylindrical, about 1 in. (2.5 cm.) long, with a bare base. The direction in which they point is irregular. The apical areoles are almost glabrous and bear only radial spines. There are three to six, 1/2 in. (1.5 cm.) long, slender and straight or slightly contorted, and very pale yellow with a reddish-brown base. The flowers measure 1½ in. (3.5 cm.) across, the outer segments of the perianth being reddish and the double layer of inner, oblong segments yellow. As in all the species of this genus, the flowers spring from the axils of the tubercles near the apex. This plant, too, has been known for a long time: Zuccarini described it in 1837, including it among the *Mammillaria,* and a few years later it was illustrated in Pfeiffer and Otto's publication *Abbildung und Beschreibung blühender Cacteen* ("Flowering Cacti Illustrated and Described").
Cultivation Like the other species of this genus, the plant has a thick, fleshy root that needs a large flowerpot. It does not flower readily, but it is easy to grow. Propagation is by basal shoots, or by seed if not tillered plants are available.

---

54 ECHINOCACTUS GRUSONII Hildm.
Tribe Cacteae — subtribe Echinocactinae
Common name: Golden barrel cactus

Etymology The name comes from the Greek *echinos* (porcupine), because of the many strong, dense spines that grow on the areoles. The genus was established in 1827 by Link and Otto. When Karl Schumann wrote a monograph on it in 1898, it included 138 species, but most were reassigned; now it has only six species; but its name is still often used as a synonym for plants that no longer belong to it.
Place of Origin The states of San Luis Potosí and Hidalgo in central Mexico.
Description This globular plant grows very slowly; the stem of a mature specimen reaches a diameter of 32 in. (80 cm.) and a height of 3¼ ft. (1 m.), and has nearly 30 sharp ribs. The areoles are covered in yellowish down that later turns gray. They bear eight to ten radial spines about 1¼ in. (3 cm.) long and three to five central spines that reach a length of 2 in. (5 cm.). The spines are initially golden-yellow, later becoming whitish. The small, brownish flowers are yellow on the inside and appear like a crown around the apex.
Cultivation Only old plants put forth shoots, so propagation is mostly by seed. The plant grows to a diameter of 4 in. (10 cm.) in about four years. Prone to scorching, it should be sheltered from the hottest sun if grown in a pot.

55 ECHINOCACTUS INGENS Zuccarini
Tribe Cacteae — subtribe Echinocactinae

Place of Origin   Central and northern Mexico.
Description   The stem of this species grows into a thick cylinder, 5 ft. (1.5 m.) high and 4 ft. (1.25 m.) in diameter, but cultivated specimens are usually spherical or slightly elongated. The apex is very woolly. Young plants have eight ribs that later increase to more than 50. The yellow woolly areoles bear radial spines and one central spine, all of which are straight and stiff 3/4 to 1¼ in. (2 to 3 cm.) long, brown at first, becoming grayish later. The yellow flowers are 3/4 in. (2 cm.) long. There are two varieties that were considered, until a short time ago, species in their own right: *grandis* (Joseph Nelson Rose) Hans Krainz, and *palmeri* (Rose) Krainz. *Grandis* is thicker and taller than the typical species; young plants are more or less ringed with red and their areoles are divided, while in adult plants they are united. They have five or six radial spines 1¾ to 1½ in. (3 to 4 cm.) long, and only one central spine, up to 2 in. (5 cm.) long. All the spines are yellow, later becoming reddish-brown. *Palmeri,* too is thick and cylindrical, 6½ ft. (2 m.) high with 12 to 26 ribs. There are five to eight light-colored, weak radial spines and four tough, sometimes flattened central spines, arranged crosswise. All the spines are brownish-yellow when young. Both varieties come from northern Mexico.
Cultivation   The plant grows slowly, and appreciates strong sunlight. Propagation is by seed.

56 ECHINOCACTUS TEXENSIS Hopffer
Tribe Cacteae — subtribe Echinocactinae
Common names: Candy cactus, devil's head, horse crippler, monco caballo, viznaga

Place of Origin   Southeastern New Mexico and Texas and northern Mexico.
Description   This species, described by Hopffer in 1842, was segregated by Britton and Rose to form the monotypical *Homalocephala* ("having a flat head") but has since been reinstated as *Echinocactus.* It has a diameter of 12 in. (30 cm.) and a height of 6 in. (15 cm.). It has 13 to 27 prominent ribs each bearing two to six large, felted areoles; from these spring six to seven flattened, splayed out radial spines 1/2 to 1½ in. (1 to 4 cm.) long. They are reddish, becoming yellow with age and have colored rings. The single central spine is flat, up to 2½ in. (6 cm.) long and 1/3 in. (8 mm.) wide, has horizontal rings and curves downward. Scented flowers are campanulate, measure 2½ in. (6 mm.) in both width and length, and have a tube covered with thin scales. Perianth segments are notched with a spiny tip; they are scarlet and bright orange at the base and shaded from pink to off-white in the center. Flowers bloom for four days. The fruit is scarlet and globular.
Cultivation   Propagation is by seed, growth slow at first.

57 ECHINOCEREUS BAILEYI Rose
Tribe Cacteae — subtribe Echinocereinae

Etymology The name comes from the Greek word *echinos*, meaning a porcupine and *cereus*, meaning candlelike, i.e. elongate.

Place of Origin The Wichita Mountains of southwestern Oklahoma.

Description This is one of the most attractive species of this genus. The stem, which ramifies from the base, is cylindrical, 8 in. (20 cm.) or more in height and has a diameter of 3½ in. (9 cm.). There are approximately 15 slender, raised ribs, sometimes arranged spirally, bearing oval areoles. There are about 16 needle-shaped radial spines that are white at first, then become yellowish, light brown or pinkish. There are no central spines, although the longest and strongest radials, which point outward and downward and may be as long as 1¼ in. (3 cm.), at first sight might appear to be central spines. The flowers spring from near the center of the youngest areoles, which are white and woolly. They have a spiny, woolly, funnel-shaped tube and pinkish-crimson perianth segments that open wide, measuring 2½ in. (6 cm.) across. There are several varieties distinguishable by the color — white, brown or pink — of their spines, which are also weaker and longer.

Cultivation The plant does not tolerate cold, but with mild heat and an adequate winter rest period it flowers abundantly. Propagation is by seed or by basal shoots if obtainable.

58 ECHINOCEREUS BARTHELOWANUS Britton and Rose
Tribe Cacteae — subtribe Echinocereinae

Place of Origin This species was collected by Rose in 1911 on Isla Magdalena in southern Baja California, near Santa Maria Bay on the Pacific Coast. It was named after Captain Barthelow, who commanded the expedition's ship.

Description The plant puts forth a great many basal shoots that form large clusters. The stems are cylindrical, up to 8 in. (20 cm.) long and 1½ to 2 in. (4 to 5 cm.) in diameter. There are about ten more or less tuberculate ribs that are almost hidden by their numerous thick spines. The close-set areoles grow between 1/12 and 1/4 in. (2 to 5 mm.) apart and are white and felted when young. They bear a great many overlapping spines, sometimes as long as 2¾ in. (7 cm.) which are pinkish when they first appear, later turn white or yellow with a brown or black tip and finally become gray. Six central spines are barely distinguishable: they are thicker, particularly at the base, and have one spine longer than the others. The flowers are very small, measuring about 1/2 in. (1 cm.) in length with petals less than 1/4 in. (5 mm.) long. Their very prickly tube is hidden by the mass of apical spines.

Cultivation This species is not readily available commercially. It requires a long rest period, when it should be kept absolutely dry and sheltered from frost. Propagation is by shoots.

59 ECHINOCEREUS DELAETII Gürke
Tribe Cacteae — subtribe Echinocereinae

Place of Origin The southern part of the state of Coahuila, northern Mexico, in the Sierra de la Paila north of Parras.

Description This species, described by Gürke in 1909, owes its name to Franz de Laet, a Belgian cactus dealer who imported many new species. In spite of its restricted area of origin, the plant has become very popular as a cultivated species because it is small and easy to grow. Its stem is erect 4 to 12 in. (10 to 30 cm.) high, and puts forth numerous basal shoots and branches with about 20 ribs. Each areole has up to 36 yellowish, sharp radial spines that are 1/2 in. (1 cm.) in length, and four or five bristly central spines, creamy-white with a reddish tip, about 1¼ in. (3 cm.) long and more or less contorted. A great many thick, twisted, white or grayish hairs grow among the spines. They measure up to 4 in. (10 cm.) in length and cover the whole stem. The pinkish-violet flowers grow from the lateral areoles, opening outward. They measure 2¾ in. (7 cm.) in length and 2½ in. (6 mm.) in diameter.

Cultivation This plant grows well in a very sunny position in sandy, chalky soil. It requires a winter rest period at a temperature above freezing and plentiful watering in summer. It grows fairly fast and may produce several new stems in about three years.

60 ECHINOCEREUS ENNEACANTHUS Engelmann
Tribe Cacteae — subtribe Echinocereinae
Common names: Strawberry cactus, pitaya

Place of Origin New Mexico, Texas and Chihuahua in Mexico.

Description This plant puts forth many basal branches from its original stem, thus forming large clusters of semiprostrate or decumbent joints, up to 8 in. (20 cm.) long with a diameter of 2 to 2¾ in. (5 to 7 cm.). They have seven to ten tuberculate ribs with round white areoles 3/4 in. (2 cm.) apart. It usually has eight unequal radial spines that are wider at their base, about 1/2 in. (1 cm.) long, and yellowish. The single central spine is thick, brownish and 1¼ to 2 in. (3 to 5 cm.) long. Although older plants may have more radial spines, the species name, adopted by Engelmann in 1848, comes from the Greek *ennea*, (nine), and *acantha* (spine) and refers to the 8 + 1 spines on each areole. Light crimson flowers are 2 to 2½ in. (5 to 6 cm.) long and nearly 3 in. (7.5 cm.) in diameter, with oblong perianth segments that open wide. The red fruit is spherical, 3/4 in. (2 cm.) in diameter and edible: in southern Texas jam is made from it; it tastes like strawberries. There is also a cristate form of this species.

Cultivation The plant needs a strict winter rest period, strong sunshine in summer, and sandy soil. Propagation is by cuttings taken from the stem.

61 ECHINOCEREUS FITCHII Britton and Rose
Tribe Cacteae — subtribe Echinocereinae

Place of Origin Around Laredo, Texas, near the Mexican border. The species was named in honor of William Fitch, who was Rose's assistant on his journeys.

Description This species was discovered in 1913. It has a slightly cylindrical stem, 3 to 4 in. (8 to 10 cm.) high and about 2 in. (5 cm.) in diameter; it tapers at the top, giving an almost conical effect, and older plants slowly put forth a few basal shoots. The taproot is very thick. There are 10 to 14 not very prominent, rounded ribs bearing small, yellowish, close-set areoles with about 20 overlapping white radial spines. These grow flat against the stem, and are 1/4 in. (5 mm.) long. The four to six straight, brownish central spines are about 1/2 in. (1 cm.) long. Flowers grow erect near the apex and have a long, funnel-shaped tube that is spiny and hairy. Perianth segments are pink or pinkish-crimson, usually darker at the center. Overall length of the flower is 2½ to 2¾ in. (6 to 7 cm.). The pointed petals open so wide they seem almost turned inside out. The plant flowers when young, but growth is slow.

Cultivation The plant requires a very sunny position, and shelter, particularly from cold winds, in winter. It is easily grown. Propagation is by basal shoots if the plant has tillered. Plants started from seed grow very slowly but their progress can be speeded by grafting onto a rootstock.

62 ECHINOCEREUS KNIPPELIANUS Liebner
Tribe Cacteae — subtribe Echinocereinae

Place of Origin Northern Mexico, in the state of Coahuila.

Description Liebner gave this plant its specific name in 1895 when he dedicated it to Karl Knippel, a well-known cactus-dealer. The plant has a spherical or slightly elongated stem, 4 in. (10 cm.) high, and a fleshy taproot similar to a turnip. The dark green stem is fairly soft and so succulent that it sometimes becomes slightly flaccid. The five ribs, which may increase to seven with age, are fairly prominent, more so near the apex, tuberculate, with transverse grooves between the tubercles. The areoles are small, felted and white, with one to three weak bristly, curved spines. These are cream or pale yellow and with time fall off, leaving the base spineless. The pink flowers are funnel-shaped, 1¼ in. (3 cm.) long, and have segments that open very wide. They grow from lateral areoles toward the top of the stem.

Cultivation Small specimens are easily found in cultivation, but they are often difficult to recognize because their tips are hardly raised at all and the stems have no distinguishing marks. Propagation is by seed.

63 ECHINOCEREUS LONGISETUS (Engelmann) Rümpler
Tribe Cacteae — subtribe Echinocereinae

Place of Origin South of the Rio Grande del Norte in the state of Coahuila, northern Mexico.

Description The species was discovered in 1853, classified by Engelmann in 1859 as a *Cereus* and transferred to its present genus by Rümpler in 1885. It was then lost, and was rediscovered only recently. Its stem is erect, up to 8 in. (20 cm.) in height and about 2 in. (5 cm.) in diameter, ramifies from the base, and produces many tillers. There are 11 to 14 slightly tuberculate ribs with round areoles, which bear 15 to 25 slender, white radial spines. Those on the lower part of the areole are 1/2 in. (1.5 cm.) long and those on the upper part are shorter. The five to seven white central spines have dark tips and the lowest one may reach a length of 1½ in. (4 cm.). All the spines are bristly and flexible. The light crimson or lilac flowers are 2½ in. (6 cm.) long and have petals measuring about 1¼ in. (3 cm.).

Cultivation This plant is quite rare, and a certain amount of confusion surrounds it. The rediscovered species may be the same as that found in 1909 in the southern Arizona mountains near the Mexican border. It is certainly a plant from a high desert habitat needing a marked rest period and sunshine, plus frequent watering in summer. Propagation is by shoots.

---

64 ECHINOCEREUS MARITIMUS (Jones) Schumann
Tribe Cacteae — subtribe Echinocereinae

Place of Origin The northwestern coast of Baja California.

Description This species was originally discovered around Ensenada, near the U.S. border, by the amateur California botanist Marcus Jones, who described it in 1883 as a *Cereus*. It is an extremely prolific plant, forming clumps up to 12 in. (30 cm.) high and 6½ ft. (2 m.) across, possibly consisting of as many as 200 stems. The stems are spherical or cylindrical, 2 to 6 in. (5 to 15 cm.) high and 3/4 in. (2 cm.) in diameter, ramifying either from the base or from above ground. There are eight to ten ribs. The areoles, set 1/2 in. (1 cm.) apart, are round and white, becoming gray with age, and bear nine or ten straight, stiff, radial spines that are splayed out. There are usually four central spines, the upper ones being angular and the others conical, measuring more than 1¼ in. (3 cm.) in length. The flowers are about 1½ in. (4 cm.) long. The perianth segments are lanceolate but rounded at the apex. They are pale or greenish yellow in color.

Cultivation The plant does not tolerate cold well and needs ample space to grow into. It should be watered less often than other species of *Echinocereus*, but it needs a humid atmosphere and some spraying. Propagation is by basal shoots or cuttings.

65 ECHINOCEREUS PAPILLOSUS Linke

Tribe Cacteae — subtribe Echinocereinae
Common names: Yellow-flowered echinocereus, yellow-flowered alicoche

Place of Origin   South Texas, from northeast of Laredo south to Edinburg.

Description   This plant branches profusely, is usually erect, rarely semiprostrate or decumbent, and has pale green stems 9½ to 12 in. (24 to 30 cm.) long and 3/4 to 3 in. (2 to 7 cm.) in diameter. It has six to ten ribs, consisting of prominent tubercles that protrude about 1/2 in. (1 cm.) and are separated by transverse grooves. The round areoles are either white or yellow and have about seven radial spines 1/2 in. (1 cm.) long which change from white or light brown to medium brown. There is a single central spine, 1/2 to 3/4 in. (1.5 to 2 cm.) long, which is usually white or yellow with a brown base; in some plants it's brown. Flowers are 5 in. (12 cm.) in diameter. Perianth segments are yellow with a red base, spatulate, and 2½ in. (6 cm.) long. The variety *rubescens* has spines that are pink or red when new, later becoming dark brown. The densely branched variety *augusticeps* has a small stem 3 in. (8 cm.) high and 1¼ in. (3 cm.) in diameter.

Cultivation   This plant is rare in cultivation. It is sometimes grafted but it grows well on its own roots. It needs a warm winter rest period; it may become wrinkled, but it revives in the spring with heat and water. It's easily propagated by basal shoots.

66 ECHINOCEREUS PECTINATUS (Scheidweiler)
Engelmann

Tribe Cacteae — subtribe Echinocereinae
Common name: Comb hedgehog

Place of Origin   From Chihuahua in northern Mexico south to Guanajuato. Now grows from southeastern Arizona to Maverick County, Texas, at elevations up to 4,500 ft. (1,350 m.).

Description   This species was first collected by Henri Galeotti (1814–1858), director of the Botanical Gardens in Brussels, who sent it to Belgium. Its stem ramifies from the base, sometimes from above-ground, is oval-cylindrical, 6 to 8 in. (15 to 20 cm.) high, with about 20 ribs that are wide at the base. Areoles are oval and close-set. It has 20 to 25 white or pink radial spines, often with blotches or stripes of another color and—as the species name implies—pectinate: this means they are spread out laterally, and flattened with slightly divaricate tips like a small comb. There are six or more short central spines. The reddish-violet flowers are 2½ to 3 in. (6 to 8 cm.) long and have a short tube and felted, spiny areoles.

Cultivation   This species, like all *Echinocereus*, is easy to grow and is tolerant of cold if the temperature stays a little above freezing. Its winter rest period must be absolute, with only enough water to keep its roots from drying up; in summer it needs frequent watering. Growth is slow, but even young plants are attractive. Propagation is by shoots or cuttings.

67 ECHINOCEREUS PECTINATUS (Scheidweiler)
Engelmann variety **REICHENBACHII** (Tersch.) Krainz
Tribe Cacteae — subtribe Echinocereinae
Common names: lace cactus, purple candle

Place of Origin Texas, Oklahoma, southeastern Colorado, New Mexico, and northern Mexico.

Description This plant was only recently reclassed as a variety of *Echinocereus pectinatus,* by Hans Krainz; it used to be a species of its own. Both plants were described a long time ago: *Index Kewensis* dates the *Reichenbachii* variety to 1893; 50 years earlier it was in the genus *Echinocactus.* Its stem is cylindrical and solitary, ramifies to varying degrees at the base and grows up to 8 in. (20 cm.) high with a diameter of 3½ in. (9 cm.). There are 12 to 19 ribs bearing oval areoles set very close together. There are 20 to 30 spines, about 1/4 in. (5 to 8 mm.) long, aligned in two rows and radially arranged. They are curved and laterally pectinate, with the result that the tips touch or overlap the spines on adjacent ribs. They may be white, reddish or brown, but all the radial spines on each stem are the same color. One or two central spines are very similar to the radials but are often absent altogether. The flowers are about 2¾ in. (7 cm.) long, with pinkish-violet segments that open wide and a short, hairy tube. They sometimes reopen for a second day, and may be scented.

Cultivation The variety has the same requirements as the species, but it may be propagated from basal shoots.

68 ECHINOCEREUS PENTALOPHUS (de Candolle) Lemaire
Tribe Cacteae — subtribe Echinocereinae
Common names: Alicoche, ladyfinger cactus

Place of Origin Southern Texas to northeastern Mexico.

Description This species has several varieties that have created problems of classification ever since it was described by de Candolle in 1828. Its pale green stem is 5 in. (12 cm.) long and 3/4 in. (2 cm.) wide and throws out from its base many prostrate, decumbent, and intertwined stems. There are about five tuberculate ribs, which sometimes grow in spirals. They bear whitish, close-set areoles. There are three to six short white radial spines with brown tips. Central spines are generally absent but there may be one dark-colored spine 1/2 in. (1.5 cm.) long. Flowers, about 4 in. (10 cm.) long, have broad, reddish-violet petals that open wide. The tube bears areoles with long hairs and brown spines. The variety *procumbens,* sometimes considered a species, has prostrate stems and flowers white or yellow at the base. Another variety often thought to be a species, *ehrenbergii,* has eight to ten radial spines and one white or creamy-yellow central spine. There is also a cristate form of this variety. The name comes from the Greek *lophos* (ridge or crest), referring to its five ribs.

Cultivation The plant usually grows and flowers easily, especially the *procumbens* variety. Propagation is by cuttings.

69 ECHINOCEREUS ROETTERI (Engelmann)
Rümpler
Tribe Cacteae — subtribe Echinocereinae

Place of Origin   Texas and New Mexico near Mexico.
Description   Engelmann named the species in 1856 after
Paulus Roetter, who drew it in a book on the U.S.- Mexico border. Engelmann placed the species in the *Cereus* genus;
Rümpler removed it in 1885. The erect stem grows 6 in. (15
cm.) tall and is about 2¾ in. (7 cm.) wide; it is solitary at first,
slowly producing tillers later. It has 10 to 13 tuberculate ribs,
depressed at the base of the tubercles. Apical areoles are circular or slightly elongated, set 1/2 in. (1 cm.) apart. They bear
8 to 15 radially arranged spines up to 1/2 in. (1 cm.) long.
These are reddish when young and turn white later. There are
between one and five central spines the same length as the radials or slightly longer, thicker (particularly at the base), and
reddish-brown. The flowers appear on the lateral areoles below
the apex and are about 2¾ in. (7 cm.) long, with a spiny tube.
The outer segments of the perianth are greenish and the inner
ones are a light reddish purple. The variety *lloydii* forms taller,
thicker clumps of stems with fewer ribs. The spines are a bright
purple-red when young; ash to reddish-gray when mature. The
plant grows in Pecos County, Texas.
Cultivation   This plant likes desert conditions and does not
tolerate intense cold. Propagation is usually by seed, although
the variety should be reproduced from basal shoots.

70 ECHINOCEREUS SALM-DYCKIANUS
Scheer
Tribe Cacteae — subtribe Echinocereinae

Place of Origin   The states of Sonora and southwestern Chihuahua in northern Mexico.
Description   When Scheer named this species in 1856 he
may simply have wished to honor that great collector of cacti,
the Prince Salm-Dyck, or he may have wished to repay a com-
pliment: in 1850 the prince had named a cactus *Cereus scheeri*
(later also transferred to the genus *Echinocereus*). *Echinocereus salm-dyckianus* branches profusely from its base,
forming clusters of yellowish-green stems that are semiprostrate or decumbent, and measure up to 8 in. (20 cm.) in length
and 3/4 to 1½ in. (2 to 4 cm.) in diameter. There are seven to
nine slightly tuberculate ribs with large, pale yellow areoles
that become brown later. They bear eight or nine yellowish radial spines less than 1/2 in. (1 cm.) long, and a solitary central
spine that is slightly longer. The flowers may reach 4 in. (10
cm.) in length and have a slender, elongated tube bearing hairy
areoles and bristly white spines. The numerous segments of
the perianth are reddish-orange.
Cultivation   This species has been cultivated in Europe for a
long time; the date of its introduction is uncertain. In the mild
climate of the Mediterranean it survives perfectly well out of
doors, and grows rapidly. Propagation is by basal shoots.

71 ECHINOCEREUS SCIURUS (Brandegee) Britton and Rose
Tribe Cacteae — subtribe Echinocereinae

Place of Origin   The southern tip of Baja California.
Description   This plant was discovered near San José del Cabo by Townshend Brandegee in 1897. His wife and fellow botanist, Katherine, described it as a *Cereus* in 1904. The plant forms dense clumps measuring 24 in. (60 cm.) across. The basal shoots grow from the original stem, which is usually erect, slender, and up to 8 in. (20 cm.) high. Each joint has 12 to 17 not very prominent ribs divided into tubercles about 1/4 in. (5 mm.) long, bearing small, round, close-set areoles that are very felted when young and almost bare later. There are 15 to 18 slender, bristlelike radial spines up to 1/2 in. (1.5 cm.) long. They are straw-colored with reddish-brown tips. Several shorter, thicker central spines are the same color. The stem is almost hidden by spines. Flowers are 2¾ in. (7 cm.) long and 3½ in. (9 cm.) or more in diameter. They appear close to the apex. The buds are covered with many slender spines with brown tips. The many pinkish-violet segments of the perianth open wide. When the plant is ready to flower the apex of the stem often becomes curved, resembling the tail of a large squirrel; hence the plant's name: *sciurus* means squirrel in Latin.
Cultivation   The plant needs a certain amount of heat in winter but must be kept dry. Propagation is by basal shoots.

---

72 ECHINOCEREUS SUBINERMIS Salm-Dyck ex Scheer
Tribe Cacteae — subtribe Echinocereinae

Place of Origin   Sonora and Chihuahua in northern Mexico.
Description   This species was introduced into Europe between 1845 and 1850 and described by Scheer in 1856. It is the least spiny species of the genus. The stem is depressed-globular at first, later oval or cylindrical, 4 to 5 in. (10 to 12 cm.) high and 3½ in. (9 cm.) in diameter. The adult sometimes ramifies from the base. The pale green of the young stem changes to a bluish color, finally becoming dark green. There are usually five ribs, at most eight, that are large and slightly corrugated at the edge, with small, not very woolly areoles bearing short, yellowish spines, of which eight are radial and one central. The spines are partially deciduous, leaving three or four brown or blackish ones, or possibly none at all. Funnel-shaped flowers are 3¼ in. (8 cm.) long and of slightly greater diameter. Areoles on the slender tube bear very short white spines. The perianth opens wide and the pointed segments are brownish—later yellow—on the outside and a brighter yellow inside. The dark green fruit is 3/4 in. (2 cm.) long.
Cultivation   Rarely cultivated, this is an extremely delicate species. It needs a warm and sunny position all year. Propagation by seed is very slow; shoots are used if available.

73 ECHINOCEREUS VIRIDIFLORUS Engelmann

Forma **Chloranthus** (Engelmann) Krainz
Tribe Cacteae — subtribe Echinocereinae
Common names: Green-flowered pitaya, green-flowered torch
cactus

Place of Origin   Western Texas and southern New Mexico;
neighboring areas in Mexico.

Description   Classified as a *Cereus* in 1856 by Engelmann
and transferred to the *Echinocereus* genus in 1885 by
Rümpler, this plant has recently been recognized first as a variety and then as a form, but references to it as a species may
still be found. Its stem is globular and later cylindrical, up to 12
in. (30 cm.) high and 1½ to 2¾ in. (4 to 7 cm.) in diameter. It
has 13 to 18 ribs, often almost concealed under the profuse
spines. The round or slightly oval white areoles bear 12 to 20
overlapping bristly white radial spines, often with a red tip. It
has a few spinescent bristles, especially in the apical areoles.
There are three to five central spines up to 1 in. (2.5 cm.) long,
initially pointing outward and later downward, arranged in a
straight row. They are white or red, often with contrasting
bands of color around the stem. Their color is actually very
variable, and the plant is mainly grown for them, since the
brownish-green flowers are only 1 in. (2.5 cm.) long, their slender segments remaining almost closed.

Cultivation   Adults ramify rarely, so propagation is by seed.

---

74 ECHINOFOSSULOCACTUS ALBATUS (Die-

trich) Britton and Rose
Tribe Cacteae — subtribe Echinocactinae

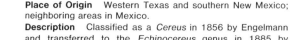

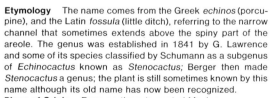

Etymology   The name comes from the Greek *echinos* (porcupine), and the Latin *fossula* (little ditch), referring to the narrow
channel that sometimes extends above the spiny part of the
areole. The genus was established in 1841 by G. Lawrence
and some of its species classified by Schumann as a subgenus
of *Echinocactus* known as *Stenocactus;* Berger then made
Stenocactus a genus; the plant is still sometimes known by this
name although its old name has now been recognized.

Place of Origin   From northern to central Mexico.

Description   The stem is a bluish-green sphere, depressed at
its spiny, white-woolly apex; with age it elongates. There are
about 35 slender ribs with sharp, undulating edges, depressed
at 1/2 in. (1.5 cm.) intervals where areoles appear. There are
about ten bristlelike, silky, radial spines, 1/2 in. (1 cm.) long,
cream-colored and partially erect; from one to three may be
missing from upper areoles. The four central spines are much
thicker, longer, and usually darker: they are straight except for
the uppermost one, which is 2 in. (5 cm.) long, flat, and often
curved backward. Funnel-shaped flowers are 3/4 in. (2 cm.)
long with yellow, lanceolate perianth segments.

Cultivation   Needs sun and careful watering. Sometimes
grafted onto other stock to hasten growth. Propagation by seed.

75 ECHINOFOSSULOCACTUS CAESPI-TOSUS
Backeberg
Tribe Cacteae — subtribe Echinocactinae

Place of Origin Mexico.
Description This species is one of the few members of the genus to put forth basal shoots. It does so as a young plant, becoming densely branched. The spherical stem is rather small, with about 27 corrugated, sharp-edged ribs, swollen where the areoles grow. The latter are round and thickly felted around the apex, later becoming almost bare. There are three spines on the areoles of the upper part of the plant: two are conical and curved upward while the central spine is flattened, yellowish, about 3/4 in. (2 cm.) long and 1/12 in. (2 mm.) wide. On the older part of the plant there are four small white radial spines, and another central spine appears below the others, pointing downward; it is curved, flat, and the same length as the upper central spine. The flowers are about 1/2 in. (1 cm.) long and have white segments with a greenish base.
Cultivation In its natural surroundings the plant tends to be larger than cultivated specimens. It likes strong sunshine and does not tolerate intense or prolonged cold. It should not be watered at all in winter. It may be propagated by seed but, since it tillers early, it is simpler to use shoots.

---

76 ECHINOFOSSULOCACTUS COPTONO-GONUS (Lemaire) Lawrence
Tribe Cacteae — subtribe Echinocactinae

Place of Origin Hidalgo and San Luis Potosí in Mexico.
Description Unlike all other members of the genus, this species has a small number of large, angular ribs that are wide at the base. The stem is solitary to begin with but puts forth basal shoots later on; it is spherical, slightly flattened at the apex, gray-green or bluish green, up to 4 in. (10 cm.) high and more than 4 in. (10 cm.) across. It has 10 to 14 ribs that protrude 1/2 in. (1.5 cm.) and have sharp, notched edges. The areoles are set about 3/4 in. (2 cm.) apart and are covered with an abundance of white felt when young but become bare later. There are three to five thick, straw-colored spines with transverse stripes. The upper ones point upward, are to varying degrees curved and flat. This is particularly true of the central spine, which may reach a length of 1 ½ in. (4 cm.); the others are shorter. The lower spines are cylindrical, point downward, and are about 1/2 in. (1.5 cm.) long. When young all the spines may be reddish. The flowers grow from or around the apex. They are 1 ¼ in. (3 cm.) long and have whitish perianth segments; the inner ones are numerous, linear-oblong, crimson or light reddish-violet in the center and white at the edges.
Cultivation This species is slightly harder to grow than others in the genus. It should be partially shaded from the sun. Propagation is by seed or from shoots, if any are available.

77 ECHINOFOSSULOCACTUS CRISPATUS
(de Candolle) Lawrence
Tribe Cacteae — subtribe Echinocactinae

Place of Origin   The state of Hidalgo in Mexico.
Description   This species, described by de Candolle in 1828 as *Echinocactus*, was transferred to its present genus by Lawrence in 1841. Most authors think it was inadequately described, but its name is accepted as valid. Its stem is initially globular, later becoming elongated-spherical with a height of 6 in. (15 cm.) and a diameter of about 3¼ in. (8 cm.). It is dark green, and has 25 to 35 slender, regularly corrugated ribs with a sharp edge. Old plants may have even more ribs. Areoles are oval, white, and very woolly, though glabrous later. They are set far apart at 1¼ to 1½ in. (3 to 4 cm.) intervals, but because they occur irregularly along the ribs, they appear to be closer-set. There are seven to eight radial spines. Upper ones are pale yellow and flat — in particular the spine in the center, which points upward and is 3/4 in. (2 cm.) long; lower spines are white and about half as long. The single central spine is straight and rigid, brown (paler at its base), and 3/4 in. (2 cm.) long. Flowers are about 1½ in. (3.5 cm.) long. Outer perianth segments are white with a violet median dorsal stripe; the inner ones are light crimson with a purplish central stripe.
Cultivation   Propagation is by seed. This may produce plants with varying characteristics.

78 ECHINOFOSSULOCACTUS LAMEL-LOSUS
(Dietrich) Britton and Rose
Tribe Cacteae — subtribe Echinocactinae

Place of Origin   The state of Hidalgo in central Mexico.
Description   This plant was described in 1847 by the German botanist Albert Dietrich. All members of the genus have compressed, lamella-like ribs, but in this species they are especially compressed. The stem is at first globular then elongates to 4 in. (10 cm.) in height and about 3½ in. (8 cm.) in diameter. The apex is flattened. There are 35 slender, corrugated and irregularly wrinkled ribs bearing small white areoles that are felted when young. It has four or five lower radial spines that are short, curved, yellow on the youngest areoles and grayish on the older ones. It also has three upper spines that are white with brownish tips; the two lateral ones are thick and curved toward the plant, the central spine measures 1¼ in. (3 cm.) or more in length and is very wide and flat. It is scored crosswise. In older plants there is also a straight rigid central spine, pointing outward, about 1½ in. (4 cm.) long, and conical or slightly triangular. Flowers spring from the center of the plant and are 1½ in. (4 cm.) long. The segments of the perianth are flesh-pink and crimson on the inside.
Cultivation   This plant needs sunshine, sandy soil and very careful watering. Most specimens tiller rarely and only when quite old, so propagation is generally by seed.

79 ECHINOFOSSULOCACTUS VAUPELIANUS

(Werdermann) Tieg. and Oehme
Tribe Cacteae — subtribe Echinocactinae

Place of Origin Mexico.

Description This species was discovered a few decades ago and classed as *Echinocactus* by Werdermann, who named it after the botanist Vaupel: his assessment was obviously based on a young specimen with no distinguishing characteristics. One of the least spectacular species in terms of spine shape, it tillers more readily than most. Its globular stem is around 4 in. (10 cm.) high and across and has a woolly, spiny apex. It has about 35 slender, deeply notched corrugated ribs. Areoles are at first covered with white felt. There are 12 to 25 slender, almost transparent white radial spines about 1/2 in. (1 to 1.5 cm.) long, straight or slightly curved, and radially arranged, overlapping each other above the ribs. There are one or two central spines, growing one above the other, which are more than 2¾ in. (7 cm.) long. They are sharp and needlelike, sometimes flattened, pointing upward at first and then outward, brownish-black at their apex and somewhat reddish lower down. The flowers are 3/4 in. (2 cm.) long, often remain squeezed between the apical spines, and have creamy-white segments with a dark median stripe on the outside.

Cultivation It needs very sandy soil and less watering than normal for the genus. Propagate by the shoots of adult plants.

---

80 ECHINOFOSSULOCACTUS WIPPERMAN-NII

(Mühlpf.) Britton and Rose
Tribe Cacteae — subtribe Echinocactinae

Place of Origin The state of Hidalgo in Mexico.

Description This species has a dark green, spherical stem that becomes elongated, reaching a height of 6 in. (15 cm.) and a diameter of about 3¼ in. (8 cm.); its apex is flat and slightly woolly. It has about 35 slender, slightly corrugated ribs; there may be from 25 in younger plants to 40 in older ones. Areoles on the sharp edges of the ribs are round, white and woolly when young and later glabrous; they have 18 to 22 white radial spines, sometimes brown at the base, which are bristly, slender and spread wide. The lowest ones reach a length of 1/2 in. (1.5 cm.). There are usually four erect central spines; three upper ones are flat, thicker at their base and lightly scored crosswise; the lower one is straight and conical. The brownish-black spines are from 3/4 in. to 2½ in. (2 to 6 cm.) long. The yellowish flowers are funnel-shaped, about 1/2 in. (1.5 cm.) long; inner segments of the perianth have a brown median line down their back. It's unclear whether the plant described in 1846 (maybe two years earlier) as *Echinofossulocactus spinosus* is the same species.

Cultivation This plant is not commonly found in cultivation because most people prefer more distinctive forms with brighter-colored spines. Propagation is by seed.

81 ECHINOMASTUS MACDOWELLII (Rebut)
Britton and Rose
Tribe Cacteae — subtribe Echinocactinae

Etymology The name comes from the Greek *echinos* (porcupine) and *mastos* (breast), referring to the plant's stem.

Place of Origin Coahuila and Nuevo León in Mexico.

Description Although this plant has been known since 1894, it is not widely cultivated — partly because it is rather difficult to grow. Most available specimens have been grafted, yet of all the species of the genus, this one grows best on its own roots. Its stem is spherical and slightly depressed, measuring about 2¾ in. (7 cm.) in height and 4 in. (10 cm.) in diameter. The apex is densely covered with yellow felt. There are about 25 ribs that are scarcely perceptible for two reasons: they are almost totally separated into rhomboidal tubercles measuring about 1/4 in. (5 mm.), and the entire stem is covered by a mass of spines which hide it almost completely. The areoles are white and woolly, bearing 20 to 25 white, slender, radial spines, almost 1¼ in. (3 cm.) long, which radiate in all directions and overlap. There are three or four central spines, 3/4 to 1¾ in. (2 to 4.5 cm.) long, thicker and heavier at the base. They are straw-colored, almost transparent at the tip and dark at the base. The pink or red flowers, which are unlikely to appear in cultivation, are funnel-shaped and 1½ in. (4 cm.) long.

Cultivation Propagation is by seed, but it is best to graft young plants onto different stocks early if one wishes to speed up their growth. Moderate watering is required.

82 ECHINOPSIS CALORUBRA Cárdenas
Tribe Cacteae — subtribe Echinocereinae

Etymology The name comes from the Greek *echinos*, porcupine, and *opsis*, appearance, because the plant's appearance suggests a hedgehog rolled up into a ball.

Place of Origin At an altitude of 6,000 ft. (1,900 m.) in the province of Valle Grande, department of Santa Cruz, Bolivia.

Description This species was described by the Bolivian botanist Martin Cárdenas in 1957. It is spherical, depressed at the apex, and reaches a diameter of 5½ in. (14 cm.) and a height of about 2½ in. (6 to 7 cm.). The light green stem turns reddish bronze in places as a result of sun or cold. It has 16 ribs divided into elongated tubercles with white, felted areoles, set 3/4 in. (2 cm.) apart in the depressions between the tubercles. There are 9 to 13 straight or slightly curved radial spines of unequal length. The single central spine is erect and 1 in. (2.5 cm.) long. All spines are yellowish, later becoming gray and partly brown at their tips. Flowers are 6 in. (15 cm.) long. The outer perianth segments are green outside and reddish inside; the upper part of the inner segments is bright orange, shading to pink lower down. Backeberg moved this species to his genus *Pseudolobivia* but since this has now been abolished the plant's original name remains valid.

Cultivation Adult plants tiller profusely, so it may be propagated from basal shoots. It tolerates low temperatures.

83 ECHINOPSIS HAMATACANTHA Backeberg
Tribe Cacteae — subtribe Echinocereinae

Place of Origin   The province of Salta in northern Argentina.
Description   This cactus has been introduced comparatively recently and was classified by Backeberg first as an *Echinopsis* and later as a *Pseudolobivia;* since the latter has been abolished, the plant has reverted to its original name. It is hemispherical and very much flattened, measuring 6 in. (15 cm.) in diameter and only 2¾ in. (7 cm.) in height. It has a bright green epidermis and up to 27 ribs, which are wide at the base and have long, sharp tubercles and large felted areoles between each tubercle. There are 8 to 15 yellowish or light brown spines, 1/6 to 1/2 in. (4 mm. to 1 cm.) or more long. One of the central spines in particular is easily distinguishable from the others: it points toward the apex of the plant and is curved or hooked. The white flowers are up to 8 in. (20 cm.) long, and scented. The fruit is green and 1½ in. (4 cm.) long.
Cultivation   The plant puts out numerous tillers, so propagation from basal shoots is both quick and easy. It does not tolerate frost.

84 ECHINOPSIS HAMMERSCHMIDII Cárdenas
Tribe Cacteae — subtribe Echinocereinae

Place of Origin   The department of Santa Cruz in Bolivia.
Description   The stem is a glossy green, globular at first, becoming slightly cylindrical later, reaching a height of 4 in. (10 cm.) and a diameter of 3½ in. (9 cm.). It may be solitary, or tillered with numerous basal branches. There are 12 to 15 almost smooth ribs with a sharp edge that becomes dented and finally tuberculate, bearing whitish-gray, felted areoles. There are eight or nine radial spines, less than 1/2 in. (1 cm.) long, and a longer central spine. All the spines are gray and thickened at the base. The flowers are white. The spherical or oval fruits are dark green and 1 in. (2.5 cm.) long. This species has been introduced only fairly recently, and when cultivated outside its original surroundings is probably very variable.
Cultivation   Propagation is either by basal shoots taken from old, tillered plants, or by seed.

85 ECHINOPSIS HYBRID "Red Paramount"

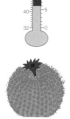

Description This hybrid is highly prized for its abundant, brightly colored flowers. The stem is globular at first, becoming cylindrical later, and is a dark green that takes on a bronze hue in sunshine. The numerous, fairly prominent ribs, bearing eye-catching areoles covered with white hairs and spines, are arranged spirally near the apex. The outer perianth segments of the flowers are white, shaded with pink, while the inner ones are a brilliant red that contrasts with the yellow of the stamens. The plant puts forth many tillers, which assume a prostrate habit.

Cultivation During the plant's winter rest period the temperature should be slightly above freezing. Considerable sunlight is necessary in summer. The soil should be very well drained, but the substratum should be a little damper than usual and should consist of one-third well-rotted leafmold and a little phosphate fertilizer to encourage the plant's flowering potential. Propagation is only from shoots.

---

86 ECHINOPSIS KERMESINA (Krainz) Krainz
Tribe Cacteae — subtribe Echinocereinae

Place of Origin Probably Argentina, but this is uncertain.

Description This species may still be referred to under the name *Pseudolobivia kermesina,* a genus created by Backeberg that has now been abolished. The plant has a large, dark green, hemispherical stem that easily grows to more than 6 in. (15 cm.) in diameter. There are 15 to 23 straight ribs, divided into tubercles by horizontal grooves in which round, white, felted areoles are set. There are 11 to 16 slender, subulate radial spines, about 1/2 in. (1 cm.) long. They are stiff and sharp, initially yellow with a brown tip, becoming gray later. There are four to six central spines that point outward. They are straight or curved slightly backward, as much as 1 in. (2.5 cm.) long, and the same color as the radial spines although darker when young. The flowers are 7 in. (18 cm.) in length with a long tuberculate tube bearing white, felted areoles. The diameter of the perianth when in full bloom is about 3½ in. (9 cm.). The segments are wide and blunt at their apex, and are a pinkish-crimson varying in shade from light to very dark. The unscented flowers are as ephemeral as those of the rest of the genus, but are very beautiful.

Cultivation The plant tolerates low temperatures, and requires strong sunshine with frequent watering in summer. Propagation is by seed.

87 ECHINOPSIS LONGISPINA (Britton and Rose)
Backeberg
Tribe Cacteae — subtribe Echinocereinae

Place of Origin Beteween La Quiaca and Tilcara in the province of Jujuy, northern Argentina, near the Bolivian border.
Description The plant was discovered near La Quiaca in 1917, growing from fissures in the rocks at 11,500 ft. (3,450 m.). The bluish-green stem is spherical at first and later cylindrical, and may grow 10 in. (25 cm.) tall and 4 in. (10 cm.) in diameter. It has 25 to 50 ribs deeply incised between the tubercles, which are 3/4 in. (2 cm.) long. Each areole bears 15 spines. Radials are hard to tell from the central spines. They range from slender to thick, are conical with a wider base, and are irregular in length, the longest 3¼ in. (8 cm.) or more. They are flexible and curved upward, and those on new parts of the plant have a hooked tip. Their color varies from yellowish to brown. Flowers are 4 in. (10 cm.) long, funnel-shaped, and have a long, slender, curved tube covered with long white hairs. Perianth segments are short and white. The variety *nigra* has a stem that grows to 12 in. (30 cm.) and has 20 ribs with 1½ in. (4 cm.) tubercles, brown or blackish spines when young but later gray, and flowers with a larger tube.
Cultivation The plant tolerates cold. In summer it should either be allowed only a few hours in the sun or be placed in semishade. Propagation is by seed.

---

88 ECHINOPSIS MAMILLOSA Gürke variety RITTERI (Boedecker) Ritter
Tribe Cacteae — subtribe Echinocereinae

Place of Origin The department of Tarija in southern Bolivia.
Description This variety is often confused with the typical species. The glossy green stem is a flattened sphere with a height of 5 in. (12 cm.) and a diameter of 4 to 10 in. (10 to 25 cm.). There are from 18 to 32 ribs with prominent, rounded, slightly curved tubercles. Areoles are set in the depressions between the tubercles. There are 12 to 15 radial spines, from 1/2 to 1 in. (1 to 2.5 cm.) long on old plants. Three to eight central spines are thicker and more numerous than those borne by the species, and are yellowish with dark tips. Flowers are 5¼ to 6 in. (13 to 15 cm.) long and 3 in. (8 cm.) in diameter. They appear from the sides of the stem and have a long green tube with woolly scales. Perianth segments are white, slightly shaded with pink. Other varieties, named after Bolivian villages near which they were found, have more spines. The variety *orozasana*, described by Ritter in 1965, is more spherical and flowers early. Flowers have a longer tube, and brown hairs, and the inner segments of the perianth are white.
Cultivation The plant tolerates fairly low temperatures but it needs protection from cold winds and should be placed in a sunny position. Very porous soil and frequent watering in summer are required. Propagation is by seed or basal shoots.

89 ECHINOPSIS MULTIPLEX (Pfeiffer) Zuccarini
Tribe Cacteae — subtribe Echinocereinae

Place of Origin   Southern Brazil.
Description   First placed in the *Cereus* genus in 1837 by
Pfeiffer, Zuccarini moved it to *Echinopsis* in 1839. Pfeiffer
mentioned a variety *monstrosus* in his *Enumeratio Diagnostica
Cactearum*. The typical form of the species is often cultivated
due to its beautiful scented flowers. It normally has a densely
tillered stem with many basal shoots and lateral joints. The
young stems are globular, elongating later to a height of 6 in.
(15 cm.) or more. It has 12 to 15 ribs with a wide base and
sharp edge bearing large, white, woolly areoles. There are
about ten yellowish-brown radial spines nearly 3/4 in. (2 cm.)
long and two to four central spines, which are darker in color
and twice as long. Flowers, which appear readily, are 8 in. (20
cm.) long and 4¾ in. (12 cm.) in diameter and have a long scaly
tube with gray hairs. They are an almost transparent mauvish-
pink, and are ephemeral and scented. One of the many varieties and forms of this species is *floribunda,* which has more
flowers in the summer. *Picta* has yellow-spotted flowers. The
cristate forms, one of which is illustrated opposite, are highly
prized by collectors because they, too, are very floriferous.
Cultivation   This plant tolerates cold well if it is kept in a
sheltered position. Propagation is by basal shoots. To obtain
more flowers, the clump should be thinned from time to time.

---

90 ENCEPHALOCARPUS STROBILIFORMIS
(Werdermann) Berger
Tribe Cacteae — subtribe Echinocactinae

Etymology   The generic name comes from the Greek *en* (in),
kephale (head), and *karpos* (fruit), because first the flowers
and then the fruit appear at the apex of the stem. The specific
name refers to the shape of its tubercles, which are reminiscent
of the scales on the strobilus—or cone—of a conifer. The
genus is monotypical, although it is very similar to *Ariocarpus*.
Place of Origin   Nuevo León and Tamaulipas in Mexico.
Description   The plant has a large, compressed taproot, and
a spherical stem, 1½ to 2½ in. (4 to 6 cm.) in diameter, completely covered with spirally arranged overlapping tubercles.
They are flat and convex on the inside and carinate on the outside; the base is woolly, and on new growth the inner portion of
the pointed apex bears small, oval, woolly areoles. While the
new growth continues, these areoles have a few short, more or
less pectinate spines. With age, the areoles disappear and the
oldest tubercles have a bare, blunter apex. The brilliant flowers
are reddish-purple, about 1¼ in. (3 cm.) long, with greenish
outer segments and incised or curly inner segments.
Cultivation   Old plants put forth basal shoots, but growth is
slow; propagation is mainly by seed. It does not tolerate cold,
and requires excellent drainage and moderate watering.

91   EPIPHYLLUM X ACKERMANNII

Tribe Cacteae — subtribe Epiphyllinae

Etymology   The name comes from the Greek *epi* (upon) and *phyllon* (leaf): the plant's flowers spring from stems which look like leaves. Link put it in the *Phyllocactus* genus in 1931, but this was later rejected in favor of the present name, established in 1812 by Adrian Hardy Haworth.

Place of Origin   A horticultural hybrid probably developed in England.

Description   Haworth described the plant as a species; it had been sent to him by Ackermann (hence its name) as a Mexican plant. However, as early as 1832 P. C. Van Geel classed it as a hybrid of a *Cereus*, which would make it one of the oldest hybrids. One of its parents was probably *Heliocereus speciosus*. Specimens are variable because they are the result of further crossing. In general, however, the main stem is erect and semiligneous. The many flat joints have scalloped edges, are weak or occasionally fairly stiff, triangular or almost cylindrical. Areoles, appearing on the scallops along the edge, are felted and sometimes bristly or bear small spines, particularly on new growth. The perianth segments of the large, irregular day-blooming flowers are scarlet.

Cultivation   Since it is hardy and very floriferous, this plant is widespread. To flower abundantly, it needs a period of rest in a cool, dry atmosphere during winter, and very well-lighted semishade in summer. It is easily propagated by cuttings.

---

92   EPITHELANTHA MICROMERIS   (Engelmann)

Weber ex Britton and Rose
Tribe Cacteae — subtribe Echinocactinae
Common names: Button cactus, mulato

Etymology   The name comes from the Greek *epi*, above, *thele*, nipple, and *anthos*, flower: the flowers spring from the apex of the tubercles.

Place of Origin   From western Texas into southern New Mexico and northern Mexico.

Description   This species is the only member of the genus suggested by Weber in 1898 and erected by Britton and Rose in 1922. The plant has fibrous roots and a depressed globular stem that elongates with age and may ramify from the base, forming small clusters. The stem reaches a height of 3 in. (8 cm.) and a diameter of 1/2 to 2½ in. (1.5 to 6 cm.). The tubercles are very small, and so are the many spirally arranged white spines which cover the entire stem (*micromeris* comes from the Greek; it means made up of small particles). Spines are only 1/12 in. (2 mm.) long: those on the new areoles are longer but eventually break off. The small flowers are white or pale pink. The long red berries are edible. The *greggii* variety is hardier; *densispina* and *rufispina*, have brown spines.

Cultivation   Growth is extremely slow, and cultivated plants rarely tiller. They are therefore mainly propagated by seed. Their potting soil should have about 20 percent lime added.

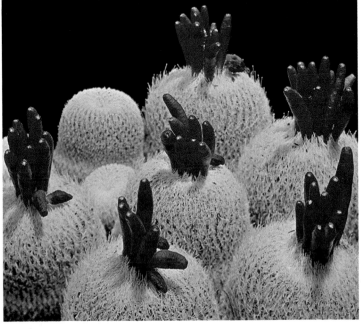

93 ERYTHRORHIPSALIS PILOCARPA (Loefgr.)
Berger
Tribe Cacteae — subtribe Rhipsalidinae

Etymology The name comes from the Greek *erythros*, red, and *Rhipsalis:* it has red fruit and resembles the pendant stems of *Rhipsalis*. It differs in that its flowers have a bristly tube, not a bare ovary, and its fruit is larger with bristly areoles.

Place of Origin The states of São Paulo and Rio de Janeiro in Brazil.

Description This epiphytic plant forms large clusters, its pendant branches giving way to a series of new whorled stems. Branches and stems are not round; they have faint ribbing noticeable only because it bears small areoles with three to ten bristles but no spines. Each stem is up to 5 in. (12 cm.) long and 1/4 in. (5 mm.) in diameter. It ends in an apical areole from which the flower appears. The buds are very bristly; their styles often emerge before the buds open. The scented flowers are up to 1 in. (2.5 cm.) across. Their tube is only 1/12 in. (2 mm.) long and has areoles with a few bristles. The flowers have a double corona of perianth segments: outer segments are triangular and pinkish; inner ones are white with pinkish tips and open wide. The wine-red fruit is spherical, measures 2/5 in. (12 mm.) and has small, bristly areoles.

Cultivation The plant needs very strong light but no direct sunshine. Propagation is by stem cuttings.

---

94 ESCOBARIA SNEEDII Britton and Rose
Tribe Cacteae — subtribe Cactinae

Etymology It is named after two Mexican naturalists, the Escobár brothers, and is similar to *Coryphantha;* indeed several of the latter's species have been transferred to it. The tubercles have a narrow groove leading away from the areoles, but the flowers are smaller and the fruit and seeds are different.

Place of Origin The plant was discovered in 1920 by J. R. Sneed in the Franklin Mountains between El Paso, Texas, and Las Cruces, New Mexico.

Description The plant forms dense clumps of up to 50 segments. The cylindrical stem is 2½ in. (6 cm.) high and only 1/2 to 3/4 in. (1 to 2 cm.) in diameter. The numerous tiny roundish tubercles protrude only 1/8 in. (approx. 3 mm.) and are practically hidden by an enormous number of small spines, about 1/4 in. (5 mm.) long, which grow in tufts of 20 on each tubercle. They are very close-set and overlap. White or off-white, the longest spines on the apex have brown tips or are reddish all over. The very small flowers, measuring only 1/2 in. (1 cm.) in length, appear near the apex from the tubercle-groove and are pink or pale yellow.

Cultivation This strange little plant is easy to propagate from basal shoots, but it is not very widespread and seems to be rare even in its natural habitat. It requires a sunny position and a strict rest period.

95 ESCOBARIA STROBILIFORMIS (Poselger)
Boedecker
Tribe Cacteae — subtribe Cactinae

Place of Origin   Southwestern Texas, southern New Mexico, and across the border into Mexico.
Description   Poselger classified this plant as *Echinocactus strobiliformis* in 1853; it is sometimes still called *Escobaria tuberculosa*, which was superseded by its present name. It should not be confused with *Encephalocarpus strobiliformis*. The specific name of both is derived from the plants' similarity to a pine cone due to their raised slanting tubercles. The stem of *Escobaria strobiliformis* is cylindrical, 7 in. (18 cm.) high with a diameter of 2½ in. (6 cm.), and it tillers to form clumps of basal shoots. Tubercles are arranged regularly in spirals, slant upward, and protrude 1/4 in. (6 mm.). The narrow, felted groove on the upper part of the tubercle is the prolongation of the apical areole. There are 20 to 30 white radial spines, 1/6 to 1/2 in. (4 to 15 mm.) long and needle-shaped. The five to nine central spines are brown or have a blackish tip, are somewhat thicker and longer, and the lowest is often curved backward. Flowers are 1 in. (2.5 cm.) across, with lilac-colored outer segments and pale pink inner ones. The species is variable; there are numerous named varieties.
Cultivation   The plant does not tolerate frost or intense, persistent cold. Propagation is from basal shoots.

96 ESPOSTOA GUENTHERI (Kupper) Buxbaum
Tribe Cacteae — subtribe Cereinae

Etymology   This name commemorates Nicolas Esposto, a Peruvian botanist at the National School of Agriculture in Lima.
Place of Origin   In the valley of the Río Grande de Lipex in the Andes of southern Bolivia, very near the Chilean border.
Description   The plant has an erect stem, 6½ ft. (2 m.) high, which ramifies from its base, forming large clusters. The stems have a diameter of 3¼ to 4 in. (8 to 10 cm.). Their 12 to 17 rounded ribs have shallow transverse grooves above the small, round areoles. The latter are larger and closer set near the apex, where they are densely covered with cream-colored felt. In young plants the 15 or so spines cannot be differentiated. As a plant develops, it acquires 25 spines from 1/4 to 1/2 in. (5 to 15 mm.) long. One of these is a thicker, longer central spine. All the spines are yellow, but the radials pointing downward are fine, silky, and more slender than those pointing upward. A cephalium appears on the side of the stem in the flower-bearing area, extending down for about 20 in. (50 cm.) below the apex. Its areoles bear thick, yellowish-white down 1/6 in. (4 mm.) long, and 20 to 25 shiny, yellowish-brown bristles. The flowers, 3¼ in. (8 cm.) long and 1¼ in. (3 cm.) in diameter, have a semicylindrical tube with pinkish, silky hairs. The perianth segments are cream-colored or very pale yellow. The flowers bloom at night.
Cultivation   Propagation is by cuttings.

97 ESPOSTOA LANATA (von Humboldt, Bonpland and Kunth) Britton and Rose
Tribe Cacteae — subtribe Cereinae

Place of Origin Northern Peru. For many years after the first description of the plant in 1823, the boundaries between Peru and Ecuador were uncertain, so the plant was given as a native of the latter.

Description This species, almost arborescent, has a definite, ramifying trunk up to 13 ft. (4 m.) high. Branches spread out from the upper part of the green stem and are 1 ½ to 2 ½ in. (4 to 6 cm.) in diameter, possibly 4 in. (10 cm.) on older plants. They initially grow almost horizontally and become erect later. There are 20 to 30 low, rounded ribs with close-set, white, circular areoles bearing numerous short, sharp radial spines that are yellowish, often with reddish-brown tips. There are at most two tough central spines pointing outward. They are yellow with a reddish tip and 2 to 3 ¼ in. (5 to 8 cm.) long. On the youngest parts of the plant most spines are often hidden by long silky, white hairs. The flower-bearing region on the upper part of the branches has a longer vertical cephalium, which is prominent even though its base is sunken. It is hairy and whitish, bearing white, nocturnal flowers 2 in. (5 cm.) long. The variety *sericata* has no long central spines.

Cultivation It grows slowly, tolerating half-shade and full sun, needing mild heat in winter. Propagation by cuttings.

---

98 ESPOSTOA MELANOSTELE (Vaupel) Borg.
Tribe Cacteae — subtribe Cereinae

Place of Origin Along the Pacific coast of western Peru, from the Río Sana in the north to Pico in the south (between approximately 7° and 16° S), at altitudes between 2,600 and 7,800 ft. (800 and 2,400 m.).

Description This plant was formerly known as *Pseudoespostoa melanostele* Backeberg, but that genus is no longer accepted. The stem ramifies from the base, has joints 4 in. (10 cm.) in diameter and grows to a height of about 6 ½ ft. (2 m.). There are about 25 low, tuberculate ribs bearing close-set areoles covered by a dense mass of hairs when young; later the hairs become sparser and softer. Radial spines are difficult to distinguish from central spines; all are yellowish, numerous, slender and almost bristlelike, less than 1/4 in. (3 mm.) long, interspersed with thicker, golden spines up to 1 ½ in. (4 cm.) long. All spines become blackish, hence the name *melanostele*, (black column). The lateral cephalium indicating the flower-bearing region is superficial rather than originating from a depression in the stem; it is covered with brownish-white down, and never bears bristles. Flowers springing from it are white and more than 2 in. (5 cm.) long, with a slightly hairy tube. Given the plant's vast area of distribution, the species is variable, some forms have more hairs or shorter spines.

Cultivation Propagation by cuttings. Needs heat in winter.

99 ESPOSTOA RITTERI Buining
Tribe Cacteae — subtribe Cereinae

Place of Origin   Along the Río Marañón in northern Peru.
Description   This is an almost arborescent plant that reaches
13 ft. (4 m.) in height. It ramifies profusely. The dark green
branches are 2¾ in. (7 mm.) in diameter. Each stem has 18 to
22 ribs with transverse depressions between which large,
white, felted areoles appear very close-set bearing slender,
white hairs, 3/4 to 1¼ in. (2 to 3 cm.) long and dense towards
the apex. It has about 25 slender, short radial spines, mostly
reddish-brown though they may be yellowish or whitish. There
is a single central spine, from about 1/4 to 3/4 in. (7 mm. to 2
cm.) long and pointing outward or downward, which is blackish-brown or reddish on young stems, and grayish-white on the
older part of the stem. On small plants grown from seed this
spine is slender and brownish-red. A long cephalium appears
on the upper part of the stem that bears the floriferous areoles;
it extends downward from the apex, and consists of a mass of
yellowish woolly hairs from among which white flowers appear.
The latter are about 3 in. (8 cm.) long and have a tube covered
with long white hairs. The red globular fruit is sparsely covered
with small scales bearing a few white bristles.
Cultivation   Plants found in cultivation are normally small
specimens grown from seed; they are unlikely to flower, but
they may show the beginnings of a cephalium.

---

100 ESPOSTOA ULEI (Gürke) Buxbaum
Tribe Cacteae — subtribe Cereinae

Place of Origin   The mountains of the Chique-Chique district
in the northern part of the state of Bahia, Brazil.
Description   When Britton and Rose discovered this plant in
1917 they created the monotypic genus *Facheiroa*. (*Facheiro*
is the Brazilian word for cacti.) Its current name was given by
Gürke in honor of the German botanist Oskar Ule. Like other
monotypic genera, it was reclassified in a much larger genus.
The almost arborescent plant has an erect trunk about 5 to
16½ ft. (1.5 to 5 m.) tall and about 5 in. (12 cm.) in diameter.
This is light green in young plants and becomes gray-green
later. It has 15 to 20 tuberculate ribs protruding about 1/2 in.
(1 cm.) and bearing felted areoles. All spines are brown: there
are 10 to 15 radials about 1/2 in. (1 to 1.5 cm.) long and three
or four central spines often almost twice that length. On one
side of the stems near the apex is a cephalium up to 8 in. (20
cm.) long, consisting of a mass of brown or reddish hairs measuring 1¾ in. (4.5 cm.), but no bristles. Flowers appear from the
middle of the cephalium and are 1½ in. (4 cm.) long and 3/4 in.
(2 cm.) across. The tube is covered with small scales and
brown hair 2/5 in. (1 cm.) long; perianth segments are white.
The fruit is pear-shaped.
Cultivation   Almost never cultivated. Propagation is by seed
or branch cuttings.

101 EULYCHINIA SPINIBARBIS (Otto) Britton and Rose
Tribe Cacteae — subtribe Cereinae

Etymology This genus was created in 1860 by Philippi; he combined the Greek *lychnia*, candelabrum, and *eu*, good, since almost all these species have an erect stem and candelabrum-shaped branches.

Place of Origin Central Chile, near Coquimbo on the Pacific.

Description This species was described and placed in the genus *Cereus* by C. Otto in 1837. It is almost arborescent and may reach a height of 13 ft. (4 m.), although it often grows to no more than 6½ ft. (2 m.) even in its natural surroundings. It has a very ramified stem. The stems measure about 3 in. (7.5 cm.) in diameter and have 12 or 13 rounded, parallel ribs. Areoles are large and scarcely felted, with about 20 sharp spines that are light brown or whitish with a brown tip, the radials being easy to distinguish from the centrals. The central spines may reach a length of 6 in. (15 cm.) while the others, most of which point outward, vary in length, reaching a maximum of nearly 3/4 in. (1.8 cm.). Flowers are 1¼ to 2½ in. (3 to 6 cm.) long and almost the same measurement across. The short tube bears small scales with long brown woolly hairs growing from the axils. Inner perianth segments are white or pink and pointed, opening wide when the flower is blooming.

Cultivation This plant is very seldom cultivated. It needs sunshine and a moist atmosphere. Propagation is by cuttings.

102 FEROCACTUS ACANTHODES (Lemaire) Britton and Rose
Tribe Cacteae — subtribe Echinocactinae
Common name: California barrel cactus, desert barrel cactus

Etymology The generic name comes from the Latin *ferus* (wild or fierce), because of its terrible prickles.

Place of Origin The deserts of California, southern Nevada, southwestern Arizona, and northern Baja California.

Description This generally solitary plant initially has a globular stem later becoming cylindrical-columnar up to 10 ft. (3 m.) tall, with up to 27 ribs bearing large, close-set, yellowish areoles especially felted when young. Spines are white, pink or red. There are about 13 radials, 1½ in. (4 cm.) long, variegated in color or striped, cylindrical, sharp, slender, and sometimes bristlelike. Of the four central spines, the upper and lower ones are flattened, slender, more or less curved but never hooked, and about 4 in. (10 cm.) long. Flowers are yellow or bright orange and campanulate, growing from the upper part of the young areoles near the apex. Including their purple-scaled tube, they are 1½ to 2½ in. (4 to 6 cm.) long and usually slightly more across. The variety *lecontei* is shorter and slenderer; its area extends into the Mexican state of Sonora.

Cultivation Cultivated forms are smaller, but just as spiny and colorful. They need strong sun, mild winter heat, and rich but porous and well-drained soil. Propagation is by seed.

103 FEROCACTUS COLORATUS Gates
Tribe Cacteae — subtribe Echinocactinae

Place of Origin   Baja California, Mexico.
Description   The stem of this species is globular at first, becomes cylindrical later; in the plant's natural habitat it may reach a height of 3¼ ft. (1 m.) and a diameter of 12 in. (30 cm.), although in cultivation it is notably smaller. There are 13 to 20 wide, blunt ribs bearing large, elongated areoles that look exceptionally large on younger parts because they are covered with thick white felt. This gradually disappears with age, until the areoles are glabrous. There are 10 to 14 radial spines that are white, long and slender; bristlelike, straight or slightly curved or contorted; and splayed out laterally so they almost overlap. There are about seven to nine central spines, and even more on large specimens. They are thick, sharp and straight; flattish, scored transversally, and up to 2 in. (5 cm.) long. The lowest is hooked and much wider than the others. They are bright red when young, later becoming brownish or brownish-red. The flowers are straw-colored, but have a large red or orange median stripe that stands out as their dominant color. The fruit is yellow.
Cultivation   This plant has fairly recently been introduced, and is still difficult to find on the market. It needs a great deal of sunshine and a complete rest in winter, suffering if the cold becomes intense. Propagation is by seed. Growth is slow.

104 FEROCACTUS EMORYI (Engelmann) Orcutt
Tribe Cacteae — subtribe Echinocactinae
Common name: Coville barrel cactus

Place of Origin   From southern Arizona to Sonora in Mexico.
Description   This species is still generally known as *Ferocactus covillei*. Britton and Rose named it after its discoverer F. V. Coville; it probably includes more than one variety. In its natural habitat the stem, solitary and spherical, becomes a cylinder varying from about 5 ft. (1.5 m.) to 6½ ft. (2 m.) tall or more, with 22 to 32 slender ribs protruding 1½ in. (4 cm.) and more or less tuberculate to begin with. Throughout this genus the tubercles of young plants are prominent, having not yet combined to form continuous ribbing. Areoles are set far apart and are at first covered with white or brown felt, becoming close-set and glabrous in old specimens. They have five to eight subulate radial spines, somewhat curved, and 1¼ to 2½ in. (3 to 6 cm.) long. The central spine, always solitary, is very variable, being straight, curved or doubled over at its tip and often hooked. It is more or less flat and 1¼ to 3 in. (3 to 8 cm.) long. All the spines vary from red to white and are scored transversally. Flowers are up to 2½ in. (6 cm.) long, with a short tube and red, yellow-striped, or yellow perianth segments. In Mexico the pulp is sliced and candied.
Cultivation   It doesn't tolerate frost and needs much sun. Propagation is seed, which increases its variability.

105 FEROCACTUS FLAVOVIRENS (Scheidweiler)
Britton and Rose
Tribe Cacteae — subtribe Echinocactinae

Place of Origin   Near Tehuacán in the state of Puebla, south-central Mexico.

Description   The plant's stem, solitary and spherical at first but later elongated, branches very readily, forming large clumps of stems, depressed at their apex, which are 12 to 16 in. (30 to 40 cm.) high and 4 to 8 in. (10 to 20 cm.) in diameter. There are usually 13 ribs, raised about 3/4 in. (2 cm.), with sharp edges. The oval areoles, felted near the apex and almost glabrous lower down, are set between slight swellings in the ribbing. There are 14 slender radial spines, pointing outward, as much as 3/4 in. (2 cm.) long, and four central spines of which the lowest is the longest, measuring from 2 to 3¼ in. (5 to 8 cm.) in length. This points upward at first, downward later. All the spines are reddish at first. Then they turn a fairly light brown and eventually gray. Some of them even turn yellowish. The flowers are 1½ in. (4 cm.) long and funnel-shaped, with a scaly tube and lanceolate, red perianth segments.

Cultivation   Although this plant is easy to grow, it is one of the less attractive species of the genus and therefore is not very widespread. Propagation is by seed, or from shoots if a tillered plant is available.

106 FEROCACTUS GATESII Lindsay
Tribe Cacteae — subtribe Echinocactinae

Place of Origin   Baja California, Mexico.

Description   Although it is spherical when young, this plant later becomes cylindrical and reaches a height of nearly 5 ft. (1.5 m.) and a diameter of 12 in. (30 cm.). There are 30 to 32 raised, slightly lumpy ribs bearing long, light-brown, felted areoles that become bare with age. There are 16 radial spines; the four central spines form a cross and are flattened at the sides, reaching a width of about 1/8 in. (3 mm.). The lowest, which is also the longest, measures 2¾ in. (7 cm.) and is not hooked. The central spines and some of the laterals are scored transversally, while others are slender and bristlelike. The red flowers are 2½ in. (6 cm.) long and the same width when open.

Cultivation   Like all plants from Baja California, this species must be kept very dry during its rest periods, and needs strong sunshine and a certain degree of heat. Propagation is by seed.

107 FEROCACTUS GRACILIS Gates
Tribe Cacteae — subtribe Echinocactinae

Place of Origin   Near San Fernando in northern Baja California, Mexico.
Description   The specific name of this plant no doubt refers to the fact that, in its natural habitat its cylindrical stem may grow to a height of nearly 10 ft. (3 m.) and a diameter of no more than 12 in. (30 cm.). When young, however, the stem is still spherical and far from slender. There are 24 ribs on an adult plant, but as with all members of the genus many of them develop after the plant has become cylindrical, so that a young specimen may have only 12 or so. The elliptical areoles are large, felted near the apex and bare lower down, with five radial spines pointing in all directions. These are white, slender, and 1 to 1½ in. (2.5 to 4 cm.) long, overlapping with those on adjacent ribs. There are from 7 to 13 central spines that are thick, red, and ringed, becoming black on older plants. They are all conical except the upper one, which is flattened at both sides, and the lower one, which is very wide and hooked. The flowers are 1½ in. (4 cm.) long, and their straw-colored segments have a reddish-brown median line. The fruit is oblong and yellow.
Cultivation   This plant needs sunshine and a soil that is not too rich in humus but has plenty of mineral salts. The salts heighten the color of the spines. Propagation is by seed.

---

108 FEROCACTUS HAMATACANTHUS (Mühlpf.)
Britton and Rose
Tribe Cacteae — subtribe Echinocactinae
Common names: Turk's head, visnaga

Place of Origin   Texas, New Mexico and northern Mexico.
Description   The plant's stem is spherical, later globose-cylindrical, as tall as 24 in. (60 cm.), with about 13 tuberculate ribs. In old plants tubercles are low and wide, and separated by transverse grooves. Areoles are large and set 1¼ in. (3 cm.) apart. Floriferous areoles near the apex have extra 1/12 to 1/6 in. (2 to 4 mm.) nectar-bearing glands. Soft at first, once they bear nectar they become hard and spinescent. There are 8 to 12 radial spines 1/2 to 2¾ in. (1 to 7 cm.) long, sometimes rather flattened. There are also one to four straight central spines; the lowest is up to 4¾ in. (12 cm.) long, sometimes slightly flattened, and hooked (*hamatus* means hooked or curved in Latin). All spines are brownish-red, later gray. Yellow flowers are 3 in. (8 cm.) long, and often red on the inside. The edible fruit, 3/4 to 2 in. (2 to 5 cm.) long, is brown or brownish-gray and has some scales; it opens at its base to allow the seeds to escape. The variety *sinuatus* has more deeply incised ribs and all yellow flowers.
Cultivation   The plant flowers when it is young, and is easy to grow, but it must be sheltered from intense cold. The stem will ramify if damaged. Propagation is generally by seed.

109 FEROCACTUS HERRERAE Ortega
Tribe Cacteae — subtribe Echinocactinae

Place of Origin   The western Sierra Madre in the states of Durango, Sinaloa and Sonora, Mexico.

Description   Like many other members of the genus, this species is spherical when young and cylindrical later, reaching up to 6½ ft. (2 m.) in height, although usually much less than this in its cultivated form. There are 13 or 14 tuberculate ribs bearing white or light gray areoles that reach a length of 3/4 in. (2 cm.) on adult plants. There are eight radial spines, two of which are white while the others are more or less striped with red. The single central spine is hooked at first, becoming erect later. From the edge of each areole there also grow eight slender, contorted bristles about 1¼ in. (3 cm.) long. The flowers are funnel-shaped and are 2¾ in. (7 cm.) long and across when they are open. The perianth segments are reddish with yellow edges.

Cultivation   This species is a fairly recent introduction and not yet in wide cultivation. It needs summer sunshine, does not tolerate cold in winter and should be kept almost completely dry. Propagation is by seed.

---

110 FEROCACTUS LATISPINUS (Haworth) Britton and Rose
Tribe Cacteae — subtribe Echinocactinae

Place of Origin   Central and eastern Mexico.

Description   This widespread species was first described by Haworth in 1824. The grayish-green stem is spherical or compressed-spherical, reaching a height and diameter of 16 in. (40 cm.); sometimes it elongates. The 8 to 14 ribs on a young stem increase to 21 or more on an adult. They protrude ½ to ¾ in. (1 to 2 cm.) and are notched between the raised portions, which later become low, blunt tubercles. Large areoles initially bear short whitish down which they lose later, and are set 1¼ to 1½ in. (3 to 4 cm.) apart with six to ten white or pinkish slender radial spines, scored transversally 3/4 to 1 in. (2 to 2.5 cm.) long. The four or more thicker central spines, more colorful than the radials, vary from yellow to red. They are straight, point outward, and are more than 1¼ in. (3 cm.) long; the lowest, which points downward, is very flat, curved at the tip, and hooked. Flowers are campanulate, have a tube covered with elongated scales and perianth segments sharp at their apex and white or pink, varying to crimson or violet. The oblong fruit is 1½ in. (4 cm.) long with minute seeds.

Cultivation   Different forms are found on the market; spines vary in thickness or brightness of color because it's propagated by seed. This method of reproduction is very easy but slow.

111 FEROCACTUS ROBUSTUS (Pfeiffer) Britton and Rose
Tribe Cacteae — subtribe Echinocactinae

Place of Origin Valley of Tehuacán in the state of Puebla in south-central Mexico.

Description The plant branches thickly at its base with hundreds of stems that form clumps 3¼ ft. (1 m.) high and nearly 10 ft. (3 m.) wide. Each stem is about 8 in. (20 cm.) in diameter. There are about 8 ribs, raised when young but indistinct in shape when mature. Its edges are slightly corrugated. Areoles are brown on new growth, later gray. Spines are variable in number as well as in length, but generally there are 14 radials. The upper ones are bristlelike, often overlapping with those on adjacent ribs, while the lower ones are light-colored and point downward. The average number of central spines is four. They measure up to 2½ in. (6 cm.) long and are sometimes flat, the apical spines being red or brown, the basal spine darker. The flowers are about 1½ in. (4 cm.) long and across. The tube is covered with large rounded scales at its apex and the inner perianth segments are slender, lanceolate and yellow. The scaly oval fruit is about 1 in. (2.5 cm.) long.

Cultivation This plant is easily propagated from the stems that form around its base and often on the main stem. It also grows easily from seed, enjoying relatively rapid growth. Although less prolific when pot-grown, it comes to need a lot of room.

112 FEROCACTUS STAINESII (Andot) Britton and Rose
Variety **PRINGLEI** (Coulter) Backeberg
Tribe Cacteae — subtribe Echinocactinae

Place of Origin North-central Mexico. The species is found in San Luis Potosí, the variety in Coahuila and Zacatecas.

Description Backeberg made *Ferocactus pringlei* a variety of *Ferocactus stainesii;* earlier authors, following Britton and Rose, had classified them as different species. The type of the species is nearly 5 ft. (1.5 m.) tall and about 24 in. (60 cm.) in diameter. It is globular initially, columnar later and branching from the base; its growth is slow. The stem has about 18 raised ribs depressed between the rounded tubercles that bear large areoles 1/2 in. (1 cm.) across and set about 1½ in. (4 cm.) apart, with short yellow down that later turns gray. The five or more radial spines are curved, 3/4 in. (2 cm.) long, and interspersed with white bristles. Four central spines, forming a cross, are somewhat flattened and longer, the uppermost one being curved. All spines are red at first, later turning yellowish and then gray. Orange flowers are campanulate and about 1½ in. (4 cm.) long. The rare variety *pringlei* has nine radial spines and long, straw-colored bristles. Flowers are red on the outside and yellow inside. The fruit is yellow, dehiscent, and 1½ in. (4 cm.) long.

Cultivation Propagation is by seed.

113 FEROCACTUS WISLIZENI (Engelmann) Britton and Rose
Tribe Cacteae — subtribe Echinocactinae
Common names: Candy barrel cactus, fishhook barrel cactus

Place of Origin This species has a vast area of distribution: from El Paso County, Texas, across New Mexico to Maricopa and Pima counties, Arizona, and from Chihuahua and Sonora along the Gulf of California as far as Sinaloa in Mexico.

Description The stem is spherical at first but becomes columnar with age, reaching a height of 6½ ft. (2 m.). It is usually single but may put forth secondary stems if the apex is damaged. There may be as many as 25 ribs on adult specimens. They protrude about 1¼ in. (3 cm.) and bear elliptical areoles up to 3/4 in. (2 cm.) long, covered with brown felt and slightly sunken. Except for flower-bearing areoles in the apical region, they are set unusually far apart. Radial spines are often absent in young plants. When they do appear, they are slender and bristlelike, measuring up to 2 in. (5 cm.) in length. There are several tough, subulate central spines, scored transversally, whose color varies from white to red. One is much thicker than the others — as much as 6 in. (15 cm.) long, flattened and markedly hooked at its apex. The campanulate flowers are 2 to 2½ in. (5 to 6 cm.) long with a short tube. Outer perianth segments are green and the inner ones vary from an orange-yellow to red. The fruit is yellow, about 2 in. (5 cm.) long.

Cultivation Its growth is not rapid, but it may reach a good height in cultivation. It needs strong sun. Propagation by seed.

114 FRAILEA CASTANEA Backeberg
Tribe Cacteae — subtribe Echinocactinae

Etymology The genus was named after the Spaniard Manuel Fraile, born in 1850, who was in charge of the cactus collection for the U.S. Department of Agriculture.

Place of Origin From southern Brazil to northern Uruguay.

Description This species, which is often referred to by the synonym *Frailea asterioides*, owes its specific name to its stem color, which is usually brown, although it may be reddish green. The stem is a flattened sphere with 10 to 15 almost flat, slightly rounded ribs separated by narrow linear grooves. Along the center of the ribs is a row of very close-set areoles covered with felt that is scarcely visible and generally not white. It has from 7 to 11 minutes spines, reddish at first, becoming black later, very close-set on the lower part of the areole. The flowers are 1½ in. (4 cm.) long and across and have yellow segments. The ovary and the base of the tube bear conspicuous wool and brown bristles. In all the species of this genus the flowers often do not open at all, and the seeds are produced inside them through self-fertilization. This species, reminiscent of an *Astrophytum*, is very variable both in color and the length of its spines; it sometimes appears slightly tuberculate.

Cultivation Although this plant will grow well on its own roots, it is often grafted on other stock. It needs both warmth and shade in summer. Propagation is by seed.

115 FRAILEA GRAHLIANA (Haage) Britton and Rose
Tribe Cacteae — subtribe Echinocactinae

Place of Origin Around Paraguari in southern Paraguay, and the provinces of Misiones and Entre Rios in Argentina.
Description This species puts forth a great many basal shoots. The greenish-brown stem is spherical, somewhat flattened and depressed at its apex, with a diameter of 1 ¼ to 1 ½ in. (3 to 4 cm.). There are 13 slightly raised ribs divided into rounded tubercles 1/12 in. (2 mm.) high. Each tubercle bears an oval or elliptical areole with 9 to 11 subulate spines that are less than 1/4 in. (5 mm.) long, slightly curved backward, and yellow when young. The flowers are about 1 ½ in. (4 cm.) long and across, and have yellow perianth segments. The fruit measures less than 1/2 in. (1 cm.) in diameter and is yellowish, with small reddish-brown scales, yellowish hairs and minuscule yellow bristles. It seems that from time to time this species produces even smaller fruit directly from its buds, bypassing altogether the blooming of its flowers and the formation of their anthers. The variety *rubrispina,* described by Yoshio Ito, has reddish-brown spines. It is probably a Japanese cultivar.
Cultivation Propagation is by seed or from shoots if tillered plants are available. The plant does not tolerate cold, and needs at least partial shade during the summer.

116 GYMNOCALYCIUM BRUCHII (Spegazzini) Backeberg
Tribe Cacteae — subtribe Echinocactinae

Etymology The name derives from the Greek *gymnos,* meaning bare, and *kalyx,* meaning involucre or bud, since its floral buds are bare. The genus is exclusively South American.
Place of Origin The province of Córdoba in Argentina.
Description This species is very variable. It is still often called by the synonym *Gymnocalycium lafaldense,* but this may have referred to a different, albeit very similar species. It tillers profusely, forming dense cushions about 1 ¼ in. (3.5 cm.) high and 2½ in. (6 cm.) across. There are about 12 low ribs divided into rounded tubercles, with only slight raised ''beaks'' (see Entry No. 118) beneath the areoles or none at all. Areoles are close-set, sunken and felted. They bear 10 to 15 radially arranged spines that are slender and bristlelike, white with a brown base, 1/4 in. (5 mm.) long, and somewhat curved inward. Central spines are often absent, or there may be one to three that are straight, darker and brownish. The flowers are 1 ¼ to 2 in. (3 to 5 cm.) long, varying in form from a fairly narrow funnel shape to a broad bell shape. The tube is short with only a few scales, while the perianth segments vary from pale to bright pink, and often have a darker line down the middle.
Cultivation Propagation by shoots is advisable, since plants raised from seed may be very variable.

117 GYMNOCALYCIUM CALOCHLORUM (Boe-decker) Ito
Tribe Cacteae — subtribe Echinocactinae

Place of Origin   Argentina.
Description   This small plant tillers profusely and has de-pressed, spherical, cushionlike stems, measuring 2½ in. (6 cm.) in diameter and 1½ in. (4 cm.) in height. There are about 11 tuberculate ribs. Each areole bears up to nine curved, close-set radial spines almost 1/2 in. (1 cm.) long, while cen-tral spines are altogether absent. The flowers are 2½ in. (6 cm.) long and have pale pink perianth segments. They grow from the youngest areoles near the apex of the plant and never open completely, remaining permanently semi-erect. The spe-cies is variable. The principal named varieties are *proliferum*, recognizable because it has larger stems that are a darker green or glaucous, and flowers that open wide and have out-ward-curved brownish-white, pink or white segments that are often pink at the base; and *roseiacanthum*, which is a much smaller variety with glaucous green stems half as big as those of the species, round yellowish areoles bearing contorted, pinkish spines, and large white flowers with red bases. The lat-ter variety originates the in Sierra de Córdoba.
Cultivation   The plant can be easily propagated from basal shoots. It does not tolerate intense cold, but prefers cool tem-peratures and shady positions when the sun is at its hottest.

---

118 GYMNOCALYCIUM DENUDATUM (Link and Otto) Pfeiffer
Tribe Cacteae — subtribe Echinocactinae
Common name: Spider cactus

Place of Origin   Throughout Paraguay and Uruguay, from southern Brazil to the province of Misiones in northern Argen-tina.
Description   The plant's stem is globular-spherical, 4 in. (10 cm.) across, with five to eight low, broad ribs. In the typical species, these have virtually no tubercles, but the majority of cultivated plants are hybrids with tuberculate ribs. If tubercles are present, the tubercles have the slightly rounded promi-nence, beneath the sunken areoles and above transverse grooves, characteristic of many species of this genus. This was described by Karl Schumann as a "chin"; it may also be called a "beak." Areoles, which are somewhat woolly, have only one to five slender, yellowish radial spines, about 1/2 in. (1.5 cm.) long, contorted and pointing sideways or downward. The flow-ers are 2 to 2¾ in. (5 to 7 cm.) long and have a slender tube and numerous white perianth segments tapering to a point. The *roseiflorum* variety has pink segments.
Cultivation   This species is easy to cultivate, as are the nu-merous natural or artificial hybrids that derive from it. It toler-ates low temperatures but not intense cold. Propagation is from basal shoots.

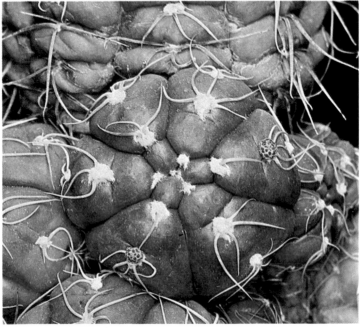

119 GYMNOCALYCIUM GIBBOSUM (Haworth)
Pfeiffer
Tribe Cacteae — subtribe Echinocactinae

Place of Origin Southern Argentina, in the province of Río Negro and Chubut between latitudes of 40° and 45° south.
Description This species, described by Haworth as a "cactus" in 1812, has been renamed by many authors since then because it has many varieties. The typical species has a spherical stem that reaches a height of 24 in. (60 cm.) and a diameter of 6 in. (15 cm.), and is a glaucous or dull green. It seldom puts forth shoots. There are 12 to 19 ribs with extremely prominent tubercles that have very pronounced "beaks" and are divided by deep transverse grooves. The slightly sunken areoles are gray and bear seven to ten somewhat curved, radial spines, pointing outward. These are pale brown with a reddish base. There are one to three central spines of the same color. All the spines vary in length, the longest reaching 1¼ in. (3 cm.). The flowers are large, 2½ to 2¾ in. (6 to 7 cm.) long, and the perianth segments are shaded from white to pink. Some of the varieties put forth basal shoots readily. The variety *nobile* has a larger, spherical stem, with more numerous, longer, overlapping spines that are white with a red base.
Cultivation It tolerates cold but not frost. Its native habitat is the pampas, very hot in summer, so it requires sun. Propagation is by shoots or seed, depending on the variety.

---

120 GYMNOCALYCIUM HORSTII Buining
Tribe Cacteae — subtribe Echinocactinae

Place of Origin In the Sierra Encantadas near Cacapava do Sul in the Brazilian state of Rio Grande do Sul in southern Brazil.
Description The plant has a glossy light green globular stem about 4½ in. (11 cm.) across, ramifying from the base. There are five to six ribs that are fairly smooth, sometimes slightly tuberculate, with three large, felted, roughly oval areoles on each rib. There are about five light yellow spines, all radial, set far apart and slanting outward; one, up to 1½ in. (3 cm.) in length, points downward. The flowers are 4¼ in. (11 cm.) long and across, with a tube covered by small pink scales, and pointed perianth segments varying in color from lilac to creamy white with a pink meridian stripe; the outer segments are dark pink. The fruit is oval and a glaucous green. It ripens very slowly and at maturity opens at the side, scattering its small seeds. The species was named in honor of Leopold Horst, who discovered it. The variety *buenekeri* differs only in that its epidermis is dark green and its flowers dark pink or red.
Cultivation The plant needs mild heat in winter and strong sunlight in summer. Propagation is by basal shoots.

121 GYMNOCALYCIUM MIHANOVICHII (Frič and Gürke) Britton and Rose
Tribe Cacteae — subtribe Echinocactinae

Place of Origin The Chaco Boreal in Paraguay. The typical species was discovered near Bahia Negra near Brazil.
Description The plant has a grayish-green or reddish spherical stem 2½ in. (6 cm.) in diameter, with about eight sharp ribs. These bear transverse prominences formed by the low tubercles, and have more or less obvious dark and light stripes. The small areoles, set 1/2 in. (1 cm.) apart, bear only five or six radial spines. These are yellowish and curved, measuring less than 1/2 in. (1 cm.) and often becoming caducous with age. Flowers, 1½ to 2 in. (4 to 5 cm.) long, vary from bell-shaped to funnel-shaped. They grow around the apex and have a scaly tube. Outer segments of the perianth are yellowish-green with a reddish tip; inner ones are markedly evaginated and are yellow, greenish or white. There are many varieties. The variety *pirarettaense* has pink flowers. There is also a red or yellow form known as *rubrum,* which is frequently seen grafted onto *Hylocereus;* the plant is exposed to gamma rays, which remove what chlorophyll it normally possesses; it then grows at the expense of the stock, gradually losing its bright color. It is impossible to get the stem or any basal shoots to take root.
Cultivation The plant prefers half-shade in summer. Propagation is by seed or basal shoots.

122 GYMNOCALYCIUM NEOCUMINGII (Backeberg) Hutchison
Tribe Cacteae — subtribe Echinocactinae

Place of Origin The Andean cordillera in Bolivia and Peru.
Description The classification of this small plant has been surprisingly complicated. It was originally classified as an *Echinocactus* in 1843; Britton and Rose then transferred it to the genus *Lobivia* and Backeberg to *Spegazzinia,* retaining the specific name *cumingii.* This later became *neocumingii* when Backeberg transferred it to his genus *Weingartia.* When this was abolished, the plant was given its present name, *Gymnocalycium,* which is still thought valid, but it may still be found under any of its former names. It has a solitary depressed-globular stem, 4 in. (10 cm.) high and 2½ in. (6 cm.) wide. There are about 18 ribs consisting of tubercles spirally arranged in rows, quadrangular at their base, flat higher up, and joined at the base. Areoles are whitish and bear 16 to 20 radial spines; upper ones are 1/2 in. (1 cm.) long and lower ones shorter. There are also two to ten thicker central spines. All spines are arranged radially and are cream-colored with a dark yellow tip, those growing around the apex being darker. The orange-yellow flowers grow laterally. More than one sometimes appears on the same areole. They are 1¼ in. (3 cm.) long.
Cultivation This plant will withstand quite low temperatures. Propagation is by seed.

123 GYMNOCALYCIUM NEUMANNIANUM

(Backeberg) Hutchison
Tribe Cacteae — subtribe Echinocactinae

Place of Origin Northern Argentina.

Description This plant has a long, conical taproot, narrowing at the neck of the short, globular stem, which reaches only 2¾ in. (7 cm.) in height and 2 in. (5 cm.) in diameter. There are about 14 ribs with transverse grooves between their compressed scarcely raised tubercles. Near the apex of the plant the tubercles have a more rounded base and are roughly hexagonal. The areoles at their apex are slightly sunken, with about six stiff, sharp radial spines pointing outward. These measure 1/2 in. (1.5 cm.) in length. Normally there is only one central spine, reaching more than 3/4 in. (2.5 cm.) in length. All the spines are dark brown or reddish-black. The flowers, which are approximately 1 in. (2.5 cm.) long and across, vary from yellow to orange. The variety *aurantium* is larger, with a dark olive-green velvety epidermis. Its areoles are covered with white felt and bear only one to four black spines, while the perianth segments are reddish on the outside and orange inside.

Cultivation This plant requires an unusually deep pot to provide ample room for the root, and very porous soil to prevent waterlogging and consequent root rot. Propagation is by seed.

---

124 GYMNOCALYCIUM OENANTHEMUM Backeberg

Tribe Cacteae — subtribe Echinocactinae

Place of origin Argentina.

Description This species owes its specific name to its often wine-colored flowers — *oinos* meaning wine, and *anthemon* flower, in Greek. The grayish or bluish green stem, a depressed sphere, widens at the base forming a hemisphere about 4 in. (10 cm.) in diameter. The 10 or 11 ribs are about 3/4 in. (2 cm.) wide at the base, with broad, angular, tubercles that are swollen lower down and have a pronounced "beak" below the oval areoles, which are covered with yellow felt. The five light gray spines are all radial; the two upper ones are shorter and thinner than the three lower ones, which are curved inward and are up to 1/2 in. (1.5 cm.) long. They may sometimes be a translucent red. The funnel-shaped flowers are large, up to 2 in. (5 cm.) long. The tube is covered with pink-edged scales. Perianth segments are typically wine red, although they can be salmon pink. The fruit is green and oval.

Cultivation This species, like many others of the genus, is not likely to rot, so its winter rest period need not be as strict as is customary. It withstands low temperatures but not intense cold (young plants are less tolerant of cold). Reduce the number of hours it spends in summer sun, shading it during the hottest parts of the day. Propagation is normally by seed.

125 GYMNOCALYCIUM PILCOMAYOENSIS
Cárdenas
Tribe Cacteae — subtribe Echinocactinae

Place of Origin The district of Potosí in Bolivia.
Description This species, described in 1964, owes its specific name to the area along the Rio Pilcomayo, where it was
found at an altitude of 7,800 ft. (2,400 m.). It may also be referred to under the name of *Weingartia pilcomayoensis;* but
this genus, in which it was first placed, has now been completely abolished. Its stem is spherical or bluntly conical, 5¼ in.
(13 cm.) high with a diameter of 5 in. (12 cm.). The color varies
from a bluish to a reddish-green. There are about 14 ribs separated into large, fully rounded tubercles that protrude 1/2 in. (1
cm.) and are 3/4 in. (2 cm.) wide at the base. The upper parts
of the tubercles bear round or elliptical gray areoles 1/2 in. (1
cm.) long. There are 12 to 15 close-set radial spines, 1/4 to
3/4 in. (5 mm. to 2 cm.) long, and spread outward. There are
also one to four central spines measuring 3/4 to 1 ¼ in. (2 to 3
cm.). Those on the upper part of the stem point upward to the
apex. All the spines are needle-shaped and thicker at their
base; they are whitish with brown or gray tips. The flowers are
1 ½ in. (4 cm.) long and have a very short, yellowish-green tube
that is scaly but glabrous. The perianth segments are yellow.
Cultivation This plant tolerates cold provided that it is kept
completely dry. It requires strong sunlight.

126 GYMNOCALYCIUM RIOGRANDENSE
Cárdenas
Tribe Cacteae — subtribe Echinocactinae

Place of Origin Along the Rio Grande (hence its specific
name) between the Cordillera de Cochabamba and the plano of
the Rio Guarayos in Bolivia.
Description This plant was fairly recently introduced and is
not yet in widespread cultivation. It has a glossy green spherical stem of an average height of about 2½ in. (6 cm.) and a diameter of up to 8 in. (20 cm.). There are about 13 ribs 1¼ in. (3
cm.) wide at their base, consisting of a series of low, wide,
conical tubercles which are well separated by transverse dividing lines. Each bears a round areole at first covered by white
felt near the apex, later becoming bare. Below the areole is a
conical, fairly slender "beak." The eight or nine spines are all
radial and up to 1 in. (2.5 cm.) long. They are slender, subulate, and sharp and are either straight or slightly curved. Those
toward the apex of the plant point upward. They are gray or
light brown with a black tip on the younger parts of the plant,
later becoming brown all over. The flowers have white perianth
segments with a red base. When adult, the plant puts forth
basal shoots.
Cultivation The plants needs mild heat in winter. Propagation is generally by seed.

127 GYMNOCALYCIUM SAGLIONE Britton and Rose
Tribe Cacteae — subtribe Echinocactinae

Place of Origin The provinces of Salta, Tucumán and Catamarca in northern Argentina.

Description The stem is solitary, globular, slightly flattened at its apex, and may reach 12 in. (30 cm.) in diameter. It is bluish-green to dark green; there are 13 to 32 ribs, depending on the plant's size. These consist of low, swollen tubercles that sometimes reach a length of 1 ½ in. (4 cm.) and are divided by transverse grooves. They have a small "beak" beneath each areole. Areoles are large, elliptical, felted when young and set 3/4 to 1 ½ in. (2 to 4 cm.) apart. They have eight to ten radial spines—as many as 15 on adult plants—which are 1 ¼ to 1 ½ in. (3 to 4 cm.) long, straight at first, curving outward later as the radial arrangement flattens. There is normally only one central spine, but with age the plant may produce several. All spines are reddish-brown or blackish. Flowers are nearly 1 ½ in. (3.5 cm.) long, with a short, scaly, funnel-shaped tube and white or pink-shaded perianth segments. The fruit is reddish, measuring 3/4 in. (2 cm.) in diameter.

Cultivation This species is very variable; since it is propagated from seed, variations are likely to increase; they are more noticeable on adult plants than on young ones. Growth is fairly rapid. The plant requires semishade, especially in summer.

128 GYMNOCALYCIUM SPEGAZZINI Britton and Rose
Tribe Cacteae — subtribe Echinocactinae

Place of Origin The slopes of the Andes near Cafayate, province of Salta, Argentina.

Description The species was described in 1905 by Spegazzini as *Echinocactus loricatus* (cuirass in Latin). Britton and Rose dedicated it to him when they reclassified it. When young, it has a depressed-globular stem that later becomes oblong and may reach 8 in. (20 cm.) tall and 7 in. (18 cm.) in diameter. The adult plant puts forth basal shoots. The epidermis may be a grayish- or bluish-green, or brownish. There are 10 to 15 ribs, sometimes more. They are wide, rounded, consisting of flat tubercles divided by transverse grooves, each of which bears a large elliptical areole above a small "beak." Areoles in the apical region are covered with a thick yellowish down; they later become gray and bare. Although there may be one downward-curving central spine, areoles generally bear only five to seven thick, light brown radial spines, just over 2 in. (5.5 cm.) long and curving obliquely downward; they are dark brown at first. Old plants sometimes produce two small upper spines that are shorter and slenderer. Flowers are 2¾ in. (7 cm.) long, with white or pink segments that are purple at the base. The species comprises many different varieties.

Cultivation Propagation is by seed or shoots.

129 HAAGEOCEREUS MULTICOLORISPINUS
Buining
Tribe Cacteae — subtribe Cereinae

Etymology   Backeberg named the genus after F. A. Haage, one of the great cactus nurserymen of his time, and included in it most of Britton and Rose's abolished genus *Binghamia*.
Place of Origin   The sand dunes between Nazca and the Pacific Ocean in the district of Ica in south-central Peru.
Description   This species, described by Buining in 1963, has a slender columnar stem growing to a height of 3¼ ft. (1 m.) and 1 ½ in. (3.5 cm.) in diameter. It is erect and ramifies from its base. It has about 15 ribs with round areoles. Initially these are almost covered by about 30 slender, bristlelike white radial spines which are less than 1/4 in. (5 mm.). The innermost part of the areole has four to eight central spines that are white with a black tip and dark base, later becoming an orange-yellow, tending to reddish and turning to grayish-white in old age— thus the plant's specific name. Flowers are nocturnal, but normally open in the afternoon and stay open for some time during the following morning. They are 3 in. (8 cm.) long, have a reddish tube and perianth segments that are reddish-brown on the outside and white on the inside. The oval fruit is crimson.
Cultivation   The plant needs warmth and sandy soil. Propagation is by cuttings.

130 HAAGEOCEREUS VERSICOLOR (Werdermann and Backeberg) Backeberg
Tribe Cacteae — subtribe Cereinae

Place of Origin   At a maximum altitude of 1,600 ft. (500 m.) in the eastern desert region of northern Peru.
Description   The plant's stem is stiff, erect, slender and columnar, nearly 5 ft. (1.5 m.) in height and 2 in. (5 cm.) in diameter in its natural habitat. It ramifies abundantly from its base, forming clusters that in the wild, amount to veritable colonies. Each stem has about 12 short, blunt ribs (old plants have more) bearing fairly close-set areoles with 25 to 30 slender, needle-shaped, straight radial spines 1/4 in. (5 mm.) long, and one or two central spines up to 1 ½ in. (4 cm.) long. The latter are yellowish at the base and dark red at the tip; the impression is that the spines are divided into rings of different colors varying from yellow to reddish-brown, or sometimes purple or russet. The nocturnal flowers have a slender tube bearing white hairs, and are about 3 to 4 in. (8 to 10 cm.) long and 2½ in. (6 cm.) across when the white segments of their perianth are wide open. The variety *aureispinus* has all-radial golden spines; *fuscus* has slender and dense dark reddish-brown radial spines; *lasiacanthus* has bristlelike radials and no central spines.
Cultivation   Growing as it does in very dry terrain, this plant needs a perfectly drained potting soil; and in view of its original habitat, it does not tolerate cold. Propagation is by cutting.

131 HAMATOCACTUS UNCINATUS (Galeotti) Buxbaum
Tribe Cacteae — subtribe Echinocactinae

Etymology The name comes from the Latin *hamatus,* hooked: the plant's central spine usually has a hooked tip.

Place of Origin Southern Texas and from the state of Chihuahua to the state of San Luis Potosí in north-central Mexico.

Description The plant has an oblong stem, about 8 in. (20 cm.) high and 2 to 2¾ in. (5 to 7 cm.) across, with about 13 tapering, deeply incised ribs with large, raised tubercles. At their apex the oval, felted areoles have a large, flat, yellow gland ringed by short yellow hair. Flower-bearing areoles have a slender groove extending down to the base of the tubercle, where flowers emerge. These glands are usually in the groove above the spines and below the flowers; they secrete nectar that attracts insects. There are seven or eight radial spines 1 to 2 in. (2.5 to 5 cm.) long; the upper ones are flat and straw-colored while the lower ones are reddish, conical and curved. There are from one to four central spines; the upper ones are tough and 1 in. (2.5 cm.) long, while the lowest may be up to 4 in. (10 cm.) long, flattened, straw-colored, reddish and hooked at its apex, and often scored transversally. The flowers are 1 in. (2.5 cm.) long, with erect, brownish-violet segments that hardly open. The variety *wrightii* has longer, red spines.

Cultivation Propagation by seed. It bears flowers in about 3 years. Sun and some winter watering are needed.

132 HARRISIA ERIOPHORA (Pfeiffer) Britton
Tribe Cacteae — subtribe Cereinae

Etymology This genus was dedicated to William Harris, superintendent of gardens and plantations in Jamaica.

Place of Origin Cuba and the adjacent Isle of Pines.

Description The main stem of this species, which ramifies prolifically, measures little more than 1½ in. (4 cm.) in diameter while reaching a height of about 3¾ ft. (3 m.). It remains erect because it becomes woody, while the segments are more or less curved or pendant. There are eight to nine rounded ribs with slight prominences in the areas of new growth, that bear white, felted areoles. There are six to nine spines that are light brown with black tips and 1½ in. (4 cm.) long. The buds, which appear near the apex of the plant on the upper part of the areole, are covered in conspicuous white wool more than 1/2 in. (1 cm.) long; this almost conceals the scales and hairs that then develop on the floral tube. The flowers are 4¾ to 7 in. (12 to 18 cm.) long. The outer perianth segments are pink or reddish while the inner ones are white. The fruit is yellow and globular, with a diameter of about 2½ in. (6 cm.).

Cultivation The plant needs warmth and a lot of sunlight; as a result, large cultivated specimens are rare. Propagation is by cuttings.

133   HATIORA SALICORNIOIDES (Haworth) Britton and Rose

Tribe Cacteae — subtribe Rhipsalidinae

Etymology In 1834 de Candolle removed this species from *Rhipsalis*, naming his new genus *Hariota* after Thomas Hariot, the sixteenth-century mathematician. Britton and Rose then added other species to the genus and and replaced it with an anagram since de Candolle's generic name was illegitimate.

Place of Origin The states of Rio de Janeiro and Minas Gerais in Brazil.

Description This small epiphytic shrub is erect with a profusely ramifying stem about 16 in. (40 cm.) tall, from which a jointed series of flattened or whorled shoots grow. At first these are swollen and barrel-shaped but later they develop a slender basal segment, usually about 1¼ in. (3 cm.) long, which is thicker where it is attached to the apex of the previous shoot. If the plant is left in a very brightly lighted place, the narrow section will be shorter, and the shoots will turn reddish. The scattered areoles nearly always remain glabrous in cultivation. The exception is the one at the apex, which is larger and more felted than the others, and bears yellow flowers just over 1/2 in. (1 cm.) long. The globoid fruit is a translucent white, reddish at its apex. This species may be mistaken for *Hatiora bambusoides*, which is similar but has less tapering, club-shaped shoots 1/6 in. (4 mm.) across at the apex, and orange flowers.

Cultivation This plant needs bright semishade, some sun and a very moist atmosphere. Propagation is by cuttings.

---

134   HELIABRAVOA CHENDE (Gosselin) Backeberg

Tribe Cacteae — subtribe Cereinae

Common name: Chende

Etymology Britton and Rose created the genus *Lemaireocereus* in 1909 to honor Charles Lemaire. Although still often referred to, it's not recognized and its members were reclassified: they did not have sufficiently uniform characteristics. Backeberg then adopted the genus *Heliabravoa* for this species to honor the Mexican botanist Helia Bravo-Hollis.

Place of Origin The states of Puebla and Oaxaca, Mexico.

Description This very large plant reaches as much as 23 ft. (7 m.) in height. It has a trunklike, profusely ramified stem, and each branch puts out additional joints, forming a dense, erect corona. The joints are about 4 in. (10 cm.) long and have seven to nine pointed ribs, becoming rounded later, which bear areoles set relatively far apart. There are two to five slender radial spines and there may be one or two central spines, although these are usually absent. All spines are yellow or brown, gray later. Flowers are funnel-shaped and 1½ to 2 in. (4 to 5 cm.) long. The scaly tube has light brown hairs, pink outer petals and white inner petals with a pale pink line down the center. The red fruit is spiny and has light brown hairs.

Cultivation Since it is sensitive to cold, it can be grown outdoors only in a mild climate and sheltered position. Propagation may be by seed, but it is easy to take cuttings from joints.

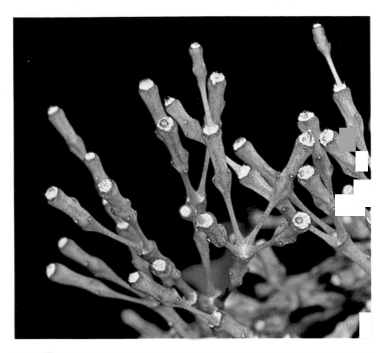

135 HELIOCEREUS SPECIOSUS (Cavanilles) Britton and Rose
Tribe Cacteae — subtribe Cereinae

Etymology The name derives from the Greek *elios*, sun; the diurnal flowers open when the sun comes out.
Place of Origin Near Mexico City in central Mexico.
Description This species was classified as a *Cereus* in 1803 by Antonio Cavanilles, director of the Botanical Gardens in Madrid. Britton and Rose transferred it in 1909 to their newly established genus. It is shrublike, with stems that are erect at first but become sarmentose or pendant later. In its natural habitat it is an epiphyte. The profusely ramified stem may be more than 3¼ ft. (1 m.) long. Reddish new growth later turns dark green. It may have three to five ribs, but it commonly has four. The raised ribs are notched where areoles are borne. These are wide, woolly and set 1/2 to 1¼ in. (1 to 3 cm.) apart. There are initially five to eight spines, but these become more numerous later. They are stiff and pointed, yellowish or brown, and up to 1/2 in. (1.5 cm.) long. The crimson flowers are about 6 in. (15 cm.) long, with many perianth segments measuring from 3¼ to 4 in. (8 to 10 cm.). The stamens and style droop. There are many varieties with flowers of different colors, and the species has often been crossed with various *Epiphyllum* resulting in plants with magnificent flowers.
Cultivation It needs semishade and should spend winter at a temperature above 50° F (10° C.). Adults flower readily; scented flowers last several days. Propagation is by cuttings.

---

136 HYLOCEREUS UNDATUS (Haworth) Britton and Rose
Tribe Cacteae — subtribe Hylocereinae

Etymology The name comes from the Greek word *yle*, meaning forest.
Place of Origin This plant is cultivated and seminaturalized in all tropical countries, but its true place of origin is unknown.
Description The plant is known mainly as *Cereus triangularis*, given by de Candolle to the Linnaean species *Cactus triangularis*, but these are two different species. The *Cereus undatus* described by Haworth was cultivated in China and sent to England, its origins unknown. Britton and Rose created the genus *Hylocereus* by separating more widely cultivated species from the Linnaean species, which is native to Jamaica and is smaller, more spiny, and seldom cultivated. Stems are long, climbing or pendant, thickly ramified and 2¾ in. (7 cm.) in diameter. Their shoots usually have three slender, prominent ribs whose corrugated edges become horny. Areoles are set far apart and bear one to three short spines. Nocturnal flowers are 12 in. (30 cm.) long and have greenish-yellow evaginated outer segments and erect white inner segments. The red fruit is 4 in. (10 cm.) long, scaly, and edible.
Cultivation It needs a mild climate, much space, and supports for roots to cling to. Propagation is by cuttings. Delicate species are grafted onto small rooted cuttings as stock.

137 ISLAYA MINOR Backeberg
Tribe Cacteae — subtribe Echinocactinae

ETYMOLOGY This plant is named after the small town of Islaya, Peru, situated on the Pacific coast among the foothills of the western cordillera in the department of Arequipa.

Place of Origin The foothills of the Andes near the town of Mollendo, department of Arequipa, southern Peru.

Description This plant has a solitary, globular stem, about 5½ in. (13 cm.) high, 2¼ in. (7 cm.) in diameter, and depressed at its apex. There are about 17 ribs. They bear close-set areoles densely covered — particularly when young — with whitish-gray felt. There are 20 or more slender, sharp, radial spines that are about 1/4 in. (6 mm.) long, black at first, later turning gray like the four central spines, which are thick, arranged in a cross and almost 3/4 in. (2 cm.) long. The stem's apical part is almost completely covered by silvery-gray felt. The flowers grow from the middle of the felted area. They are about 3/4 in. (2 cm.) in diameter and vary from gold to very light, greenish yellow. The red hairy fruit, initially globular, becoming elongated when ripe. The flower's withered perianth and a few bristles persist at the apex of the fruit.

Cultivation Growth is very slow, partly because the plant can be propagated only by seed. Development may be speeded up by grafting plants onto a different stock as soon as possible.

---

138 LEPISMIUM CRUCIFORME (Vellozo) Miquel
Tribe Cacteae — subtribe Rhipsalidinae

Etymology The name comes from the Greek *lepis,* scale, because of the scale at the base of each areole.

Place of Origin Southern Brazil, Argentina, and Paraguay.

Description Since the Brazilian botanist José Vellozo described this plant as *Cactus cruciformis* in 1825, it has undergone many changes of name both generic and specific. Some of these names are still used to describe the many varieties of the species. The plant is an epiphyte but is also able to grow as a creeper from crevices in rocks, developing numerous aerial roots. The typical species is mainly pendant, up to 23 in. (60 cm.) long, and has triangular shoots that are somewhat winged and notched. Felted, bristly, whitish areoles grow in the depressions. The white or pinkish campanulate flowers grow embedded in the areoles, leaving a scar upon them later. The fruit is purple. The principal varieties, sometimes considered separate species, are *anceps,* which has more or less flat shoots and pale lilac-colored flowers; *cavernosum,* scarcely ramified with shoots that are sometimes flat and very woolly, often reddish areoles; and *myosurus,* which has pinkish-red flowers.

Cultivation The plant requires a very well lighted position but no direct sunlight, very humusy soil and a semi-rest period after flowering. Propagation is by shoot cuttings placed in damp peat and sand.

139   LEPISMIUM PARADOXUM   Salm-Dyck
Tribe Cacteae — subtribe Rhipsalidinae

Place of Origin   The state of São Paulo in Brazil. The plant is even commonly found on the outskirts of the city.

Description   This species was first described by Salm-Dyck in 1837, but he then renamed it *Rhipsalis paradoxa* in 1845. This name was retained for many years, but the original name was eventually reverted to because of botanical differences. In its natural habitat the plant is an often shrublike epiphyte that hangs from trees, reaching a length of 3 to 17 ft. (1 to 5 m.). It has numerous short joints, each growing from its predecessor in pairs or in whorls. Cultivated plants are much smaller. The joints are triangular in cross-section and approximately 2 in. (5 cm.) long. The apex of one triangular joint adjoins the flat base of another like the links of a chain. Each rib has an areole at its apex. The flower-bearing areoles are very woolly, with the ovaries embedded in them, leaving a permanent scar in the center. On new growth the areoles are often accompanied by a small, more or less round bract. The flowers are solitary, white, and 3/4 in. (2 cm.) long. The berries are reddish.

Cultivation   Propagation is by cuttings, which root readily in sand and damp peat. A well-lighted but shady position and winter warmth with no marked rest period are needed.

---

140   LEUCHTENBERGIA PRINCIPIS   Hooker
Tribe Cacteae — subtribe Echinocactinae

Etymology   Hooker named the plant in 1848 in honor of Eugène de Beauharnais, Duke of Leuchtenberg.

Place of Origin   Northern and central Mexico.

Description   The genus comprises this one distinctive species. It has a large taproot and a cylindrical stem that in old age becomes bare and corky at the base, from which it sometimes ramifies. Tubercles are long, triangular, flat on upper parts and carinate on lower parts; grayish-green, often reddish along the sharp edges; and truncated at the tip, where gray, felted areoles appear. Tubercles are woolly at their base and grow upward, spreading out at an oblique angle except for erect ones in the center. Old plants may reach a height of 19½ in. (50 cm.) with 4 in. (10 cm.) tubercles. They resemble a small *Agave*. The spines are blunt, slender and flexible. On adult plants there are as many as 14 radials, 2 in. (5 cm.) long, and one or two central spines, which are longer. Young plants normally have only three or four radial spines. In the course of time the basal tubercles die and disappear. The large, funnel-shaped flowers are yellow with reddish outer segments.

Cultivation   The plant needs a deep flowerpot and strong sun. It does not tolerate frost. Propagation is usually by seed or by shoots from old plants. It is possible, though not easy, to persuade single tubercles, used as cuttings, to take root.

141 LOBIVIA ARGENTEA Backeberg
Tribe Cacteae — subtribe Echinocereinae

Etymology The name of the plant is simply an anagram of Bolivia. The plant is found only in the Andes in Peru, the Bolivian tableland, and northern Argentina. The genus, established by Britton and Rose, originally comprised 20 species previously classified as *Echinopsis* and *Echinocactus;* it now includes over 70, following new discoveries.

Place of Origin The department of Oruro in Bolivia.

Description This species tillers to form large clumps of stems up to 4 in. (10 cm.) high with a diameter of 6 in. (15 cm.); they are a glossy or grayish-green and have 24 ribs that with age curve and diverge. The ribs are tuberculate with sharp edges. The areoles, which appear in the depressions between the tubercles, are oval and felted and become obliquely arranged as the ribs grow farther apart. There are 14 radial spines 3/4 in. (2 cm.) long, and a central spine reaching 3 in. (8 cm.); all the spines are dark to begin with, later becoming a pinkish white. The inner perianth segments of the funnel-shaped flowers are slender and open wide. They vary from a delicate silvery white to a pinkish lilac.

Cultivation This species is not commonly cultivated. Propagation is from basal shoots.

142 LOBIVIA AUREA (Britton and Rose) Backeberg
Tribe Cacteae — subtribe Echinocereinae

Place of Origin The Sierra de Córdoba in the province of the same name, Argentina.

Description This plant has a dark green globular or elongated stem reaching a height of 4 in. (10 cm.) and a diameter of 1½ to 2½ in. (4 to 6 cm.). The stem puts out many basal and lateral offshoots. There are 14 to 15 sharp-edged ribs separated by deep grooves. Areoles are brown on young plants. The ten or so radial spines are white, 1/2 in. (1 cm.) long and point outward. The one to four central spines are thicker, sometimes flat, about 1¼ in. (3 cm.) long, and brown with yellow tips. Flowers are nearly 4 in. (10 cm.) long. Buds are covered by long silky hairs and grow laterally from the center of the stem. The tube is slightly curved, funnel-shaped, slender and a greenish white, with pale green scales red at the base, with white and black down. The numerous perianth segments, measuring 3 in. (8 cm.) across when opened out, are lemon yellow and bright yellow inside. There are several varieties. One of these, *fallax,* has a grayish-green stem; all the spines are black at first; and the yellow flowers turn pink before they wither.

Cultivation This hardy plant, easily grown, needs strong sun and dry soil. It's propagated by cuttings or basal shoots.

143 LOBIVIA BACKEBERGII (Werdermann) Backeberg
Tribe Cacteae — subtribe Echinocereinae

Place of Origin   At an altitude of 11,800 ft. (3,600 m.) near La Paz, Bolivia.

Description   This small, spherical plant has a diameter of 1¾ to 2 in. (4.5 to 5 cm.). In time it may become oblong. It puts forth a great many shoots. There are about 15 ribs divided by slightly oblique grooves and not quite spirally arranged. The areoles grow in depressions on the sharp edges of the ribs. They are woolly when young and set 1/2 in. (1 cm.) or more apart. There are three to seven spines, all radials, which vary from 1/4 to 2 in. (5 mm. to 5 cm.) in length. The longest grow more or less obliquely and are often curved. All the spines are brown initially, turning gray with age. They may have hooked tips. The flowers grow from the upper part of the stem and are about 1¾ in. (4.5 cm.) long. The inner segments of the perianth are crimson with a bluish sheen and a white base. The scaly brown tube bears white hairs.

Cultivation   This species is easy to cultivate but needs a strict rest period. It suffers in summer if the heat is extreme, so it is wise to shade it during the hottest hours of the day, particularly in climates enjoying very hot sunshine. Propagation is by basal shoots.

---

144 LOBIVIA BOLIVIENSIS Britton and Rose
Tribe Cacteae — subtribe Echinocereinae

Place of Origin   The Bolivian tableland, near Oruro in the department of the same name.

Description   The plant has a globular stem about 4 in. (10 cm.) in diameter. In time it becomes oval and puts out about six basal shoots, all barely cylindrical and slightly curved upward. There are about 20 ribs with corrugated edges formed by the depressions between the low, elongated tubercles, which bear areoles set about 1/2 in. (1 cm.) apart. Each areole has six to eight brown, slender, pointed, flexible spines up to 3½ in. (9 cm.) long. The difference between radial and central spines is virtually imperceptible. The flowers are red.

Cultivation   The typical species is difficult to find, since the plant tends not to do very well in cultivation. This is probably because it needs fairly cool surroundings, even in summer. Propagation by shoots from old plants should produce specimens better suited to their environment.

145 LOBIVIA CINNABARINA (Hooker) Britton and Rose
Tribe Cacteae — subtribe Echinocereinae

Place of Origin   At an altitude of about 11,100 ft. (3,400 m.) in the Bolivian Andes, near Punata and Rio Chaparé in the department of Cochabamba.

Description   The name of this species, given by Hooker to an *Echinocactus*, comes from the Greek *kinnabari*, meaning cinnabar or the vermilion coloring extracted from sulfide of mercury, which the ancients called dragon's blood. Its flowers are, of course, red. The stem is spherical, 6 in. (15 cm.) in diameter with a depressed apex; it later becomes cylindrical and may put out basal shoots. It has about 20 spirally arranged ribs with raised tubercles between which the areoles appear. They bear 10 to 14 outward pointing radial spines 1/2 in. (1 cm.) long and two to five thicker and longer central spines. They are all somewhat curved, brown at first, turning grayish later. The campanulate flowers are varying shades of crimson, 1¼ in. (3 cm.) long and 1½ in. (4 cm.) across, with a short tube that is green and scaly. They remain open for two days. Some confusion surrounds this species because, after its original discovery, it was lost and rediscovered by Cárdenas in a form with smaller flowers than those originally described. Backeberg named the later version *Lobivia neocinnabarina*.

Cultivation   The plant withstands cold but not strong summer sun. Propagation is by seed or cuttings.

146 LOBIVIA FAMATIMENSIS (Spegazzini) Britton and Rose
Variety **OLIGACANTHA** Ito
Tribe Cacteae — subtribe Echinocereinae

Place of Origin   Spegazzini classed this species as *Echinocactus* in 1921. Its name is obviously erroneous, since the plant was found on the Sierra de Famatina in the province of La Rioja, Argentina, extending to the province of Jujuy.

Description   This variable species comprises many varieties. The typical species has an oval stem about 1½ in. (4 cm.) high and 1¼ in. (3 cm.) in diameter which is solitary or tillered. When grafted, the plant becomes cylindrical, growing to 6 in. (15 cm.). There are 18 to 24 low tuberculate ribs bearing close-set areoles. The many short, whitish, intersecting spines cover the stem. Flowers grow on the upper part of the stem and are generally 1¼ to 1½ in. (3 to 4 cm.) long, with a scaly, woolly tube. The many segments of the perianth vary from cream to red, with many intermediary shades depending on the variety. The *oligacantha* variety has only a few long spines and forms part of a group described by Yoshio Ito in 1963. Other varieties are *haematantha*, with blood-red flowers; *albiflora*, with white flowers; and *densispina*, which has bristlelike radial spines and seven brown central spines.

Cultivation   These plants flower profusely, particularly when grafted. They need protection from frost and strong summer sun. Propagation is by seed, or shoots from tillered plants.

147 LOBIVIA MISTIENSIS (Werdermann and Backeberg) Backeberg
Tribe Cacteae — subtribe Echinocereinae

Place of Origin Misti volcano, department of Arequipa, southern Peru.

Description The plant has a large taproot. The bluish-green stem is spherical, flattened at the apex, and solitary at first, ramifying in old age. It has 25 to 30 ribs, raised about 1/4 in. (5 mm.), divided into elongated protuberances. Oval, white, felted areoles appear in the oblique incisions between the protuberances. Central spines are not clearly differentiated from the radials; in fact, there often seem to be only radial spines, although many areoles bear some that grow from the center. There are seven or eight spines or sometimes more, splayed out or slightly curved upward, up to 2 in. (5 cm.) in length, the lowest generally being shorter than the others. When young, they vary from brown or blackish to red; then they turn grayish. Flowers are 2 to 2½ in. (5 to 6 cm.) long, sometimes reaching 3 in. (8 cm.). The outer perianth segments are reddish-brown while the inner ones are often pink but may vary from orange-yellow to red. They are slender with a pointed apex.

Cultivation It requires acid rather than calcareous soil since its natural habitat is volcanic ground. The flowerpot must be large enough to accommodate its thick roots. Propagation is mainly by seed or the shoots from old plants.

148 LOBIVIA PENTLANDII (Hooker) Britton and Rose
Tribe Cacteae — subtribe Echinocereinae

Place of Origin The slopes of the Andes and the plateaus of southern Peru and northern Bolivia.

Description This plant has an almost cylindrical, darkish green stem that ramifies abundantly from its base to form large clusters. Each stem has about 15 prominent ribs with sharp edges and oblique depressions at the point where the fairly large, white areoles grow. With age, they turn brown. There are 7 to 12 radial spines of markedly different lengths, varying from 1/2 to 1¼ in. (1 to 3 cm.). They are splayed out, more or less curved, and yellowish brown. Central spines may be absent altogether, but usually there is one (and occasionally on older stems there are more). It may be straight and point outward or curve upward. It measures up to 1¼ in. (3 cm.) in length. The flowers grow laterally and are about 2 in. (5 cm.) long. The funnel-shaped tube bears hairs, spines and short, triangular scales. The perianth segments are reddish-orange toward the tip and lighter, almost pink toward the base, and are always more or less erect. The plant is very variable. Salm-Dyck included it in *Echinopsis* in 1846, and a great many varieties have been attributed to it. Today only a few varieties are recognized: *albiflora* has white flowers; *forbesii* has dark red flowers; and *ochroleuca* has yellow flowers.

Cultivation Propagation is by basal shoots.

149 LOBIVIA REBUTIOIDES Backeberg
Variety **KRAUSSIANA** Backeberg
Tribe Cacteae — subtribe Echinocereinae

Place of Origin Northern Argentina.
Description This tiny plant has a spherical stem only 1/4 in. (2 cm.) in diameter, but it tillers abundantly, forming cushion-like clumps. The small stems are bluish-green and, unlike those of other species, they never turn dark or bronze-colored if exposed to sun or cold. The root is napiform and similar to a carrot. The 12 or so low, very slender ribs are very slightly tuberculate. The areoles bear nine or more extremely short whitish, very slender radial spines, and one or two central spines that are thicker, darker, slightly swollen at the base and fairly long. The flowers are about 1½ in. (4 cm.) long and across. The perianth segments are bright red with a greenish base inside. The variety *kraussiana* has brilliant yellow petals that open to lie completely flat, reaching a diameter of 4 in. (10 cm.). The flowers of the variety *sublimiflora* are larger than those of the typical species and are salmon-pink with a crimson sheen and a pink base inside. The variety *citriniflora* has lemon-yellow flowers.
Cultivation This species has only recently been introduced and is not easily found in the market. It tolerates cold if kept dry, and requires a lot of sunlight. Propagation is by cuttings.

---

150 LOBIVIA ROSSII (Boedecker) Boedecker and Backeberg
Tribe Cacteae — subtribe Echinocereinae

Place of Origin Bolivia.
Description Boedeker originally classified this species as an *Echinopsis* but later transferred it to its present genus. The plant is initially spherical, becoming elongated with age and putting forth several basal shoots measuring 2¾ in. (7 cm.) or more in diameter. There are 18 ribs having elongated, ax-shaped tubercles. The tubercles are oblique, with four to six pointed, sharp radial spines that are reddish or gray with a dark tip. The upper ones measure 2½ in. (6 cm.) and are longer than the lower ones. Central spines are absent. The flowers are about 1½ in. (4 cm.) long, and are orange with a green base inside. This species is also very variable, having many varieties and forms, with flowers of different shades. The variety *boedekeriana* has red flowers with a light yellow center; the variety *walterspielii* (considered by Boedeker to be a separate species) has crimson flowers with larger petals; the variety *carminata* has crimson flowers and spines that intersect; and the flowers of the variety *salmonea* are salmon-pink.
Cultivation This species is fairly rare. It tolerates cold, but, like most of the genus, prefers semishade to intense summer sunshine. Propagation may be by seed but the varieties must be reproduced by cuttings or shoots.

151 LOBIVIA SHAFERI Britton and Rose
Tribe Cacteae — subtribe Echinocereinae

Place of Origin   This plant was discovered in 1916 by J. A. Shafer, from whom it takes its name, on the Sierra de Ambata near Andalgalá, province of Catamarca, Argentina.
Description   The stem is initially globular, later becoming cylindrical, reaching a height of 2¾ to 6 in. (7 to 15 cm.) and a diameter of 1 to 1 ½ in. (2.5 to 4 cm.). It is densely covered with spines, and tillers rather untidily, putting out somewhat elongated basal joints. There are about ten very flat ribs bearing close-set areoles, each of which has 10 to 15 sharp, needlelike radial spines. These are white or brown and about 1/2 in. (1 cm.) long. There are several central spines, one of which is much longer than the others; it reaches 1¼ in. (3 cm.). The funnel-shaped flowers appear laterally from hairy buds. They are 1¾ to 2½ in. (4 to 6 cm.) long; have a large tube covered with linear scales with long white hairs at their base; and have a corona of short petals varying from pale to bright yellow.
Cultivation   This species is difficult to find, and it is not easy to cultivate because it shrinks from scorching summer heat. The shoots of an already acclimated plant have a better chance of success than those grown from seed.

---

152 LOPHOCEREUS SCHOTTII (Berger) Britton and Rose
Tribe Cacteae — subtribe Cereinae
Common name: Senita cactus

Etymology   The name comes from the Greek *lophos,* crest; the plant's stems have a very spiny, bristly apex.
Place of Origin   Southern Arizona and the states of Sonora and Baja California, Mexico.
Description   The plant tillers and forms large clusters of stems as tall as 16½ to 23 ft. (5 to 7 m.) with a diameter of 2½ to 4 in. (6 to 10 cm.). Five to nine ribs have woolly, whitish areoles bearing about five conical spines nearly 1/2 in. (1 cm.) long, dark at first though turning grayish. Later, it also bears one central spine. When stems are about to flower, the upper part develops larger areoles with about 20 sharp bristles that are straight, brownish-gray and almost brushlike. White or reddish nocturnal flowers are 1½ in. (4 cm.) long. More than one appears upon each areole, growing from among the bristles at right angles to the stem. Various types of stem fasciation sometimes cause "monstrous" forms. The variety *mieckleyanus* (illustrated at right) is heavily fasciated and has variable, irregular ribs with no spines, only a few bristles. Flowers are pink. This species grows only in Baja California.
Cultivation   It tolerates severe aridity if it already has large colonies of stems. Propagation by cuttings; growth is slow.

153 LOPHOPHORA LUTEA (Rouh.) Backeberg
Tribe Cacteae — subtribe Echinocactinae

Etymology The name derives from the Greek word *lophos*, meaning a crest, and *phoreo*, meaning I carry, due to the plant's spineless areoles covered in woolly tufts. Lemaire placed it in *Anhalonium*, a genus he created but which is no longer recognized.

Place of Origin Mexico.

Description For a long time this genus was thought to include the single species *Lophophora williamsii*; today, however, two other species belong to it as well as several varieties of *L. williamsii*. An exact classification has not yet been achieved, however, for several reasons: the plants do not grow in abundance and are distributed over a vast area; restrictions are placed upon their cultivation and possession; and research can be carried out only into plants grown from seed, which are consequently subject to a certain degree of variability. Even the words "solitary" or "tillering" mean little, since some plants put out shoots at a very early age while others delay until they are very old. This species, which may also be found under the name *Lophophora ziegleri*, is very similar to *Lophophora williamsii*; it has scarcely tuberculate ribs divided by winding grooves, yellowish down, and larger, pale yellow flowers.

Cultivation It does not tolerate frost and needs full sun in summer. As in the rest of the genus, it grows very slowly.

---

154 LOPHOPHORA WILLIAMSII (Lemaire ex Salm-Dyck) Coulter
Tribe Cacteae — subtribe Echinocactinae
Common names: Peyote, whiskey cactus, mescal button

Place of Origin Hidalgo, Starr, Zapata and Brewster counties, Texas, southward across the Rio Grande.

Description Like all the species of the genus, this plant has a large taproot. The grayish-green stem is round, soft and fleshy, tillering to a varying extent depending on the variety, and only 2 to 4 in. (5 to 10 cm.) high with a depressed apex. Tubercles are rounded, barely raised, often almost indistinct, set on eight to ten low ribs. Areoles bear minute spines when the plant is very young. Later they are covered with conspicuous felted tufts that are denser at the apex. Small pink flowers emerge from the apex. They have only a few perianth segments and a funnel-shaped tube. There are several varieties. *Caespitosa* is a cultivar obtained from a local form that tillers abundantly, forming small cushions. The variety *decipiens* is smaller. When adult, its ribs are divided into conical tubercles. The variety *pentagona* has only five ribs, where the variety *texana* may have as many as 14. There is also a form with pinkish-violet flowers that was once classified as *Lophophora jourdaniana*.

Cultivation Tillered plants may be propagated from their shoots, but generally they are reproduced through seed. The plant tolerates cold provided it is perfectly dry, but not frost.

155 LOXANTHOCEREUS AUREISPINUS (Ritter)
Buxbaum
Tribe Cacteae — subtribe Cereinae

Etymology Backeberg invented the name of this genus, using the Greek words *loxos,* slanting, and *anthos,* flower: its flowers grow obliquely. He included in the genus some Peruvian plants which now have been moved to *Borzicactus* by some authors. The name has, however, been retained for this Bolivian species (originally named *Winterocereus* by Backeberg).

Place of Origin Near Rio Wapacani to the north of Santa Cruz, Bolivia.

Description The plant is pendant with a slender stem, up to 5 ft. (1.5 m.) long and 1 in. (2.5 cm.) in diameter, ramifying from its base. It has about 16 ribs depressed between round areoles covered with brown felt. Each areole bears about 30 slender, golden radial spines and 20 longer and tougher yellow central spines. All spines are flexible and cover the stem almost entirely. Flowers are borne laterally and last several days, staying open at night. They are about 2 in. (5 cm.) across and are curved. The two parts of the perianth are very different: outer segments are wide, evaginated, and orange-red; inner ones are much shorter, white or pink, and curve toward the filaments, which are almost enclosed by them.

Cultivation This plant is still quite rare. It is advisable to protect it from cold, although presumably it tolerates it well.

156 MACHAEROCEREUS ERUCA (Brandegee) Britton and Rose
Tribe Cacteae — subtribe Cereinae

Etymology The name comes from the Greek *macaera,* dagger: the longest spine is knifelike. The specific name derives from the Latin word *eruca,* meaning caterpillar.

Place of Origin Magdalena Island and Llano de la Magdalena, Baja Caifornia.

Description Stems of the plant are prostrate except for their slightly raised tips. They grow about 10 ft. (3 m.) long and take root as they creep, ramifying further and eventually covering a huge area. Sometimes plants separate from the parent stem and spread out around it, leaving it to die. There are about 12 ribs bearing large areoles set 3/4 in. (2 cm.) apart. Each areole bears about 20 pale gray or white spines of unequal length. Outer ones are short and subulate; inner ones are larger and flat. One semi-central spine is 1½ in. (3.5 cm.) long, is much wider than the others. Flowers are 4 to 5 in. (10 to 12 cm.) long, with a 4 in (10 cm.) tube. The lower part of this is scaly and felted with spines. Perianth segments are cream-colored, sometimes with a pink base. When the scarlet fruit ripens its spines fall off.

Cultivation This plant, which is seldom cultivated, needs very sandy soil and should be placed in a semiprostrate position so that it may creep. Propagation is by cuttings.

157 MACHAEROCEREUS GUMMOSUS (Engelmann) Britton and Rose
Tribe Cacteae — subtribe Cereinae

Place of Origin   Baja California and coast of Sonora and adjacent islands.
Description   The stem is initially erect, up to 3¼ ft. (1 m.) long and 1¾ to 2½ in. (4 to 6 cm.) in diameter. It ramifies from its base, putting out semi-erect branches that ramify again, forming a large shrub 20 to 23 ft. (6 to 7 m.) across. It has eight low, blunt ribs with large areoles 3/4 in. (2 cm.) apart. There are 8 to 11 radial spines 1/2 in. (1 cm.) long, and three to six flat and thick central spines, one of the lower ones much wider than the others and up to 1½ in. (4 cm.) long, pointing outward at first and downward later. All spines are blackish when young, later paler and whitish. Flowers are 4 to 5½ in. (10 to 14 cm.) long, and have a long, slender tube, the lower part of which is woolly, spiny and scaly. Perianth segments are a purplish red. Fruit is round and spiny with a scarlet epidermis; spines fall off when it is ripe. The reddish pulp is sour but edible, its local name being *pitahaya agria*. The sap in the stem is poisonous, although presumably not to human beings, since the natives use its pulp to kill their fish.
Cultivation   Seldom cultivated, it needs little water and is easily propagated by cuttings if adult plants are available.

---

158 MAMMILLARIA ALBICANS (Britton and Rose) Berger
Tribe Cacteae — subtribe Cactinae

Etymology   The genus was established by Haworth in 1812 and comes from the Latin *mamilla* (or *mammilla*), meaning breast, because of the plant's conical tubercles.
Place of Origin   Baja California, the islands of Santa Cruz and San Diego and the southern part of the Gulf of California.
Description   This species has been described only very briefly; probably other varieties and even other species should be in it. Craig attributes *Mammillaria slevinii,* found on the nearby island of San José, to it. The plant is globular at first and cylindrical later, 8 in. (20 cm.) high and 2½ in. (6 cm.) in diameter. It tillers profusely. The close-set tubercles are conical and wide at the base, bearing very woolly white areoles near the apex, which gradually becomes almost bare. There are numerous white, slender radial spines splayed out laterally, almost pectinate, and long enough to overlap adjacent spines. The several central spines are straight, stiff and slender, and spread outward. They are often brown or blackish (especially in the center) or pale with a brown tip. The fruit is red, club-shaped, and 1/2 to 3/4 in. (1 to 2 cm.) long. *Mammillaria slevinii,* shorter and solitary, has white and pink flowers.
Cultivation   The plant, sold under different names, does not tolerate cold. Propagation is by seed or shoots.

159 MAMMILLARIA BOCASANA Poselger
Tribe Cacteae — subtribe Cactinae

Place of Origin The state of San Luis Potosí and the surrounding area in north-central Mexico. The plant's specific name refers to where it was discovered, the Sierra de Bocas.
Description Poselger described this plant in 1853. Since then its hardiness and the ease with which it can be propagated by shoots have made it one of the most commonly cultivated species. The stem is a light or dark bluish-green, globular, measuring 1 ½ to 2 in. (4 to 5 cm.) in diameter. It tillers thickly, forming large clusters. The more or less conical tubercles are slender, raised about 1/4 in. (5 mm.) and arranged spirally. There are sometimes very fine white hairs around their base. The areoles are round or very slightly oval. There may be as many as 30 radial spines. They measure 3/4 in. (2 cm.) in length, and consist of white, silky, bristlelike hairs usually arranged somewhat untidily. Normally there is a single central spine, although as many as three may appear on old specimens; they are 1/4 to 1/3 in. (5 to 8 mm.) long, yellow or yellowish-brown, and at least one of them, usually the lowest, is hooked. The plant flowers readily and profusely, but the flowers are small. The inner perianth segments are a creamy yellow with a reddish median stripe. The fruit is red and long.
Cultivation The plant tolerates cold if kept completely dry, and requires strong sunlight. Propagation is by shoots.

160 MAMMILLARIA BOMBYCINA Quehl
Tribe Cacteae — subtribe Cactinae

Place of Origin Mexico (place of wild origin unknown).
Description The plant's specific name derives from the Latin adjective *bombycinus,* meaning silky, because the thick white down covering the young areoles at the plant's apex resembles silk. The stem is initially simple, becoming clustered later. It reaches a height of 6 to 8 in. (15 to 20 cm.) and a diameter of 2 to 2½ in. (5 to 6 cm.). The close-set tubercles are conical or cylindrical and spirally arranged, with a very woolly base that sometimes also bears one or more bristles. The areoles are also woolly when young, but in time they lose everything but their numerous spines. There are 30 to 40 white, slender but rigid radial spines, from 1/12 to 1/2 in. (2 mm. to 1 cm.) long, radiating in all directions. There are two to four central spines. If there are four, they are arranged in a cross, and the side thorns measure 3/8 in. (1 cm.), the upper one is shorter, and the lower one is 3/4 in. (2 cm.) long, stronger, decidedly hooked and points downward. Their color contrasts with that of the other spines, since although they are white at their base they are a reddish brown for most of their length. The flowers are small, 1/2 in. (1.5 cm.) long and across, with slender, lanceolate segments that are light crimson. The variety *flavispina* has yellow central spines.
Cultivation It needs some heat. Propagation by shoots.

161 MAMMILLARIA HAHNIANA
Tribe Cacteae — subtribe Cactinae

Place of Origin The state of Querétaro, Mexico, at altitudes below 6,500 ft. (2,000 m.)

Description This species may be distinguished by its long white hairs. The stem is spherical at first, measuring 4 to 5½ in. (10–14 cm.) in diameter, and then tends to become elongated and cylindrical. Adult specimens produce several spherical or cylindrical basal shoots, forming a dense cluster of plants. The stem of an adult plant beneath the spinescent down is light green. It contains milky juice. The flexible, white radial spines are borne in groups of 20–30. The stiff central spine is white with a reddish-brown tip and is ⅙ in. (4 mm.) long. The tubercles bear 20 white, flexible hairs which are 1½ in. (4 cm.) long. The plant produces a corona of bright purplish-red flowers, 1/2 to 3/4 in. (1.5–2 cm.) long and 1/2 in. (1.5 cm.) across. The species has two varieties: *giselana* has few hairs, while *werdermanniana* has white hairs up to 1 in. (25 mm.) long. The American common name for *Mammillaria hahniana* is "old lady cactus."

Cultivation In very hot climates this plant prefers some shade in summer, at least around noon. It is propagated by seed or from shoots taken from mature plants.

---

162 MAMMILLARIA CAPUT-MEDUSAE Otto
Tribe Cacteae — subtribe Cactinae

Place of Origin Near Metztitlán in the northeastern part of the state of Hidalgo, Mexico.

Description For a long time this species was considered a variety of *Mammillaria sempervivi*, or synonymous with it. Otto described it in 1837, but all subsequent authors until Backeberg in 1966 refused to recognize the validity of the species, which has only recently been reestablished. The plant tends to be solitary, although it sometimes puts forth basal shoots. Its stem and size are very similar to those of *Mammillaria sempervivi*, but its tubercles differ in that they are conical and quadrangular at the base and their lower corner is somewhat carinate. White, bristlelike radial spines, 1/12 to 1/8 in. (2 to 3 mm.) long, appear on the young areoles but are almost never persistent, falling off very soon. There are four central spines, pinkish-white at first and grayish later, measuring about 3/16 in. (5 mm.) long and arranged in a cross. The flowers are about 3/4 in. (2 cm.) long and have pinkish segments with a red median dorsal stripe.

Cultivation Too much sun turns the epidermis reddish. Propagation is by seed.

163 MAMMILLARIA CARNEA Zuccarini
Tribe Cacteae — subtribe Cactinae

Place of Origin   The states of Hidalgo, Guerrero, Puebla and Oaxaca, Mexico.

Description   The plant's greenish stem is spherical at first, later cylindrical, reaches a height of about 4 in. (10 cm.), and tillers by putting out basal shoots. Tubercles are quadrangular, rhomboid-pyramidal, raised about 3/8 in. (1 cm.) and arranged in 8 to 13 spirals. Their base is initially yellowish and woolly, becoming bare. New areoles are felted, but quickly become glabrous. Radial spines are absent and often replaced by a few bristles. The four central spines are stiff, sharp, straight or slightly curved and point downward—particularly the bottom one, which measures 1/2 to 1 ½ in. (1.5 to 4 cm.); the others vary from 3/16 to 3/4 in. (5 mm. to 2 cm.) long. All spines are first reddish, later flesh-colored with a black tip. Small flowers sprout from the base of the tubercles in a circle around the apex and are pale pink, the tip of their segments darker. There are several varieties. *Cirrosa* has apical spines that are almost as curly as ivy tendrils. The spines of *longispina* are all longer, and the tubercles of *subtetragona* have rounded corners, while all the spines are brown or whitish with a brown base and tip.

Cultivation   Propagation is by seed. Or shoots can be used from old plants, particularly in the case of varieties.

164 MAMMILLARIA CELSIANA Lemaire
Tribe Cacteae — subtribe Cactinae

Place of Origin   From the state of San Luis Potosí southward to the state of Oaxaca, central Mexico.

Description   The bluish-green stem is globular at first, becoming cylindrical later, and is about 4 ½ in. (12 cm.) high with a diameter of 3 in. (8 cm.). The adult plant proliferates through basal shoots. The conical tubercles, raised by about 1/4 in. (6 mm.), are arranged in numerous compact spirals. Their base is covered with white down, which is dense on new growth and conspicuous at the apex. Areoles are small, round and felted. There are 20 to 30 radial spines, just over 1/4 in. (7 mm.) long, slender, white and sharp. The four to six central spines are just over 1/4 in. to 1/2 in. (7 mm. to 1.5 cm.) long except for the lowest one, which is as much as 1 in. (3 cm.) long. They are stiff and very sharp and vary from pale to dark yellow with brown tips. Flowers appear from the axil of the tubercles in a wide circle around the apex and are about 3/8 in. (1 cm.) long. Outer perianth segments are usually reddish; inner ones are lanceolate and vary from scarlet to crimson. The red fruit is oval and clings for a very long time to the withered remains of the corola. This plant was first described in 1839.

Cultivation   This plant is easy to grow. It prefers some shade at least during the hottest hours of the summer. Propagation is by basal shoots or seed.

165 MAMMILLARIA COMPRESSA de Candolle
Tribe Cacteae — subtribe Cactinae

Place of Origin From San Luis Potosí southward to Querétaro and Ixmiquilpán in central Mexico.

Description This plant is also known by its old name, *Mammillaria angularis*. It is very variable, and many of its varieties have been classified. The typical species has a globular stem and tillers to form hemispherical cushions. Later, however, it often becomes cylindrical, and in some forms may reach a height of 8 in. (20 cm.). The tubercles are short and thick, slightly angular, and compressed laterally. Their base is thickly covered by woolly white down and silvery bristles. The areoles are woolly at first but later retain only their spines. There are four to six radial spines, reddish when young, later turning white and then gray with a brown tip. The lowest is as much as 2¾ in. (7 cm.) long, pointing outward and downward. The somewhat rare flowers are a pinkish violet or purple with a lighter border. The light red fruit is 3/4 in. (2 cm.) long with brownish seeds. The variety *fulvispina* has axils that are just a little woolly and five yellowish-brown spines. The variety *longiseta* is tougher and taller, very woolly with long bristles; it has seven long white spines.

Cultivation The plant is propagated from shoots. It grows well in either sunshine or semishade.

166 MAMMILLARIA ELONGATA de Candolle
Tribe Cacteae — subtribe Cactinae

Place of Origin The state of Hidalgo in Mexico.

Description This plant's name changed several times after de Candolle described it in 1828. About 100 years ago it was transferred by Buxbaum to his new genus *Leptocladodia,* but its original name is firmly established. Its slender, cylindrical stems are 2¼ to 6 in. (6 to 15 cm.) long, with a diameter of 1/2 to 1½ in. (1.5 to 3.5 cm.). They form dense clumps, in which some stems are erect and others semiprostrate. Tubercles are conical and slender with a slightly woolly or glabrous base. The small, round areoles bear about 20 short radial spines of varying shades of yellow, spread out in a star pattern. Central spines are usually absent, although some varieties have one to three that are 3/8 in. (1 cm.) long or more. The pale yellow flowers are 1/2 in. (1.5 cm.) long. There are many cultivars. *Obscurior* has slender stems and the spines, which are dark at the base, form a brown circle around the areole. *Stella-aurata* has one slender central spine; all spines are yellow with a dark tip. *Subcrocea* has pale yellow spines with brown or red tips, and *Tenuis* has much thinner but erect stems.

Cultivation This plant is widely grown because it is small, easy to cultivate and to propagate from shoots, and grows rapidly. It is very vulnerable to rot, however, and should be kept absolutely dry throughout the autumn and winter.

167 MAMMILLARIA FRAILEANA (Britton and Rose) Boedecker
Tribe Cacteae — subtribe Cactinae

Place of Origin This plant was discovered by J. N. Rose in 1911 on the small islands of Pichilinque, Cerralbo and Santa Catalina, off Baja California in the Gulf of California.

Description The plant's stem is cylindrical, tillers from the base when adult and is fairly short, reaching only 4 to 6 in. (10 to 15 cm.) in height. The tubercles are conical, broad at the base and not very prominent. Their axils are glabrous or have a few bristles. There are 10 to 12 radial spines, approximately 3/8 in. (1 cm.) long, slender, needle-shaped, reddish-brown at first, later turning white, and radiating outward. There are three or four somewhat thicker central spines up to 3/8 in. (1 cm.) long, dark brown when young and lighter later. One of the spines is hooked. The flowers measure 1 in. (3 cm.) or more across when open wide, and have pink perianth segments that are darker in the center. The elongated, club-shaped fruit is pinkish-lilac or red, and its seeds are black.

Cultivation This plant is not very widely cultivated, partly because it needs a certain amount of heat in winter and a moist atmosphere. The soil, however, should be perfectly drained, kept dry during the plant's rest period, and watered with extreme caution at other times. Propagation is from basal shoots.

---

168 MAMMILLARIA GRACILIS Pfeiffer
Tribe Cacteae — subtribe Cactinae

Place of Origin The state of Hidalgo in Mexico.

Description This is another small plant that has been widely cultivated. The small stem is cylindrical, 4 in. (10 cm.) high, and tillers profusely both through basal shoots and lateral branches. New stems are often semiprostrate or twisted. Tubercles are about 3/16 in. (5 mm.) long and a little less across and have a slightly woolly base. There are 12 to 14 bristlelike radial spines 1/6 to 1/3 in. (5 to 9 mm.) long, cream-colored but later white, and arranged in a star pattern. There are three to five central spines, up to 1/2 in. (1.5 cm.) long and varying from light to dark brown. Flowers are 2/3 in. (1.7 cm.) long and 1/2 in. (1.3 cm.) across. The lanceolate perianth segments are pale yellow or whitish. The fruit is 3/8 in. (1 cm.) long and bright orange. Young shoots have lower tubercles bearing radial spines firmly attached to the epidermis and no central spines; the shoots detach themselves and fall off easily. The variety *fragilis*, even more common than *M. gracillis* and often considered a species, is smaller and has white central spines with a brown tip. The variety *pulchella* is more slender, with fewer, partly brown radial spines and no central spines.

Cultivation It is easy to cultivate and to propagate by shoots or cuttings, but these do not flower for the first three years. The plant tolerates moderate cold, provided it is kept dry.

169 MAMMILLARIA GUELDEMANNIANA Backeberg
Tribe Cacteae — subtribe Cactinae

Place of Origin Near Alamos in the state of Sonora, Mexico.
Description This plant has a light grayish-green stem that is globular at first, becoming cylindrical later, reaching a height of 4 in. (10 cm.) and a diameter of about 2 in. (5 cm.). It becomes shrublike by putting out numerous basal shoots. The tubercles, which are rather soft and fleshy, are rounded toward the apex and quadrangular, wide and glabrous at the base. The areoles bear about 20 radial spines that are slender, whitish, and about 3/16 in. (5 mm.) long, and one very short central spine measuring 1/12 in. (2 mm.). This is conical, sometimes hooked, and fairly dark. The flowers are small and campanulate with a diameter of 3/8 in. (1 cm.). The petals are white with a pink edge and a crimson throat. The variety *guirocombensis* has been found over a much larger area in southern Sonora, the northeast corner of Sinaloa, the southwest corner of Chihuahua and on the slopes of the western Sierra Madre, at higher altitudes. It has one to three reddish-brown central spines almost 3/8 in. (1 cm.) long. One spine is hooked. The flowers are bigger and open wider and the scarlet fruit produces black seeds.
Cultivation The variety is easier to find than the typical species. It tolerates moderate cold as long as it is dry. Propagation is by seed, or from basal shoots if available.

170 MAMMILLARIA KEWENSIS Salm-Dyck
Tribe Cacteae — subtribe Cactinae

Place of Origin This species was first sent to Kew Gardens in England with no indication of its place of origin; in 1850 Salm-Dyck described a specimen he had cultivated. It is now known that it comes from the central plateau of Mexico.
Description The plant's spherical stem becomes cylindrical, measuring about 5 in. (12 cm.) tall and 3½ in. (9 cm.) in diameter. Tubercles are conical, short, and wide at the base, which bears persistent white, curly down. The apical areoles are woolly when young but later become bare. The four to six spines are all radial, curved, and arranged in a star pattern. The upper ones are 1/4 to 1/2 in. (6 to 12 mm.) long while the lowest, which is thick and sharp, reaches a length of 1 in. (3 cm.). In time their color changes from a reddish to a blackish brown, becoming lighter later. The funnel-shaped flowers are about 1/2 in. (1.5 cm.) long and have pointed perianth segments that are a dark purplish pink, particularly in the center. The greenish fruit, 3/4 in. (2 cm.) long, may become pinkish and has brown seeds. The variety *albispina*, better known in horticultural circles as *spectabilis*, has white spines.
Cultivation This slow-growing plant tolerates cold but not frost. Like all species unprotected by spines, it is vulnerable to scorching if it is not exposed to the sun gradually after spending a winter under shelter. Propagation is by seed.

171 MAMMILLARIA LENTA Brandegee
Tribe Cacteae — subtribe Cactinae

Place of Origin Near Viesca and Torreón in the southwestern part of the state of Coahuila, Mexico.

Description This plant, which tillers from its base, forming thick clumps, is peculiar in that it ramifies from its apex, which divides dichotomously. Each stem is light green or yellowish and measures 1 to 2 in. (3 to 5 cm.) in diameter, usually remaining hemispherical and wider than it is tall. The tubercles are slender and conical, arranged in dense spirals. Their base is woolly and sometimes has one bristle. The areoles bearing the spines are glabrous, white, and felted near the apex only. There are 30 to 40 bristly white radial spines 1/12 to 1/2 in. (2 to 5 mm.) long, which are arranged in numerous concentric circles. They are slender, fragile, sometimes almost transparent, and overlap to a greater or lesser extent, practically hiding the whole of the stem. There are no central spines. The flowers are whitish and have pointed perianth segments. They are followed by red berries 3/8 in. (1 cm.) long.

Cultivation This species grows particularly slowly, so where possible it should be propagated from basal shoots. The plant prefers semishade and, in winter, mild heat. It should be sprayed occasionally to preserve the delicate beauty of the spines.

172 MAMMILLARIA MARNIERIANA Backeberg
Tribe Cacteae — subtribe Cactinae

Place of Origin The mountains surrounding Santa Ana in the state of Sonora, Mexico.

Description This species was dedicated by Backeberg to Julien Marnier-Lapostolle, who established a magnificent private botanical garden, where succulents take pride of place, at Les Cèdres, his villa near Cap Ferrat. The plant has a slightly cylindrical stem, solitary at first, later ramifying by means of numerous basal shoots. The stem is about 4 in. (10 cm.) high with a diameter of 2½ in. (6.5 cm.) and an almost flat apex. The tubercles are conical, small, set very close together, and arranged in dense spirals. Their base is glabrous. The areoles at their apex bear about 30 radial spines that are about 1/3 in. (8 mm.) long, slender, straight, and not hooked, and one fairly thick central spine only 1/12 in. (2 mm.) long. All the spines are white, although somewhat brownish at their base. The campanulate flowers are large for their genus, measuring 1/2 in. (1.5 cm.) long and 1¼ in. (3.5 cm.) across. The perianth segments are evaginated, slightly rolled outward, and are pink, crimson, or purple.

Cultivation This species has been fairly recently introduced and is difficult to find on the market. It prefers some heat in winter and a warm, sunny position in summer. Propagation is by seed.

173 MAMMILLARIA MAZATLANENSIS Schumann
Tribe Cacteae — subtribe Cactinae

Place of origin On the coast around the town of Mazatlán, in the state of Sinaloa, northwestern Mexico.

Description This plant was described in 1901. It grows in the hills near the sea, forming large clusters of small oblong stems, up to 5 in. (12 cm.) high and 1½ in. (4 cm.) in diameter at the most. The tubercles of the grayish-green stems are arranged in loose spirals; they are wide at the base and protrude by about 1/8 to 1/4 in. (3 to 5 mm.). The base of the tubercles is bare or slightly felted, sometimes bearing a few bristles. The apical areoles are woolly and round. There are 13 to 15 radial spines on an adult plant. They are white, stiff, needle-shaped, and 3/16 to 3/8 in. (5 mm. to 1 cm.) long. There are three or four sharp central spines, or as many as six on old plants, and they are thicker and longer than the radial spines. One may be hooked. Brown in color, those near the stem's apex are darker with a white base, and point outward. The flowers grow on the upper part of the plant from the axil of the older tubercles. They are about 1½ in. (4 cm.) long, with oblong perianth segments that are varying shades of crimson. The fruit is red, reddish or sometimes brownish, club-shaped and 3/4 in. (2 cm.) long.

Cultivation It needs heat in winter and should be sprayed during its winter rest period: unlike the desert species, it prefers a fairly humid atmosphere. Propagation is by shoots.

174 MAMMILLARIA MICROCARPA Engelmann
Tribe Cacteae — subtribe Cactinae
Common names: Fishhook cactus, pincushion cactus, sunset cactus

Place of Origin From western Texas, southern New Mexico and Arizona to the states of Chihuahua and Sonora in Mexico.

Description The plant is rather small, in cultivation growing to less than 4 in. (10 cm.) although in its natural habitat it may reach 6¼ in. (16 cm.). The dark grayish-green stem, which measures a maximum of 2¼ in. (6 cm.) in diameter, tends to be solitary, but occasionally tillers. Its small tubercles are conical or slightly oval and its axils lack hairs and bristles. The stem is completely covered with radial spines 3/16 to 3/8 in. (5 mm. to 1 cm.) long that overlap with those on adjacent areoles. They are slender and white or yellow with a brown tip; there are generally 20 to 30 on each areole. There is usually only one central spine, but there may be three or four, in which case upper spines are close-set and the lower one is hooked. They are initially red, becoming a blackish brown later, and reach nearly 3/4 in. (2 cm.) in length. The flowers are pink with a darker median line and measure about 1½ in. (4 cm.) across. There are one or two local varieties in Arizona that have golden-yellow central spines, or brown hooked spines.

Cultivation Because propagation by seed is slow, it's often grafted onto other stock; this improves its flowering potential.

175 MAMMILLARIA OCCIDENTALIS (Britton and Rose) Boedecker

Tribe Cacteae — subtribe Cactinae

Place of Origin Mexico. The plant was discovered on the Pacific coast near Manzanillo, in the state of Colima. Later it was found farther north on the coast in Nayarit and Sinaloa.

Description This species tillers and ramifies abundantly, producing slender cylindrical stems up to 6 in. (15 cm.) high with a diameter of 3/4 to 1 in. (2 to 3 cm.). The conical tubercles, which are completely hidden by the numerous spines, sometimes bear a few spines but no wool at their base. The 12 to 18 radial spines, 1/8 to 1/3 in. (3 to 8 mm.) long, are flattened, radiate in all directions and overlap. They are slender and needle-shaped and vary from white to yellowish with a brown tip. There are four to five central spines measuring 3/16 to 3/8 in. (5 mm. to 1 cm.) long. These are reddish-brown, stiff and needle-shaped; and one of them—usually the lowest—is hooked. The flowers are 3/8 in. (1 cm.) long and are lightly scented. The perianth segments are a fairly dark crimson or violet, and very much evaginated. The variety *monocentra* bears a single reddish-brown central spine, 1/4 in. (7 mm.) long, which may be straight, curved or hooked.

Cultivation In its natural habitat this plant grows among rocks in the sunshine, so it needs gravelly and perfectly drained soil. Propagation is by shoots.

176 MAMMILLARIA PLUMOSA Weber

Tribe Cacteae — subtribe Cactinae

Place of Origin The state of Coahuila in northern Mexico.

Description This small plant tillers very profusely, forming small cushions that cover the calcareous rocks and gravelly slopes in which it grows. Its stem is spherical, pale green and 2¾ in. (7 cm.) in diameter. It has soft cylindrical tubercles arranged in numerous spirals. Each tubercle has a white, woolly axil and small round areoles bearing up to 40 white radial spines. The latter are 1/8 to 1/4 in. (3 to 7 mm.) long, soft and feathery and cover the stems entirely. Central spines are absent. Often a few of the spines are bent or twisted, thus forming an even denser covering. The flowers are small, rarely exceeding 3/8 in. (1 cm.) long and across. They are white, greenish at the base, with a fairly narrow red or brown median stripe that is sometimes indistinct. The plant does not flower regularly or prolifically, but is nonetheless very attractive, being cultivated mainly for its strange resemblance—particularly when it has tillered—to balls of cotton wool. It is often confused with *Mammillaria lasiacantha*, which has even more numerous, bristlelike spines, tubercles with a glabrous base, and a grayer epidermis.

Cultivation The plant requires strong sunlight and very well-drained soil, and should be kept fairly dry from November till April. Propagation is by shoots.

177 MAMMILLARIA PROLIFERA Haworth
Tribe Cacteae — subtribe Cactinae

Place of Origin   Cuba and Haiti in the West Indies.
Description   Miller named this plant *Cactus proliferus* in 1768; in 1812 Haworth put it in his new genus *Mammillaria*. The plant is spherical or oblong and only 2¼ in. (6 cm.) high with a diameter of 1½ in. (4 cm.). It tillers to form colonies that often measure 25 in. (60 cm.) across. The tubercles are soft, conical, slender, just over 3/16 in. (5 mm.), and arranged in a few spirals. Long, hairlike bristles grow from the base of the tubercles to above their tip. Areoles are somewhat woolly toward the apex of the stem. They bear a great many radial spines, from 3/16 to 3/8 in. (5 mm. to 1 cm.) long, which are white and bristlelike; and five to ten central spines, about 1/3 in. (8 mm.) long, slender, radially arranged, and pale yellow with a darker tip. Flowers appear around the center of the plant at the base of the oldest tubercles. They are about 1/2 in. (1.5 cm.) long and the inner perianth segments are large, fairly erect and pale yellow with a reddish-brown median stripe. Withered remains of the perianth cling to the scarlet or orange 3/8 in. (1 cm.) long fruit. The variety *multiceps*, often considered a separate species, has a slenderer stem and originates in southern Texas and northern Mexico. Its common names are hair-covered cactus and grape cactus.
Cultivation   The plant is easily propagated from shoots.

---

178 MAMMILLARIA PSEUDOPERBELLA Quehl
Tribe Cacteae — subtribe Cactinae

Place of Origin   This species, described by Quehl in 1909, has a fairly large area of distribution in Mexico: from the state of Querétaro across central Mexico to the state of Oaxaca on the Pacific coast.
Description   The plant's stem is usually solitary but ramifies occasionally, producing a few basal shoots. It is spherical at first, becoming slightly cylindrical later, with a depressed apex that appears completely white. The stem reaches a diameter of 6 in. (15 cm.) and may, with age, become suberized at its base. The tubercles are short and conical and are arranged in numerous, very close-set spirals. Their axils are fairly woolly, and the apical areoles bear from 20 to 30 radial spines which are 1/8 in. (3 mm.) long, white, slender, silky and arranged laterally on each side of the tubercle. There are two central spines; the upper one is erect and about 1/4 in. (5 mm.) long, while the lower one is shorter; they are both brownish with a darker tip. The flowers are small and crimson. The fruit is a light red.
Cultivation   The plant is easy to cultivate. It does not tolerate intense cold, but tolerates some cold if kept dry. It is propagated by seed. Sometimes old plants divide at their apex, ramifying dichotomously—to form two distinct joints—but the removal of one of these joints may prove fatal to the plant.

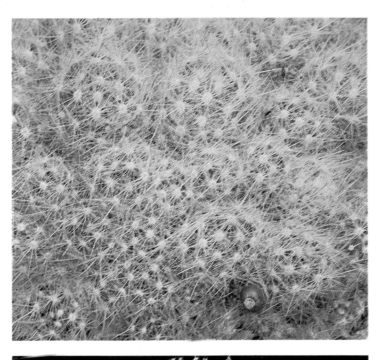

179 MAMMILLARIA SCHIEDEANA Ehrenberg
Tribe Cacteae — subtribe Cactinae

Place of Origin   Central Mexico.
Description   The German Ehrenberg named this species in 1838. The plant is spherical with a somewhat flattened apex. It is about 1½ to 2 in. (4 to 5.5 cm.) in diameter and puts out many basal shoots, forming dense clusters. The fairly soft tubercles are conical-cylindrical and about 3/8 in. (1 cm.) long, arranged in low spirals and have bristlelike hairs at the base. Areoles bear a great many radial spines that are very slender, 1/12 to 1/5 in. (2 to 5 mm.) long, arranged in close-set concentric circles. They are interspersed with bristlelike hairs that are yellow at the base and that overlap with those on adjacent areoles, giving the stem a festooned appearance. There are no central spines. Flowers are 3/4 in. (2 cm.) long and white or cream-colored, with notched inner perianth segments. The cylindrical berries are red. There are various forms of this species with spines and bristles that are entirely white, entirely yellow, or yellow at the corona.
Cultivation   This plant may have either fibrous roots or a long taproot. This latter must be given plenty of room when the plant is repotted. The species is hardy in milder climates, but needs to be protected from intense cold. Its shoots do not root easily, and the plant is therefore often grafted onto other stock or propagated by seed.

---

180 MAMMILLARIA SEMPERVIVI de Candolle
Tribe Cacteae — subtribe Cactinae

Place of Origin   The states of Hidalgo and Vera Cruz in central Mexico.
Description   In 1828 de Candolle named this species, which, with its fairly long and very conspicuous tubercles set close together in a large number of spirals, reminded him of the *Sempervivum* (houseleek) of the European mountains. The plant is solitary at first and later tillers slowly. It is spherical with a very depressed apex and reaches a height of about 2¼ in. (6 cm.) and a diameter of 2¾ in. (7 cm.). The tubercles are pyramidal, slightly angular, about 3/8 in. (1 cm.) long, with a very woolly base, particularly on the flower-bearing area. The areoles are small and felted in the center of the stem, gradually becoming glabrous. Three to seven white radial spines, only 1/8 in. (3 mm.) long, appear only on new growth. There are usually two central spines that are stiff, short—the longer of the two measures 3/16 in. (5 mm.)—nearly conical, somewhat curved, and reddish-brown when young, soon turning white. The flowers grow from the axils of adult tubercles. The outer segments of the perianth are normally greenish while the inner ones are white with a red central line. Occasionally the flowers may be yellowish or pink.
Cultivation   The plant needs mild heat in winter and protection from sun in the summer. Propagation is by seed or shoots.

181 MAMMILLARIA SPHACELATA von Martius
Tribe Cacteae — subtribe Cactinae

Place of Origin   In the mountainous region of southern Mexico, in the states of Oaxaca and Puebla, near Tehuacán.

Description   According to Buxbaum, this plant no longer belongs to *Mammillaria* but to the new genus *Leptocladodia* (meaning "having a slender stem"), established by Buxbaum. However, since the old name has remained in common use and is retained in many texts, we have preferred to use it, too. The plant's specific name, which was attributed to it by Martius in 1832, derives from the Greek word *sphakelos,* meaning dry or parched, and is perhaps due to the appearance of the stems in old age: they cease to be erect and their grayish-green epidermis is covered with white spines. The plant has cylindrical, greenish-gray stems up to 8 in. (20 cm.) in length but only a maximum of 1 in. (3 cm.) in diameter. They are often twisted and branch very readily, forming dense clumps. The small, conical tubercles have a woolly, bristly axil; at their apex the areoles bear 10 to 15 slender radial spines that are white with a red tip, turning brownish later. There is usually one central spine — although there may be two or three — similar to the radial spines. The flowers are a more or less dark red.

Cultivation   The plant grows very slowly and is likely to rot. It therefore requires scant watering. It does not tolerate frost. Propagation is by basal shoots.

182 MAMMILLARIA SPINOSISSIMA Lemaire
Tribe Cacteae — subtribe Cactinae

Place of Origin   Mexico. This plant has an enormous area of distribution, extending from the states of Hidalgo, Morelos and Puebla in central Mexico to the Pacific Coast.

Description   Lemaire named this plant in 1838; it has probably been renamed more than any other plant because of its enormous variability — particularly in terms of its spines. Today these names are attributed to the plant's many varieties or are used as synonyms. The stem is cylindrical, becoming columnar when adult, reaching a height of 12 in. (30 cm.) and a diameter of 4 in. (10 cm.). It is almost always described as solitary, but it may at this age ramify from its base. Tubercles are conical-oval, slightly angular, 1/6 to 1/4 in. (4 to 5 mm.) high, with woolly, bristly axils, and are arranged in numerous spirals. Areoles are woolly at the apex, later glabrous. There are 20 to 30 radial spines pointing in all directions; they are bristlelike, as much as 3/8 in. (1 cm.) long, and mainly white. The 7 to 15 central spines measure up to 3/4 in. (2 cm.) long, and are needle-shaped, flexible, rarely sharp, and vary widely from white to ruby-red, or yellowish-brown to reddish-brown. The flowers are 3/4 in. (2 cm.) long and have pinkish-brown outer segments with crimson inner segments.

Cultivation   The plant's natural variability is increased by propagation from seed. Only old plants tiller, but not always.

183 MAMMILLARIA THERESAE Cutak
Tribe Cacteae — subtribe Cactinae

Place of Origin This species was discovered in 1966 by Theresa Bock growing at an altitude of 7,200 ft. (2,200 m.) in the state of Durango, northern Mexico; it was later named *theresae* in her honor by Ladislaus Cutak, a botanist from Bucovina, Romania, who became a naturalized American and a specialist in succulents at the Saint Louis Botanical Gardens.
Description This small plant has a cylindrical stem which is often solitary but which may ramify. It is olive-green, but if well cultivated will become red or purple. Its tubercles are small and slender, with round, woolly areoles bearing numerous whitish radial spines, barely 1/12 in. (2 mm.) long, and nine central spines. The reddish-violet flowers have a slender tube and may reach a length of 1½ in. (4 cm.). The black seeds are minute.
Cultivation The plant probably tolerates a certain amount of cold but, in view of its small size, it should be grown separately and with a few precautions. It is easily propagated from seed.

---

184 MAMMILLARIA TROHARTII Hildmann
Tribe Cacteae — subtribe Cactinae

Place of Origin Mexico.
Description The stem of this species is initially solitary and then proliferates by putting forth a great many basal shoots, forming large clusters. It is dark green tending to bluish-green. Each stem grows to approximately 2¼ in. (6 cm.) in diameter, has a depressed apex and large conical tubercles that are somewhat angular and raised about 3/16 in. (5 mm.). The tubercles have a glabrous base on new growth, though later developing thick white down. In contrast, the areoles are felted at first but become bare later. They bear four to five white radial spines with brown tips; these are short, except for the lower ones, which may reach a length of nearly 1/3 in. (8 mm.). The single central spine is brownish, much longer and stiff, straight or slightly curved, and in time it falls off, leaving the tubercle almost spineless. The red flowers grow from the axil of the adult tubercles, emerging from the middle of the down.
Cultivation This species is not easy to identify since there are many others like it — probably the result of either natural or artificial hybridization. As in the case of all barely spinescent cacti with an unprotected epidermis, the greatest care must be taken to prevent scorching of the plant when it is exposed to sunlight — particularly after its rest period. Propagation is from shoots.

185 MAMMILLARIA WOBURNENSIS Scheer
Tribe Cacteae — subtribe Cactinae

Place of Origin   Guatemala.
Description   The plant's name refers to Woburn Abbey in England, where there was once a large cactus collection. In 1845 Scheer described a specimen at Kew Gardens, and in 1908 F. Eichlam rediscovered it and named it *Mammillaria chapinensis*, which is still in use. The stem is spherical, later oval-oblong, reaches 8 in. (20 cm.) high and 3 in. (8 cm.) in diameter. In time it puts out shoots and ramifies to form large clusters. The conical, blunt tubercles exude large quantities of latex when they are injured. Some ten white bristles grow from their woolly base. The eight or nine radial spines are about 1/4 in. (4 to 5 mm.) long and creamy-white with reddish tips. One to five central spines vary in length up to 3/4 in. (2 cm.). They are dark brown at first, later yellowish with a brownish-red tip. The flowers appear from the base of the tubercles to form a corona around the apex, or just below it. They are about 3/4 in. (2 cm.) long and have yellow outer perianth segments with a reddish-brown median dorsal stripe. Inner segments are plain yellow. The plant's skin color may vary; it is often reddish. It is then known as the *rubescens* variety.

Cultivation   In its natural habitat this species grows under bushes; it therefore needs semishade. It does not tolerate cold. Propagation is by cuttings or shoots.

---

186 MAMMILLARIA ZEILMANNIANA Boedecker
Tribe Cacteae — subtribe Cactinae

Place of Origin   Near San Miguel Allende in the state of Guanajuato, central Mexico.
Description   This very floriferous species tends to have a solitary stem that occasionally puts forth shoots when older. It is oval or somewhat cylindrical, about 2¼ in. (6 cm.) high and 1½ in. (4 cm.) across. The tubercles are oval or nearly cylindrical, 1/4 in. (5 mm.) long, with a bare base and an areole at their apex. The areoles are woolly when young, bearing 15 to 18 radial spines that are white, very slender, 3/8 in. (1 cm.) long and radially arranged. There are four reddish-brown central spines that are nearly 1/3 in. (8 mm.) long. One is a little longer than the others and hooked. The flowers are 3/4 in. (2 cm.) across. Their color varies from lilac to violet or a reddish purple. The small green fruits have black seeds.

Cultivation   Normal growth conditions: porous soil, a winter rest period at a temperature a little above freezing, and summer sunlight. Propagation is by seed, since it is difficult to obtain tillered plants.

187 MATUCANA COMACEPHALA Ritter
Tribe Cacteae — subtribe Echinocactinae

Etymology This plant takes its name from a village in central Peru, high up in the western cordillera northeast of Lima, where the typical species was discovered.

Place of Origin The eastern slopes of the Cordillera Blanca in the department of Ancash, northern Peru.

Description The plant has a cylindrical stem that generally reaches a length of 29½ in. (75 cm.), although in its natural habitat it may grow even longer, with a diameter of 3 in. (8 cm.). There are about 25 very close-set, obviously tuberculate ribs. The areoles bear 15 to 20 radial spines that are 1/2 in. (1.5 cm.) long, more or less hairlike, and splayed outward. Thicker central spines point obliquely upward (although occasionally one points downward) and are more or less curved. They vary from 3/8 to 1½ in. (1 to 4 cm.) in length. All the spines are white. The flowers are red, as in most species of the genus, and are nearly 2¼ in. (5.5 cm.) long, with an irregular curved perianth. The fruit is greenish.

Cultivation This plant is seldom cultivated because, as with all Andean species, the hours of summer sunshine in temperate regions are excessive. Plants should therefore be placed in a southeasterly position during the summer. Propagation is by cuttings or seed if available.

188 MATUCANA PAUCICOSTATA Ritter
Tribe Cacteae — subtribe Echinocactinae

Place of Origin Between the Pacific coast and the Cordillera Negra in the province of Huarás, department of Ancash, Peru.

Description The plant's stem is hemispherical, reaching a height of up to 5½ in. (14 cm.) and about half that in diameter. It has 7 to 11 ribs measuring 1/4 to 1/2 in. (7 mm. to 1.5 cm.) high and across, bearing conical, raised tubercles with grayish areoles set about 3/8 in. (1 cm.) apart. There are four to eight radial spines, measuring 3/16 to 1 in. (5 mm. to 3 cm.) long, and one central spine (which is often absent). All the spines are chestnut brown when young, becoming gray with age. The irregular flowers are 2¼ in. (6 cm.) long, more than half their length consisting of a tube bearing long white hairs. The segments of the perianth are dark crimson with a more or less conspicuous violet border. The green fruit is absolutely spherical and has a few hairs; its seeds, hardly longer than 1/25 in. (1 mm.) are brown. The species may still be found under the name of *Submatucana*, one of Backeberg's genera that is no longer accepted.

Cultivation This species has been fairly recently introduced. In cultivation it is more likely to be found grafted onto other stock to accelerate its growth, although it grows perfectly well on its own roots. It tolerates cold when adult. Propagation is by seed.

189 MATUCANA WEBERBAUERI (Vaupel) Backeberg

Tribe Cacteae — subtribe Echinocactinae

Place of Origin The eastern slopes of the central cordillera near Chachapoyas, capital of the department of Amazonas, northern Peru.

Description The stem of this plant is a depressed sphere with a height of about 2¾ in. (7 cm.) and a diameter of 6 in. (15 cm.). It has 21 tuberculate ribs. The tubercles are rounded and fairly close-set. The areoles are elliptical and bear about 30 straight spines radiating in all directions. They are brown, turning black later, the longest measure 1½ in. (4 cm.). The flowers are tubular, slightly funnel-shaped, and just over 2 in. (5.5 cm.) long. The tube is covered with pointed, lanceolate scales, and the perianth segments are lemon yellow. This color is peculiar to the species, all the other members of the genus having flowers that are various shades of red or violet. In 1913 Vaupel described this species as an *Echinocactus*, and it may still be found under this genus.

Cultivation In their natural habitat all the species of *Matucana* grow among rocks. Hence they need perfectly drained soil and cannot tolerate moisture around their roots. Propagation is by seed.

190 MATUCANA YANGANUCENSIS Rauh and Backeberg

Tribe Cacteae — subtribe Echinocactinae

Place of Origin The Cordillera Blanca in Ancash, Peru.

Description The plant has a spherical stem 4 in. (10 cm.) or more in diameter, and it tillers when adult, producing basal shoots. There are 27 ribs with quite close-set areoles that are felted when young. They bear many thick 3/8 in. (1 cm.) long radial spines, yellowish-brown on new growth, turning whitish with age. The one or two needle-shaped central spines are up to 1 in. (2.5 cm.) long and yellowish-brown. Flowers are 2¼ in. (6 cm.) long and 1 in. (2.5 cm.) across with reddish-violet perianth segments. There are many varieties: *Albispina* has pectinate overlapping radial spines and longer central spines; all the spines are white. Flowers are crimson. *Fuscispina* has a solitary stem and dark brown central spines 1 in. (3 cm.) long. *Longistyla* has a larger spherical stem, 23 tuberculate ribs, white radial spines with a dark base, and dark brown central spines; its flowers are red or pale crimson, with a very long style, hence its name. *Parviflora* has a short, depressed stem, and longer, thicker erect spines. Its crimson flowers are smaller and irregular. *Suberecta* may grow 8 in. (20 cm.) long. Its whitish central spines are hard to distinguish from the radials, and its flowers are red.

Cultivation When possible, it is propagated from shoots.

191 MELOCACTUS BAHIENSIS (Britton and Rose)
Werdermann
Tribe Cacteae — subtribe Cactinae

Etymology Its name, first used by Tournefort, comes from the Latin *melo,* an abbreviation of *melopepo,* which Pliny the Elder used for melon; its cephalium is rounded.
Place of Origin The state of Bahia in Brazil.
Description The plant's dark green stem is spherical at first, but in adult plants it elongates to a greater or lesser extent 4 in. (10 cm.) or more. The diameter is about 6 in. (15 cm.). There are 10 to 12 sharp, raised ribs that are 1 in. (2.5 cm.) wide at the base. Each bears six or seven whitish areoles with seven to ten radial spines 1 in. (2.5 cm.) long, and four central spines that are about 3/8 in. (1 cm.) longer. All the spines are brown. The cephalium is not very high and is covered by numerous brown or reddish bristles. From it grow small pink flowers that are followed by oblong red berries measuring 1/2 in. (1.5 cm.). This species is one of those in which the cephalium may divide on older plants. Sometimes new shoots spring from it, in turn producing a new cephalium, but this is very rare in cultivation.
Cultivation This plant is sensitive to waterlogged conditions and very prone to rot. Propagation is by seed, and growth is very slow, but it may be speeded up by grafting. Winter temperatures should never sink below 60° to 65° F. (15° to 18° C.). In summer the plant prefers strong sunlight.

---

192 MELOCACTUS CONCINNUS Buining and Bred.
Tribe Cacteae — subtribe Cactinae

Place of Origin The state of Bahia, Brazil, at an altitude of about 3,200 ft. (1,000 m.). It grows under the typical maquis or *caatinga* vegetation on rocky, sandy, very dry terrain.
Description This species was discovered in 1968. The green or bluish-green stem is a markedly depressed sphere about 4 in. (10 cm.) in height and slightly more in diameter. There are 10 to 13 sharp, tuberculate ribs with white, felted areoles embedded in transverse depressions between the tubercles. There are seven radial spines of which two are very short, four are curved and 1/2 in. (5 mm.) long, and one is 1 in. (2.5 cm.) long, tougher, and points downward. There is only one central spine, just over 3/8 in. (1 cm.) long. All the spines are reddish with a light base at first, later becoming gray with a brown tip. The cephalium is only about 1 in. (3 cm.) high, but is fairly wide, being 2¼ to 2¾ in. (6 to 7 cm.) in diameter. The youngest part is covered with thick white wool interspersed with red bristles, while the latter predominate on the older parts. The crimson flowers are about 3/4 in. (2 cm.) long and 2¼ to 2¾ in. (6 to 7 cm.) across. The fruit is red or pinkish violet. A characteristic of this genus is that the ripe fruit becomes membranous before it falls off.
Cultivation The plant's fibrous roots do not need much space. Careful watering is called for. Propagation is by seed.

193 MELOCACTUS GUARICENSIS Croizar
Tribe Cacteae — subtribe Cactinae

Place of Origin   The state of Guárico in Venezuela; hence the plant's name.

Description   This species was named fairly recently by Léon Croizat, an American botanist specializing in South American flora. It has a spherical or conical truncated stem, up to 4 in. (10 cm.) in height and about 3½ in. (9 cm.) in diameter. There are about ten ribs that are wide and blunt, with only slightly tuberculate edges when the plant is young, but more noticeable protuberances on older parts. The areoles are whitish and slightly sunken. The radial spines are indistinguishable from the central ones. There are seven to nine, almost 3/4 in. (2 cm.) long, initially slightly curved, becoming stiff later. They vary from deep yellow to dark brown. The cephalium is hemispherical, 1½ in. (4 cm.) high and 3½ in. (9 cm.) across, and covered with white hairs interspersed with red bristles.

Cultivation   Like the rest of the genus, this species requires a strict winter rest period, a sunny position in summer, and very porous soil. In winter the temperature should never drop below 60° to 65° F. (15° to 18° C.), and the plant should be sprayed if the stem shows signs of wrinkling. The chief difficulty in cultivating this genus lies in combining high temperature with low humidity during the rest period.

---

194 MONVILLEA SPEGAZZINII (Weber) Britton and Rose
Tribe Cacteae — subtribe Cereinae

Etymology   This name commemorates M. Monville, a scholar and collector of cacti in the eighteenth and mid-nineteenth century. The genus is exclusively South-American.

Place of Origin   Paraguay and northeastern Argentina, near Resistencia in Chaco province. It was discovered near Resistencia, capital of the province of Chaco, Argentina.

Description   It puts forth many basal shoots, soon becoming tillered. Erect or semiprostrate stems may reach a height of 6½ ft. (2 m.) and a diameter of 3/4 in. (2 cm.). They are a bluish green with white marbling. The three to five (usually four) raised angular ribs have deep incisions similar to indentations along the edge. They are about 1 in. (3 cm.) long at the base and bear small areoles at the apex of the protuberances. Young plants usually have three sharp, blackish spines 3/16 in. (5 mm.) long, two pointing upward and one downward. On the older parts there are five radial and one central spine, 1/2 in. (1.5 cm.) long. Flowers are borne laterally; buds point upward but curve suddenly downward when the flowers open. They are 5 in. (12 cm.) long, with a slender tube, reddish outer perianth segments and white inner ones. They bloom at night.

Cultivation   It needs semishade and a minimum winter temperature of about 50° F. (10° C.). Growth is rapid, and supports are needed for the stems. Propagation is by cuttings.

195 MYRTILLOCACTUS GEOMETRIZANS
(von Martius) Console
Tribe Cacteae — subtribe Cereinae

Etymology The Sicilian botanist Michelangelo Console chose this plant's name because of the similarity between its fruit and that of the myrtle (*Vaccinium myrtillus*).

Place of Origin The central Mexican plateau, from the state of San Luis Potosí to Oaxaca.

Description In its natural habitat this plant is almost treelike, up to 13 ft. (4 m.) tall with a well-defined trunk that produces upward-curving branches. However, plants grown from cuttings do not develop a trunk, and ramify from their base. These have a diameter of 2¼ to 4 in. (6 to 10 cm.), are a bluish green and very glaucous because of the bloom covering their youngest parts. The five to six ribs are wide at their base and bear only slightly felted areoles set far apart. There are five radial spines only about 1/12 in. (2 mm.) long. These are initially a reddish-brown. The single, blackish central spine is flattened laterally and is 3/4 to 2¾ in. (2 to 7 cm.) long. The flowers are 1 to 1¼ in. (2.5 to 3.5 cm.) across and have a very short tube and greenish perianth segments. Several flowers may appear simultaneously from each areole. The bluish fruit is globular, measuring 3/8 to 3/4 in. (1 to 2 cm.). The berries, known as *garambullos*, can be eaten fresh or dried.

Cultivation Propagation is by cuttings.

---

196 NEOBUXBAUMIA EUPHORBIOIDES
(Haworth) Buxbaum
Tribe Cacteae — subtribe Cereinae

Etymology This genus was created by Backeberg and named in honor of the Austrian botanist Franz Buxbaum.

Place of Origin Haworth described this species in 1819 as *Cereus euphorbioides,* but its place of origin was uncertain. Britton and Rose found only cultivated specimens. Backeberg said it was a native of Tamaulipas, Mexico, in the 1960s.

Description The plant's stem is columnar, erect, solitary, several meters high, and a grayish or bluish green. It has eight or nine pointed ribs and whitish, woolly areoles 3/16 to 3/8 in. (5 mm. to 1 cm.) apart. There are usually one to three large spines but on rare occasions as many as five, in which case only one of them is prominent, being 3/8 to 3/4 in. (1 to 2 cm.) long, while two shorter spines point downward. All spines are blackish or dark brown. Central spines are absent. Flowers are borne laterally below the apex and point outward. They are about 2¾ in. (7 cm.) long and slightly more across. The tube and outermost segments are wine-red; petals are pinkish-red. Flowers probably bloom at night, though not all authors agree on this point. The plant is still also known as *Cephalocereus.*

Cultivation It is easy to reproduce by seed and grow but not very attractive. Only adults produce flowers.

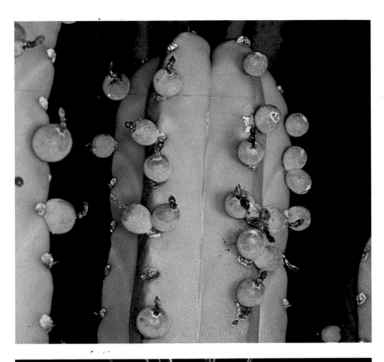

197 NEOBUXBAUMIA POLYLOPHA (de Candolle)
Backeberg
Tribe Cacteae — subtribe Cereinae

Place of Origin The valley of Tolimán and around Metztitlán in the state of Hidalgo, central Mexico.

Description De Candolle described the species in 1828 as a *Cereus*. It is still classified as a *Cephalocereus*, since Backeberg moved it to its new genus only recently. The stem is simple and columnar and in its native habitat reaches a height of 42 ft. (13 m.) and a diameter of 12 in. (30 cm.) or more. The bright green of the epidermis turns gray on the older parts of the plant. Many ribs meet at the rounded apex. They increase as the plant grows, ranging from 15 in young plants to about 50 in the largest wild specimens. Ribs have sharp edges with round areoles, which are covered with white felt on the new growth and are set less than 3/8 in. (1 cm.) apart. There are seven or eight radial spines up to 3/4 in. (2 cm.) long, pointing outward and more erect at the apex. The one central spine is longer, as much as 2¾ in. (7 cm.) on the flowering part of the plant. All spines are honey-colored with a brown tip; as they get older they turn white, eventually falling off and leaving the areoles inermous. Flowers are a darkish red, with a tube covered in fleshy scales.

Cultivation The plant is easy to grow and is pretty when young. Propagation is by seed.

198 NEOBUXBAUMIA SCOPARIA (Poselger) Backeberg
Tribe Cacteae — subtribe Cereinae

Place of Origin Around Juchitán, near the Pacific Ocean, in the states of Vera Cruz and Oaxaca, southern Mexico.

Description This species was also once included in *Cephalocereus*. The stem is columnar and up to 24½ ft. (7.5 m.) high and ramifies profusely. The green epidermis of young stems changes to gray on older parts. New joints have 12 to 15 ribs that are tuberculate toward the apex, with a wedge-shaped incision below each areole. As they grow, the tubercles become elongated and less angular. Areoles on the rounded apex are slightly felted; later they become glabrous. They bear five radial spines, nearly 3/8 in. (1 cm.) long, of which three point downward; and one thicker, central spine that is about 3/4 in. (2 cm.) long, reddish at first, later turning black and eventually whitish. The oldest branches that are capable of flowering are slenderer and have 20 to 25 low ribs and white-felted areoles set closer together. Their spines are longer, sharp, and yellow at first; those on the flowering region are brown and bristlelike. Flowers and fruit are small and reddish.

Cultivation This plant is generally cultivated more for its general appearance than for its flowers, since young specimens do not bloom. It needs a warm, sheltered position. Propagation is by cuttings from new growth or by seed.

199 NEOPORTERIA GEROCEPHALA Ito
Tribe Cacteae — subtribe Echinocactinae

Etymology This genus was named after Carlos Porter, a Chilean entomologist and naturalist. The prefix "Neo" was added because there was already a genus *Porteria*, established by Hooker, which included members of the family *Valerianaceae*. In other instances the prefix "neo" often indicates that some species have been regrouped in a new genus.

Place of Origin Chile.

Description This species has a more or less spherical stem that, with age, becomes somewhat elongated without becoming cylindrical. There are numerous tuberculate ribs with prominent tubercles and broad felted areoles. The spines are numerous, thick and bristlelike, and blackish when young, soon becoming completely white. Because they are long and grow in a disordered fashion, they overlap, hiding the stem almost completely. They grow in tufts, which makes it almost impossible to distinguish the radials from the centrals, but the outer spines are much slenderer and shorter than the inner ones. The apical flowers are 2 in. (5 cm.) long, with rather pointed crimson-pink segments with a yellow base.

Cultivation This plant is not yet widely cultivated. It grows slowly unless grafted. Propagation is by seed.

---

200 NEOPORTERIA PSEUDOREICHEANA
(Backeberg) Krainz
Tribe Cacteae — subtribe Echinocactinae

Place of Origin Chile, but the exact locality is unknown.

Description In 1900 Schumann attributed the name *Echinocactus reichei* to a plant sent to him from Santiago de Chile by Karl Reiche, and since then it has been the subject of great taxonomic confusion. The plant was later transferred to the *Neoporteria* genus. Backeberg then created a new genus, *Reicheocactus*, for a few other Chilean species, and since he could not use this specific name for his new discoveries, he called one of them *neoreichei* and the other *pseudoreicheana*. His genus was subsequently abolished, and its members transferred to *Neoporteria*. The plant is roughly cylindrical or oval. The new growth is olive green while older plants are grayish. It has up to 40 ribs that are separated into small, round, flattened tubercles set very close together. The areoles are oblong, covered with brown felt, and yellowish at their depressed apex. There are seven to nine spines that are only about 1/8 in. (3 mm.) long, close-set, slender, and more or less curved. The flowers have a very short tube, the outer perianth segments are reddish-brown while the inner ones are yellow. The species is not very floriferous and is often grafted onto other stock, in which case it grows taller and ramifies more.

Cultivation This plant is rarely cultivated. Propagation is by cuttings.

201 NEOPORTERIA SUBGIBBOSA (Haworth) Britton and Rose
Tribe Cacteae — subtribe Echinocactinae

Place of Origin On the coast of Chile near Valparaiso.
Description The plant's stem is globular when young, later cylindrical and erect, reaching a height of 12 in. (30 cm.). In its natural habitat it may grow 3¼ ft. (1 m.) high and 4 in. (10 cm.) in diameter; the stem becomes prostrate or often hangs down from the rocks on which the plant usually grows and puts forth many shoots. There are as many as 20 tuberculate ribs, raised about 3/8 in. (1 cm.). They bear close-set, wide areoles that are felted when young; on older parts they are almost glabrous. The epidermis on new growth is light green but turns grayish- or brownish-green with age. The whole plant is very spiny. There are about 24 thick radial spines, pointing sideways, and four central spines that are stiff, subulate, and up to 1 in. (3 cm.) long. All spines are initially amber-colored but become darker with a light base. Later they turn reddish-brown. Flowers are borne on the stem's apex, grouped fairly close to the center, and are about 1 ½ in. (4 cm.) long. Buds are red and almost conical, and the flower's tube bears a few bristles. The perianth segments are crimson; the outer ones open wide while those in the center are erect and remain closed, hiding the stamens until the flower withers.
Cultivation Propagation is by cuttings or seed.

202 NOTOCACTUS HASELBERGII (Haage) Berger
Tribe Cacteae — subtribe Echinocactinae

Etymology The generic name derives from the Greek *notos*, south: all 25 or so species of this genus come from South America. This species used to be included in the genus *Malacocarpus* ("having soft fruit"), established by Britton and Rose, and is sometimes known as *Brasilicactus*.
Place of Origin Not mentioned in the original description, but it appears to be Rio Grande do Sul in southern Brazil.
Description This plant is quite small and has a globular or slightly cylindrical stem that is often semiprostrate and may reach a height of 5 in. (12 cm.) and a diameter of 2 to 4 in. (5 to 10 cm.), with a depressed apex. There are 30 or more ribs consisting of low, rounded tubercles bearing small areoles covered with white down. There are 20 or more needle-shaped radial spines as much as 3/8 in. (1 cm.) long, yellowish at first and white later, which almost conceal the stem. The three to five central spines are yellow. Flowers are borne on the stem's upper areoles and have a short tube and petals that are bright red or sometimes orange. A large and hardier form of this species has wider flowers with a longer, spiny tube.
Cultivation This plant grows easily in semishade. Since it only occasionally tillers from its base, it is often propagated by seed. But since the plantlets develop slowly, they are often grafted in order to speed up the process.

203 NOTOCACTUS HORSTII Ritter
Tribe Cacteae — subtribe Echinocactinae

Place of Origin   The Sierra Geral in the state of Rio Grande do Sul, southern Brazil.
Description   This species was described in 1966 by Ritter, but a single specimen had been discovered several years earlier by Leopold Horst (hence its specific name). Although Horst made a note of its characteristics when he discovered it, he never published them. The stem reaches a diameter of 5½ in. (14 cm.) and is globular at first, later becoming elongated and cylindrical, growing to a height of 12 in. (30 cm.). In its natural habitat, the plant sometimes produces new plants up to 3¼ ft. (1 m.) away from the parent, whose woolly, white apexes hang down from the rocks where the plant grows. There are 12 to 16 straight ribs marked by small tubercles bearing white, felted areoles set about 1/4 in. (6 to 9 mm.) apart. There are 10 to 15 radial spines that are pale, 3/8 to 1 in. (1 to 3 cm.) long, and straight or slightly curved. The one to four central spines are weaker, brown, and somewhat longer. Flowers are apical and 1 to 1¼ in. (3 to 3.5 cm.) long, with a scaly tube bearing white or brown down. Perianth segments are spatulate or lanceolate, yellow at the base and orange or scarlet toward the tip.
Cultivation   Like all other plants described so recently, this species is not readily available on the market. It needs some winter warmth as well as strong sun. Propagation is by seed.

204 NOTOCACTUS LENINGHAUSII (Haage)
Berger
Tribe Cacteae — subtribe Echinocactinae

Place of Origin   Southern Brazil.
Description   The plant has a globular stem that slowly becomes cylindrical; it is up to 3¼ ft. (1 m.) tall and 4 in. (10 cm.) in diameter. It ramifies from the base, forming slightly curved clusters of stems that become erect. The apex is rounded in young plants, becomes oblique in older ones. There are about 30 low, blunt, vertical ribs bearing areoles covered with thick white wool around the apex and on the flower-bearing part of the plant. There are about 15 radial spines that are slender, bristlelike, silky, pale yellow, and 3/16 in. (5 mm.) long. Three or four golden central spines are slender, curved downward, and as long as 1½ in. (4 cm.). When the new spines grow from the center of the apex they are reddish and form a small, erect tuft characteristic of the species; they turn yellow very soon. Flowers are borne near the center of the apex and are 1½ in. (4 cm.) long and 2 in. (5 cm.) across. Outer segments of the perianth are greenish, inner ones are yellow or lemon-colored. The tube is scaly, with brown hairs and bristles.
Cultivation   It is easy but slow to grow and is often cultivated. It does not flower until it is about 8 in. (20 cm.) tall. It tolerates cold and needs a shaded position. Propagation is by seed or shoots. Cristate forms have generally been grafted.

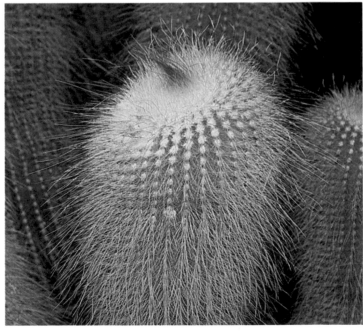

205 NOTOCACTUS MAMMULOSUS (Lemaire)
Berger
Tribe Cacteae — subtribe Echinocactinae

Place of Origin Uruguay and Argentina.
Description Lemaire first described this species in 1838 as
an *Echinocactus,* but it may still be found under the name *Malacocarpus mammulosus,* a now defunct genus created by
Salm-Dyck to which it was transferred by Britton and Rose. It
has a globular stem that elongates to a height of 4 in. (10 cm.)
with a diameter of 2¼ in. (6 cm.). It is grayish-green with a depressed, spineless apex. It has 18 to 20 ribs with prominent,
rounded tubercles between which large areoles are deeply
embedded and set about 3/16 in. (5 mm.) apart. There are 10
to 13 slender brown radial spines less than 1/4 in. (5 mm.)
long. The three or four central spines are thicker and more than
twice as long and are yellow with a brown tip. Flowers are yellow, with a tube covered with white wool and brown bristles.
This species is often confused with *Notocactus submammu-
losus,* which is similar but has only 13 ribs, about six radial
spines spread out horizontally, and two long and flat central
spines, one pointing upward and one downward, with a slender
groove along their lower part. Spines are yellow with a brown
tip, the largest having a red base when young, later turning
gray. The yellow flowers are smaller.
Cultivation Propagation by seed. It does not tolerate cold.

206 NOTOCACTUS OTTONIS (Lehmann) Berger
Tribe Cacteae — subtribe Echinocactinae

Place of Origin Southern Brazil, Uruguay, and Argentina.
Description The typical species has a dark green, flattened-
spherical stem 2 to 4½ in. (5 to 11 cm.) in diameter and eight to
ten tuberculate, rounded ribs bearing round, pubescent
areoles thickly felted when young. These are embedded in the
prominences and set 3/8 in. (1 cm.) apart. There are about 10
to 15 yellow, slender radial spines. There are usually three to
four central spines. Sometimes they are absent. They are
stronger, reddish-brown with a light tip, and about 1 in. (2.5
cm.) long. Flowers are 1½ to 2¼ in. (4 to 6 cm.) long and
across and have a woolly tube with bristles at the axil of the
scales. Perianth segments are yellow. The adult often puts
forth shoots. Principal varieties are *albispinus:* seven to nine
radial spines and one central spine, all whitish, and smaller
flowers; *brasiliensis:* more erect radial spines and shorter central ones, all brownish; *linkii:* thinner, sharper, more numerous
ribs, radial spines at first white, and smaller central spines;
multiflorus: pointed ribs, spines less than 3/4 in. (2 cm.) long,
and many small flowers; *tortuosus:* ribs arranged in spirals and
shorter, thicker radial spines and four to six central spines; and
uruguayensis: 11 large, more tuberculate ribs, no central
spines, and slender splayed out radial spines.
Cultivation Propagation is by seed or basal shoots.

207 NOTOCACTUS PURPUREUS Ritter
Tribe Cacteae — subtribe Echinocactinae

Place of Origin   The state of Rio Grande do Sul, south of the Sierra, in southern Brazil.

Description   The plant's spherical stem becomes oval later, is about 5½ in. (14 cm.) in diameter, and often puts out basal shoots. There are 14 to 18 straight, tuberculate ribs that protrude about 1/4 to 1/2 in. (7 mm. to 1.5 cm.). Tubercles on the older part of the plant become compressed and divided by deep transverse grooves. Areoles are round and white. The youngest are covered with white hairs that give the stem's depressed apex a woolly appearance and make the areoles seem larger than they are. On new growth the areoles are borne along the upper part of the tubercles and their felt extends down into the depressions. As the tubercles decrease in size with age, the areoles are set at their apex and those at the base have an almost glabrous surface. There are 7 to 15 radial spines 3/4 in. (2 cm.) long and curved or contorted, and one central 1 in. (2.5 cm.) spine that curves upward at first and downward later. All spines are yellowish or brown. Flowers grow from the center of the plant. They are funnel-shaped, with a tube bearing brown bristles, and almost 1½ in. (4 cm.) long and across. Perianth segments are pointed, narrow and crimson, hence the species name. The fruit is a reddish green.

Cultivation   Propagation is generally by seed.

208 NOTOCACTUS SCHUMANNIANUS (Nicolai)
Berger
Tribe Cacteae — subtribe Echinocactinae

Place of Origin   Southern Paraguay, near Paraguari, southeast of Asunción, and northern Argentina.

Description   This species was classified by Britton and Rose as a *Malacocarpus* and was later transferred by Backeberg to the genus *Eriocactus*. It may still be found under these synonyms. The plant is spherical at first, though with age it becomes columnar and reaches 3¼ ft. (1 m.) in height. It has numerous slender, sharp ribs that gradually multiply to 30 or more. The areoles are small, round, and set fairly close together. They are felted around the apex of the plant, which is very woolly and spiny, but they soon become glabrous. There are four to seven spines—or as many as ten on old plants—which are not distinguishable as radials or centrals. They are bristlelike, contorted or curved backward, and reddish-brown when young, turning gray later. The lowest spine, which is often caducous, measures 2 in. (5 cm.) in length. It is slightly curved and points either outward or downward. The flowers are apical, funnel-shaped, and 1½ to 2 in. (4 to 5 cm.) long. The yellow perianth segments open wide, measuring 1½ in. (4 cm.) across. They bloom for several days.

Cultivation   The plant prefers a semishaded position, or only a few hours in the sun. Propagation is by seed.

209 NOTOCACTUS SCOPA (Sprengel) Berger
Variety RUBERRIMUS
Tribe Cacteae — subtribe Echinocactinae

Place of Origin   Southern Brazil and Uruguay.
Description   The plant was described by Sprengel in 1825 as a *Cactus,* and has since been transferred to various genera. Its stem is spherical at first, becoming cylindrical later, 10 in. (25 cm.) high and 4 in. (10 cm.) across. It is almost entirely covered by soft white spines and is usually solitary, putting forth basal shoots only occasionally. There are 30 to 35 ribs that are low, blunt and have slight protuberances marked by small tubercles and areoles set just over 1/2 in. (5 mm.) apart. The latter are covered with white wool when young. There are about 40 radial spines, about 1/4 in. (5 to 7 mm.) long, very slender, white, and silky. The three or four central spines are thicker, longer, and reddish-brown. The flowers grow from the center and are about 1½ in. (4 cm.) long and across. The ovary has greenish scales, brown down and dark bristles, while canary- or lemon-yellow perianth segments open wide. There are several varieties, some of which tiller more frequently. *Ruberrimus* has crimson spines, and there is a cristate form which is much sought after by collectors.
Cultivation   The plant withstands strong sunlight, but during really hot periods it is wise to keep it in semishade. Propagation is from shoots when available, or by seed.

---

210 NOTOCACTUS SUCINEUS (Ritter)
Tribe Cacteae — subtribe Echinocactinae

Place of Origin   Rio Grande do Sul in southern Brazil.
Description   This specific name comes from the Latin *sucinum,* meaning yellow amber, because of many yellow spines that almost cover the plant's stem. The stem is spherical at first, becoming oblong later. It is a glossy green beneath the spines, has a sunken apex and measures 1 to 2¾ in. (3 to 7 cm.) in diameter. The ribs consist of a series of tubercles that protrude only about 1/2 in. (2 to 4 mm.). There are small, white, round areoles between the tubercles. They are heavily felted, particularly around the apex of the plant, where they form a corona, and bear sharp, straight spines. There are 15 to 30 amber-colored radial spines 1/8 to 1/4 in. (3 to 6 mm.) long, and 8 to 12 gold-colored central spines 1/4 in. to 3/4 in. (7 mm. to 2 cm.) long. The flowers are apical and about 1¼ in. (3.5 cm.) long and have a cylindrical tube, 3/8 in. (1 cm.) long, with a slight "beak." The perianth segments are sulfur-yellow; the outer ones are rounded while the inner ones are narrower and pointed. The fruit is entirely covered with white wool and has pink pulp and minute seeds. The plant tillers only when mature, but young, solitary specimens are very attractive, and may flower before putting forth any basal shoots.
Cultivation   Requires some warmth in winter. Propagation is by seed or shoots.

211 OBREGONIA DENEGRII Frič
Tribe Cacteae — subtribe Echinocactinae

Etymology   This plant was dedicated by the Czechoslovakian botanist Alberto Frič to Álvaro Obregón, president of Mexico, after Frič visited Mexico in 1920. The genus is monotypic, comprising this species only.

Place of Origin   On the slopes of the eastern Sierra Madre and the Sierra de Tamaulipas, near Ciudad Victoria, state of Tamaulipas in northeastern Mexico.

Description   This genus is fairly similar to the genera *Ariocarpus* and *Strombocactus*. The plant has a large taproot, and its rounded stem may reach a diameter of 5 in. (12 cm.). It consists of large, triangular tubercles, rather like leaves, arranged in overlapping spirals. The tubercles of adult plants are 3/4 to 1 in. (2 to 2.5 cm.) wide at the base. Their inner surface is flat while their outside is decidedly carinate. The cusped, somewhat everted apex bears a small areole that is felted at first, with two to four short, weak spines curved outward. The felt disappears and the spines fall off as the plant gets older. The flowers grow from the fairly flat, woolly center and are about 1 in. (3 cm.) across. The outer perianth segments are short and scalelike, while the inner ones are white or pink.

Cultivation   Propagation is by seed, and growth is slow. The plant is rare, but it is easy to cultivate if placed in full sunshine sheltered from the cold. It cannot be grafted.

---

212 OPUNTIA ACANTHOCARPA Engelmann and Bigelow
Tribe Opuntieae — subgenus Cylindropuntia
Common names: Buckhorn cholla, major cholla

Etymology   The plant's generic name refers to the city of Opus, capital of the region of Locris in ancient Greece.

Place of Origin   Arizona, Utah, Nevada and California and the state of Sonora, Mexico.

Description   This much-ramified plant gets as tall as 6½ ft. (2 m.). Its thick cylindrical trunk eventually becomes woody, as do the main branches, which grow from the trunk at an acute angle and ramify in turn. Ends of the branches are tuberculate terminal shoots about 3 in. (8 cm.) long and 3/4 in. (2 cm.) or more in diameter. Tubercles are elongated and flattened at the sides, bearing round or oval, whitish, felted areoles with short yellow glochids. There are 8 to 25 needle-shaped, dark brown spines, about 1 in. (3 cm.) long, encased in light, slender, usually straw-colored sheaths. Often only the most central spines, which are thicker and somewhat longer, are sheathed. Flowers appear only on terminal joints and are 2 in. (5 cm.) long and across when open. Perianth segments vary from yellow to red. The pear-shaped fruit has a shallow but wide umbilicus and is about 1 in. (3 cm.) long. Its upper part is tuberculate, with about 10 large spines on each tubercle.

Cultivation   Seldom cultivated, it is propagated by cuttings.

213   OPUNTIA BASILARIS Engelmann and Bigelow
Tribe Opuntieae — subgenus Opuntia
Common name: Beavertail cactus

Place of Origin   From California, Nevada, Utah and Arizona to the state of Sonora in northern Mexico.

Description   This low, shrubby, spreading plant is usually 6 to 12 in. (15 to 30 cm.) high and ramifies from the base. Its pad-shaped joints, or branches, are more or less erect or prostrate. The pads are oval, grayish- or bluish-green, slightly pubescent, often reddish round the areoles, and 5 to 8 in. (12 to 20 cm.) long. They bear many areoles covered in whitish, light brown or yellowish down, and many reddish-brown, slender glochids inclined to be caducous. Upper areoles occasionally have short spines. Flowers are 2 to 2¾ in. (5 to 7 cm.) long and are light to purplish crimson. The velvety fruit is globular-oval. Because of the huge distribution of this species, it is somewhat variable and there are several known varieties. *Cordata*, which is probably a horticultural variety, has thinner pads, of which the upper part is heart-shaped. *Longiareolata*, native to the Grand Canyon, has oblong areoles on the oldest rods, which are spatulate rather than oval, and the glochids fall off very early, leaving the areoles merely woolly.

Cultivation   It is widely cultivated for its color and because it is small. It tolerates reasonably low temperatures. It is propagated by removing and rooting the padlike joints.

---

214   OPUNTIA BIGELOVII Engelmann
Tribe Opuntieae — subgenus Cylindropuntia
Common name: Teddy bear cholla

Place of Origin   Southern Nevada, Arizona and California and the northern part of Sonora and Baja California in Mexico.

Description   This cylindrical *Opuntia* is a semishrub or miniature tree. It generally has a central stem which becomes trunk-like and many short lateral branches, of which the central ones are erect and the others horizontal or semi-erect. It grows as tall as 8 ft. (2.5 m.). Branches are light green, 2 to 6 in. (5 to 15 cm.) long with a diameter of about 2 in. (5 cm.). They are turgid, and have quadrangular tubercles 3/8 in. (1 cm.) wide at their base and equally long. Round areoles are white with yellow glochids and bear many ferocious spines. There are about ten radials up to 1/2 in. (1 to 1.5 cm.) long and about ten longer centrals. All are pale yellow and have papery, membranous sheaths. Since the spines almost completely cover the stem, the plant is a pale golden color. Flowers are borne on the tips of stems at the top of the plant. They are 1½ in. (4 cm.) long and purple, although there are also yellow-flowered forms. The fruit is yellow, pear-shaped and tuberculate. Backeberg classifies the plant under the *Cylindropuntia*.

Cultivation   It may be grown outdoors in mild climates. Propagation is by cuttings; even the fruit will root from its tubercles and produce new plants.

215 OPUNTIA BRASILIENSIS (Willdenow) Haworth
Tribe Opuntieae — subgenus Opuntia

Place of Origin   Southern Brazil, Paraguay, Argentina, Peru and eastern Bolivia.

Description   This species really belongs to a separate subgenus—Brasiliopuntia—comprising only four species. But these are rarely cultivated, and we have retained its old name to avoid confusion. These exclusively South American plants are characterized by having young joints shaped like flat disks. By contrast, the basal stem is trunklike and the main branches are more markedly cylindrical than those of other arborescent *Opuntia*. In its natural habitat the plant may reach a height of 13 ft. (4 m.) and the stem a diameter of 10 in. (25 cm.). It is erect, either glabrous or spiny, and puts forth more or less horizontal or erect lateral branches. The disks at the ends of the branches are slender, pale green, partly caducous, 6 in. (15 cm.) long and 2¼ in. (6 cm.) wide. The areoles are infrequent and bear only one or two spines 1/2 in. (1.5 cm.) long. The flowers are about 2 in. (5 cm.) long and have yellow or pale yellow perianth segments. The fruit is spherical, measuring 1½ in. (4 cm.) in diameter, and bears areoles with short spines; it is yellow when ripe. There are many varieties.

Cultivation   The plant needs winter warmth and a humid atmosphere. Propagation is by cuttings.

216 OPUNTIA CATINGICOLA Werdermann
Tribe Opuntieae — subgenus Opuntia

Place of Origin   The state of Bahia, Brazil, at an altitude of nearly 2,000 ft. (600 m.), among the maquis vegetation known as the *caatinga* (hence the plant's specific name).

Description   Maquis vegetation is always low-growing, and this plant is no exception, reaching a maximum of nearly 5 ft. (1.5 m.), although its very fleshy disk-shaped segments may be 6 in. (15 cm.) long. The large, circular, infrequent areoles bear yellowish-white or yellow glochids and five or more spines, of irregular length, that are light brown or light-colored with a dark tip, although reddish when young. They are usually borne at the center of the areole. The longest measures 2 in. (5 cm.) and points downward. The flowers have a green, slightly tuberculate tube with areoles bearing glochids and a few short spines. The perianth segments are short, red and so evaginated that the apex is curled under. This species was introduced only fairly recently and is difficult to find on the market.

Cultivation   The plant requires some winter warmth, and may be cultivated outdoors in mild climates only if it is sheltered from cold winds. Its winter rest period should be strict. It is propagated by removing a disk and rooting it in almost dry soil.

217 OPUNTIA DIADEMATA Lemaire
Tribe Opuntieae — subgenus Tephrocactus

Place of Origin   The central provinces of western Argentina.
Description   This species may still be found listed as a variety
of *Tephrocactus articulatus* (the generic name was established
by Lemaire; the specific name was given to a similar plant in
1833 by Christoph Otto). The plant is a low shrub, either erect
or prostrate, with grayish-green, more or less potato-shaped
joints that are about 2 in. (5 cm.) long and about 1 ½ in. (4 cm.)
wide. The tubercles are not very prominent except on new
growth. The raised areoles are covered with reddish-brown
glochids. There are one to four whitish spines, from 1 to 4 in. (3
to 10 cm.) long and almost 3/8 in. (1 cm.) wide, which are similar to raffia fibers, soft, curved or bent over. The flowers are
pale yellow and 1 ¼ in. (3.5 cm.) across. The fruit, which is
about 3/4 in. (2 cm.) long, never appears on cultivated plants,
but on plants in their natural habitat it probably has glochids.
Many varieties of this species exist, due to its wide distribution
area. *Calva* has almost spherical, often reddish, corrugated
joints and no spines. *Oligacantha* is very similar to the typical
species, but its spines are narrower and shorter and its flowers
are pinkish white. *Papyracantha,* which is the most attractive
variety, has white, ribbon-shaped spines that are wider and
longer. It is very similar to *syringacantha,* except that the latter
has completely spherical joints, light brown spines—real
spines are sometimes present—and white flowers. The variety
inermis (see photo opposite, below), from central Argentina, tillers, forming large clusters, and has green, cylindrical joints
that are tapered toward their apex. The areoles are white and
spineless, with light-colored or brown glochids.
Cultivation   The plant requires strong sunlight and moderate
watering. It is propagated from cuttings of joints placed on
pure, dry sand.

218 OPUNTIA ERINACEA Engelmann and Bigelow

Tribe Opuntieae — subgenus Opuntia
Common name: Hedgehog prickly pear

Place of Origin Northern Arizona, southern Utah, southern Nevada, western Colorado and southeastern California.

Description This small shrub reaches no more than 30 in. (80 cm.) in height. The stem tillers and is more or less erect or semiprostrate in habit. The padlike joints are oval or ellipsoid, 3 to 4 in. (8 to 10 cm.) long, of a variable thickness, but are usually fairly solid. There are numerous fairly large, slightly raised areoles with white felt, bearing a few yellowish glochids and a great many spines that radiate in all directions. These are white, slender and flexible but not bristly, 2 in. (5 cm.) long or sometimes more. They practically cover the whole of the epidermis. The flowers are 2¼ in. (6 cm.) long and slightly more across, with reddish-orange to yellow segments. The fruit is very spiny. The variety *ursina* is even more attractive. It is known as the grizzly bear cactus or old man prickly pear, and is a native of the Mojave Desert in California. It is smaller and more delicate than the species and has a large number of long, weak spines that are almost hairlike, brownish-white or a very pale brown, turning grayish in time. Its flowers are mostly yellow.

Cultivation The plant tolerates a certain degree of cold provided it is kept dry. It is propagated from the pads.

---

219 OPUNTIA FICUS-INDICA (Linnaeus) Miller

Tribe Opuntieae — subgenus Opuntia

Place of Origin Tropical America. Precise location is unknown. Cultivated in subtropical regions, it now grows wild in Mexico, the Mediterranean countries, and South Africa.

Description This is a shrubby plant that may become arborescent, reaching a height of 16½ ft. (5 m.). The upper part of the woody trunk is much ramified. The plant has oval or oblong padlike joints that reach a length of up to 16 in. (40 cm.) and are thick and fleshy. The areoles are small and usually lack spines, although they do have a large number of yellow glochids, most of which fall from the oldest stems. The large flowers are generally yellow, with pale yellow stamens. The fruit is the best of the edible cactus fruits. It is pear-shaped and umbilicate at its apex and has several areoles without spines but with yellow glochids. Depending on the variety, it may be yellow, reddish, red, or even striped. The juicy pulp is usually the same color as the epidermis, and it contains a large number of small, hard seeds. Since the plant is cultivated for its fruit, there are many horticultural varieties. *Asperma* has small yellow fruit containing a few tiny seeds; *lutea* produces yellow fruit; *rubra* produces red; *serotina* bears yellow fruit late in the season, until November.

Cultivation It needs perfectly drained sandy or stony soil, and strong sun. It is propagated by rooting a pad in sand.

220 OPUNTIA FULGIDA Engelmann
Variety **MAMILLATA** (Schott) Backeberg
Tribe Opuntieae — subgenus Cylindropuntia
Common name: Jumping cholla

Place of Origin   From Arizona along the Gulf of California to the Mexican states of Sonora and Sinaloa, but it occurs mostly in the western mountains of Sonora.

Description   Engelmann described this arborescent species in 1856. It grows as tall as 10 ft. (3 m.) or more and has an erect trunk 8 in. (20 cm.) in diameter and very ramified. Branches, which form a fairly compact corona, are up to 8 in. (20 cm.) long and 2 in. (5 cm.) in diameter. They are fleshy and have prominent tubercles that bear small areoles at their apex. Areoles are covered with short white or yellowish glochids, and bear as many as ten spines up to 1 ¼ in. (3.5 cm.) long. They are yellow or brownish, enclosed in a white, papery sheath. The misshapen joints are easily removed and root readily. Flowers are about 1 in. (2.5 to 3 cm.) across with a few red or light red petals. The green fruit is pear-shaped, tuberculate at first, later smooth, and is 2 in. (5 cm.) long. The variety *mamillata* has shorter spines, fleshier joints and more prominent tubercles. Backeberg classified it among *Cylindropuntia*.

Cultivation   The plant tolerates cold well if it is dry, but it needs warmth and sun in summer. Propagation is by cuttings. Even the fallen fruits put down roots from their tubercles.

---

221 OPUNTIA GOSSELINIANA Weber
Tribe Opuntieae — subgenus Opuntia

Place of Origin   Baja California and Sonora, Mexico.

Description   This shrublike plant is about 3 ¼ ft. (1 m.) high, of spreading habit, ramifying almost from its base. The disk-shaped joints are often wider than they are long, as much as 8 in. (20 cm.) across. They are thin and generally reddish. The plant forms a short trunk with many long spines. Areoles on the disks are large and yellowish, with raised clusters of yellow or brown glochids. Spines appear only on the upper part of the disks, particularly on the areoles around the edge. There are usually one to three; sometimes they are absent. They are slender, flexible, 2 in. (5 cm.) or more long, white or pale yellow, or brown when young. Flowers are yellow. The fruit, which is 1 ½ in. (4 cm.) long, globular and umbilicate, has many spineless areoles covered with glochids. Variety *santa-rita* — the purple prickly pear — is found primarily in Arizona but is also native to New Mexico, Texas and Mexico. It is much smaller, from 20 in. to nearly 5 ft. (50 cm. to 1.5 m.) high, and has bluish-green circular disks reddish at the edge and around the areoles. The latter are round, are set far apart, and bear many chestnut-colored glochids and only occasionally one brown spine. Flowers are larger and yellow with a purple ovary. It is one of the most beautiful members of the genus.

Cultivation   It doesn't tolerate cold. Propagated from disks.

222 OPUNTIA HUMIFUSA Rafinesque-Schmaltz
Tribe Opuntieae — subgenus Opuntia
Common names: Low prickly pear, smooth prickly pear

Place of Origin   This species' distribution covers the entire United States except the northwest third and Maine.

Description   This plant has had many names since Linnaeus called it *Cactus opuntia* in 1753. It may still be found under the synonyms *Opuntia vulgaris,* adopted by several authors; *Opuntia rafinesquei,* used by Engelmann in 1856; and the rarer *Opuntia compressa,* used recently by James Macbride. Linnaeus probably included two types in his species. One of these became naturalized in Europe and even grows in the Swiss mountains. It is low, of spreading, prostrate habit although it may sometimes be erect. It has flat and thin oval or disk-shaped pads 3 to 6¾ in. (8 to 17 cm.) long, with areoles set far apart and bearing yellowish-brown glochids. Spines are often absent. If present, they are borne on the areoles along the edge. One is usually conical, whitish, and up to 1 in. (2.5 cm.) long; and—on young plants especially—there are two or three small ones with a brown tip. Flowers measure 2 to 3 in. (5 to 8 cm.) across and have sulfur-yellow perianth segments with a reddish base. The fruit is pear-shaped and glabrous. A variety called *variegata* is found on the market.

Cultivation   The plant is extremely hardy. Propagation is by cuttings.

---

223 OPUNTIA LEPTOCAULIS de Candolle
Tribe Opuntieae — subgenus Cylindropuntia
Common name: Desert Christmas cactus

Place of Origin   Arizona, New Mexico, Oklahoma and Texas, stretching to Puebla, Mexico. It is invasive and very variable.

Description   The plant is shrubby, sometimes having a short trunk, and may grow up to 6½ ft. (2 m.) high. It has very slender, barely tuberculate, woody branches up to 16 in. (40 cm.) long and numerous close-set joints up to 3 in. (7.5 cm.) long growing almost at right angles to them. The barely raised tubercles bear small round areoles with an abundance of yellowish glochids and short white felt. Although they are often spineless, they usually have one spine, or sometimes two or three on the oldest parts of the plant. The spines are light-colored and up to 2 in. (5 cm.) long, and are enclosed in a sheath, which varies from off-white to yellowish to reddish-brown. The sheath is very sharp and catches easily in any fairly soft object; consequently, because the joints break off easily, a whole joint can become attached to an object. The small flowers are greenish or yellow. The fruit is globular, 3/8 in. (1 cm.) long, red or yellow, and has areoles able to produce new plants. There are many varieties with different-colored or shorter or longer spines, and brown glochids.

Cultivation   Because stems are woody, cuttings are hard to root. They should be sprayed with oil to control cochineal bug.

224 OPUNTIA LEUCOTRICHA de Candolle
Tribe Opuntieae — subgenus Opuntia
Common name: Aaron's beard

Place of Origin   The central plateau of Durango, Mexico.
Description   This large shrub is almost arborescent since in its natural habitat it develops a ramifying trunk and reaches a height of as much as 16½ ft. (5 m.). The trunk and the oldest padlike joints are covered with long white bristles. The pads are oblong and circular, 4 to 8 in. (10 to 20 cm.) long, and covered with a white pubescence, which gives them a velvety appearance. The areoles are white with yellow glochids. They are set very close together in transverse lines on young pads, and bear only one to three short white spines. As a pad increases in size, the distance between the areoles becomes greater and more irregular and the areoles bear more spines and white, spinescent or woolly bristles. The flowers are 2 to 3 in. (6 to 8 cm.) across, and have a short, tuberculate tube with areoles bearing spines and bristles. The fruit is spherical and varies from white to red or violet. It is fragrant and edible, and is sold in Mexico under the name *duraznillo*. The plant, which was described by de Candolle in 1828, is cultivated in parts of central America.
Cultivation   This plant does not tolerate cold, but if sheltered, it grows in mild climates. It is easy to cultivate in other respects. It is propagated by the pads.

225 OPUNTIA LLOYDII Rose
Tribe Opuntieae — subgenus Cylindropuntia

Place of Origin   Central Mexico.
Description   This shrub is very similar to *Opuntia versicolor* but is somewhat smaller. In its natural habitat it reaches 6½ to 9¾ ft. (2 to 3 m.) in height, with branches spreading out to a similar distance. The trunk and branches are slenderer and slightly more erect, and the cylindrical joints are shorter, attaining a diameter of about 3/4 in. (2 cm.), and have prominent oblong tubercles that often form a rhomboid pattern. Round, felted areoles appear at the thickest, most prominent part of the tubercles, near their apex, and bear brown glochids. There are generally only three spines, 1/2 in. (1.5 cm.) long, reddish and pointing outward or downward. They appear only on the preceding year's joints, new joints being inermous or bearing for a short time small, cylindrical, caducous leaves. The flowers are about 1 in. (3 cm.) long, with dark purple segments that open in the afternoon and are 1/2 in. (1.5 cm.) long. The fruit is 1 in. (3 cm.) long, yellow or orange, and slightly tuberculate.
Cultivation   This plant is rather difficult to grow, since it does not tolerate severe cold or grow well in a greenhouse. Propagation is by cuttings.

226 OPUNTIA MICRODASYS (Lehmann) Pfeiffer
Variety **ALBISPINA**
Tribe Opuntieae — subgenus Opuntia

Place of Origin   Parts of northern Mexico as far north as the states of Zacatecas and Hidalgo.

Description   The name of this species derives from the Greek word *mikros,* meaning small, and *dasys,* hairy, because of the plant's small glochids, which are likely to catch on anything. Both the species and the variety are favorites among cactus growers because they are like miniature versions of the larger *Opuntia.* The plant forms thick, much-ramified clumps about 24 in. (60 cm.) high. The pads are either oval or slightly elongated to 4 to 6 in. (10 to 15 cm.). The areoles are densely covered with yellow glochids that are pale on young parts of the plant, turn darker later. There are no spines, and the epidermis has a velvety appearance. The flowers are numerous on mature plants. They are 1½ to 2 in. (4 to 5 cm.) long, with pure yellow perianth segments that turn yellow-orange before they wither. The reddish-violet fruit is almost round. The cultivar *albispina* has white glochids that are initially as numerous as on the species, but become fewer in time. The flowers are pale yellow. There is a form called *minima,* with tiny light green pads.

Cultivation   As with all members of the subgenus, this species is easily propagated by removing a pad and placing it on almost dry sand or soil. It does not tolerate severe cold.

---

227 OPUNTIA MOLESTA Brandegee
Tribe Opuntieae — subgenus Cylindropuntia

Place of Origin   North-central Baja California.

Description   This large shrub is dangerous and difficult to handle. In its natural habitat the stems reach a height of 3¼ to 6½ ft. (1 to 2 m.), but in cultivation they seldom grow much taller than about 1½ ft. (50 cm.). Whatever their height, they ramify very little, but are fairly spread out. The joints are pale green and of varying lengths, up to about 16 in. (40 cm.). They are slender and cylindrical or somewhat club-shaped; in the latter case, they may be 1½ in. (4 cm.) across at the apex. The large, alternate tubercles are not very prominent, but they may be up to 1½ in. (4 cm.) long. Round, felted areoles are borne on the upper part of the tubercles, from which narrow, caducous leaves, less than 3/8 in. (1 cm.) long, appear. There are eight to ten straw-colored spines. The outer ones vary in length from 3/8 to 3/4 in. (1 to 2 cm.), and radiate in all directions, while the one to three spines in the center may measure 2 in. (5 cm.) and are enclosed in a slender, papery, membranous sheath that catches in anything that comes in contact with it and then detaches from the plant. The purple flowers are 1½ to 2 in. (4 to 5 cm.) across. The fruit is oval, about 1 in. (2.5 cm.) long, soft and fleshy; it may be glabrous, or have a few spines.

Cultivation   The plant is seldom cultivated. Propagation is by cuttings.

228 OPUNTIA OVATA Pfeiffer
Tribe Opuntieae — subgenus Tephrocactus

Place of Origin   The slopes of the Andes at the foot of Mount Aconcagua in the province of Mendoza in west-central Argentina; possibly also on the Chilean side of the border.

Description   The plant is low and bushy, forming compact clumps about 5 in. (12 cm.) high. Each branch has two to five egg-shaped green joints that taper somewhat at the tip and are about 1½ in. (4 cm.) long; some are absolutely spherical. Its habit is characteristic of species from high mountain habitats, since it gives protection, particularly from cold and often violent winds. Joints are tuberculate with large, low protuberances that bear a large, round, brown or pale yellow areole at the apex. Areoles have tufts of prominent, stiff, yellowish glochids. There are seven to nine spines that are sharp and straight. They vary from 3/16 to 1/2 in. (5 mm. to 1.5 cm.) long and are brownish or yellow when young; but with age they turn white or grayish and sometimes even fall off, leaving the lower part of the joint spineless. Young joints are sometimes reddish-violet, turning green as they grow. The reddish hue may be due to sudden cold spells during the growing period.

Cultivation   Various species belonging to the subgenus *Tephrocactus* are cultivated, though they are difficult to grow. They are often grafted. They can be propagated by taking cuttings from the joints.

---

229 OPUNTIA PENTLANDII Salm-Dyck
Tribe Opuntieae — subgenus Tephrocactus

Place of Origin   The Bolivian plateaus.

Description   This is a typical plant from high-altitude plateaus. It has a large number of basal shoots that ramify both sideways and upward and form low, thick, cushionlike bushes more than 3¼ ft. (1 m.) wide. Each oval or oblong joint is up to 4 in. (10 cm.) long, and 1½ in. (4 cm.) in diameter. They are tuberculate at first, becoming smooth as they grow older. The tubercles point upward and bear circular areoles covered with short down and yellow glochids at the apex. One to five spines appear irregularly on the upper part of the joints, but they fall off later, leaving the basal part inermous. Variable in color, they are usually a yellowish white or yellow, but they are sometimes light brown or reddish. The grow to 2¾ in. (7 cm.) long. The flowers are 1 in. (3 cm.) long and 2 in. (5 cm.) across, and vary from yellow to orange. The short tube bears a few woolly areoles: the upper ones have bristlelike spines that are retained by the spherical or oblong fruit, which is yellow when ripe and inedible. In 1845 Salm-Dyck described two species of *Opuntia,* one as *boliviana* and the other as *pentlandii*. These were so alike that later they were combined under the latter.

Cultivation   The plant tolerates cold, but does not thrive in the hot summers prevalent in mild climates. It is propagated from the joints.

230 OPUNTIA PHAEACANTHA Engelmann
Variety **CAMANCHICA** (Engelmann and Bigelow) Borg
Tribe Opuntieae — subgenus Opuntia
Common names: Purple-fruited prickly pear, New Mexico
prickly pear

Place of Origin It grows in Oklahoma, New Mexico, Texas
and Arizona to Chihuahua, Mexico; the variety in Kansas, Oklahoma, Colorado, Texas and New Mexico to the border.
Description Engelmann described the typical species in
1849 and in 1856 described the variety as a separate species.
Borg reunited the two. Other varieties have since been added.
This species is very widespread and is closely related to some
other species. It is low, prostrate, 3¼ ft. (1 m.) tall, and has
pads 4 to 6 in. (10 to 15 cm.) long and slightly less across.
Areoles, set far apart, bear many brown or yellowish glochids
and one to four spines, one of which grows 2¼ in. (6 cm.) long.
They are all thick, point downward and have a brown base with
a light tip. Yellow flowers are 2 in. (5 cm.) across. The red to
purple fruit is pear-shaped, tapered at its base. The variety is
lower, more prostrate and a lighter green. It has circular or
ovate pads 6¾ in. (17 cm.) long and across. It has one to
three—sometimes five—spines. These longer spines are dark
brown or reddish with a lighter tip. Glochids are brownish-yellow or green. Flowers are larger, varying from orange to
salmon pink or yellow. Fruit is oval, reddish-violet and edible.
Cultivation The plant tolerates cold but the epidermis turns
reddish in winter. It is propagated by rooting the pads.

231 OPUNTIA PICARDOI Marn.-Lap.
Tribe Opuntieae — subgenus Opuntia

Place of Origin The provinces of Salta and Catamarca in
northern Argentina.
Description This is a low, prostrate plant with padlike joints
that ramify like a chain. Its glossy green pads are oval, flat and
slightly oblique, 2¾ in. (7 cm.) long and 1½ in. (3.5 cm.)
across, with tuberculate protuberances that bear round
areoles. These are yellowish-brown and have yellow glochids
and up to ten white spines with yellow tips, ranging in length
from a few millimeters to about 3/16 in. (5 mm.). The red flowers measure 1½ in. (4 cm.) across when they are opened wide,
while the fruit, nearly 1/2 in. (1.2 cm.) long, may be yellowish
or red when ripe. The species has fairly recently been introduced and is not very common, although like most members of
this genus it has an extraordinary reproductive capacity.
Cultivation This plant is unsuitable for flowerpot cultivation,
but it may be grown outside in very mild climates, provided that
it is well sheltered from cold winter winds. It is easily propagated by removing a disk and rooting it in scarcely damp sand
or soil.

232 OPUNTIA QUIMILO Schumann
Tribe Opuntieae — subgenus Opuntia

Place of Origin   The provinces of Santiago del Estero, Tucumán, Salta and Córdoba in northern Argentina.
Description   Schumann first described this species in 1898 and adopted the local name for it. In its natural habitat the plant forms a large, very ramified shrub that may reach a height of 13 ft. (4 m.); in cultivation it rarely grows taller than 6½ ft. (2 m.). It usually develops a spiny trunk that puts out padlike joints that ramify in their turn. The pads are a bluish or grayish green, smooth, elliptical or obovate, as long as 20 in. (50 cm.), 10 in. (25 cm.) across and 3/4 to 1 in. (2 to 3 cm.) thick. Infrequent but prominent areoles are very large on the oldest parts of the plant, and have sharp white glochids. Very young pads have no spines. In time each areole bears one stiff, white spine pointing outward and 2¾ to 6 in. (7 to 15 cm.) long. On older parts of the plant up to three shorter spines may appear. Flowers measure 1½ to 2¾ in. (4 to 7 cm.), are brick-red and have a slightly tuberculate tube that tends to curve upward. The fruit varies from globular to pear-shaped, is 2¾ in. (7 cm.) long, light green or yellowish, and umbilicate at its apex.
Cultivation   This very distinctive species is not widely cultivated because its large pads take up so much room. It is able to live outdoors in a mild climate if its position is sheltered. It is easily propagated from the pads.

233 OPUNTIA RECONDITA Griffiths
Tribe Opuntieae — subgenus Cylindropuntia

Place of Origin   Near La Perla in Coahuila, northern Mexico.
Description   This species, which was described in 1913, is a dense, much-ramified shrub, 3¼ to nearly 5 ft. (1 to 1.5 m.) tall. The cylindrical stem is about 2¾ in. (7 cm.) in diameter, narrowing where each year's new growth begins. Its many shoots are easily detached. Young shoots are about 4 in. (10 cm.) long with few spines; the oldest reach a length of 12 in. (30 cm.) and a diameter of 3/4 in. (2 cm.), and are tuberculate and exceedingly spiny. Tubercles are 2 in. (5 cm.) long and about 1/4 in. (5 mm.) across and protrude because their lower part is flattened. They gradually disappear as the shoot grows older. Areoles are obovate, nearly 1/4 in. (6 mm.) long, and densely covered with yellow glochids. There are initially two to four spines, later six to ten; they are arranged obliquely and are 2 in. (5 cm.) long, gray at the base, brown toward the tip, and covered by a shiny sheath. A few short, blackish bristles appear between the spines. Flowers are purple and about 1 in. (2.5 cm.) across. The fruit is about 1¼ in. (3 cm.) long, greenish-yellow with red shading and slightly tuberculate. Backeberg classified this species under *Cylindropuntia*.
Cultivation   Although this plant is too large for normal cultivation, it could be grown outdoors in a dry, sunny position in a mild climate. Propagation is by cuttings.

234 OPUNTIA RUFIDA Engelmann
Tribe Opuntieae — subgenus Opuntia

Place of Origin Northern Mexico, and along the Rio Grande in Texas.

Description This plant is probably better known by the name *Opuntia herrfeldtii,* but its original name takes precedence and the latter is now only a synonym. The plant is often confused with *Opuntia microdasys,* variety *rufida,* but the latter has much smaller, oval pads bearing short brown glochids that are yellow in the center or at the base, and yellow flowers. The species is shrubby, erect, from 20 to 60 in. (50 cm. to 1.5 m.) high, with a short trunk. The pads are approximately circular, very wide and thick, and their gray-green epidermis has a velvety appearance. Spines are lacking altogether, but the broad, circular, raised areoles, which are close-set in diagonal lines, bear a great many reddish-brown glochids that are darker on the older pads. The flowers grow to a length of about 2 in. (5 cm.), including their ovary. The perianth segments vary from yellow to orange. The fruit is light red. The plant is so attractive that many horticultural hybrids have been developed. Some of these have tiny spines inherited from their other parent plant.

Cultivation This plant withstands cold and damp far less well than other members of *Opuntia.* It needs strong sun in summer and shelter in winter. It is quite suitable for flowerpot cultivation. It is propagated by placing pads on almost dry sand.

235 OPUNTIA SALMIANA Parment.
Tribe Opuntieae — subgenus Cylindropuntia

Place of Origin Southern Brazil, Paraguay and northern Argentina as far as Bolivia.

Description This shrublike plant can reach a height of 6½ ft. (2 m.), but in cultivation it is always smaller. It is ramified, the cylindrical stems without tubercles measuring about 1/2 in. (1 cm.) in diameter. They are rather weak and normally bluish-green, otherwise reddish. The shoots range up to 10 in. (25 cm.) long and are nearly oval. The infrequent areoles are small, white and felted, bearing numerous yellowish glochids and whitish spines up to 1/2 in. (1.5 cm.) long. Because the spines have no sheath, they are particularly unpleasant even when young. The flowers are about 1 in. (3 cm.) across, and are pale yellow or cream-colored. The fruit is about 3/8 in. (1 cm.) in diameter, scarlet or a dark, almost purplish, red, and has many areoles covered by glochids that may produce shoots capable of rooting. The shortest shoots particularly come away very easily and promptly take root in the ground. There is a variety called *albiflora* that has smaller, white flowers.

Cultivation The plant is very easily propagated from detached shoots, and is easy to cultivate if it has strong sunlight and a complete rest in winter.

236 OPUNTIA STENOPETALA Engelmann
Tribe Opuntieae — subgenus Opuntia

Place of Origin The states of Coahuila, Hidalgo and Querétaro in central Mexico.

Description The plant's specific name comes from the Greek *stenos*, narrow, and *petalon*, petal: the plant belongs to a small, anomalous group of *Opuntia* whose flowers are unisexual and have narrow perianth segments with a pointed apex. The species is low and shrubby, its principal branches often semiprostrate. The pads are obovate, from 4 to 8 in. (10 to 20 cm.) long, and grayish-green, but more often reddish, particularly the very spiny young ones. The infrequent, brown areoles are set as much as 1 in. (3 cm.) apart and bear brown glochids that grow especially densely on new growth. Basal areoles are often spineless, but the others bear two to four or sometimes more irregularly arranged spines. The longest, up to 2 in. (5 cm.), is slightly curved and points downward. All spines are blackish-brown at first, becoming gray later. The flowers are small, with a tube only 1 in. (3 cm.) long, and short, narrow, orange perianth segments. In male flowers the large style in the center is rudimentary and lacks a stigma, while in female flowers it bears a stigma with eight or nine yellow lobes. The scarlet fruit is globular and sometimes spiny.

Cultivation If sheltered, it may be cultivated outdoors in mild climates. It is propagated by cuttings taken from pads.

---

237 OPUNTIA SUBULATA (Mühlpf.) Engelmann
Tribe Opuntieae — Subgenus Cylindropuntia

Place of Origin Southern Peru. At first it was thought to be native to Chile: it was first described on the basis of specimens growing at Valparaiso, but these must have been cultivated, since it has never been found growing wild in Chile.

Description This stiff, shrublike plant grows 13 ft. (4 m.) tall in its natural habitat. Its main stem is 2½ to 4 in. (6 to 10 cm.) in diameter and puts out cylindrical lateral shoots 2¼ in. (6 cm.) in diameter, which point upward. The stem and branches are green and have long tubercles that protrude at the top and are flattened toward their base, and almost disappear in old age, when the epidermis becomes brown and suberose. White, felted areoles are borne at the apex of the tubercles. Below them, curved, cylindrical, tapering leaves appear and persist for a year or longer. There are one or two, or sometimes more, spines, up to 3 in. (8 cm.) long. These are light yellow or light brown, strong and straight. Glochids are few. Flowers are borne near the tips of the shoots; other perianth segments are small, reddish, and about 3/16 to 3/8 in. (5 mm. to 1 cm.) long. Inner segments are larger and orange or reddish-orange. The green fruit is oblong, 4 in. (10 cm.) long, and deeply umbilicate. It persists for a long time on the plant; new plants may grow from its areoles when it falls to the ground.

Cultivation Propagation is by cuttings.

238 OPUNTIA SULPHUREA Don
Tribe Opuntieae — subgenus Opuntia

Place of Origin   From the province of San Luis to that of Chubut, along the Chubut River in Argentina.

Description   This low, tillered plant forms large colonies sometimes measuring 6½ ft. (2 m.) across and between 12 and 20 in. (30 to 50 cm.) high. Its more or less erect or prostrate pads are flat, very thick, oblong or oval, 6 to 8 in. (15 to 20 cm.) long, grayish-green, green, or reddish, and have conspicuous irregular tubercles. Each tubercle bears a small areole with yellowish-red glochids and two to eight spines, up to 4 in. (10 cm.) long, splayed outward. They are usually straight but sometimes curved or contorted; thick and very sharp; and reddish or brownish-red, but often pale at first on young pads. The flowers are about 1½ in. (4 cm.) long and have sulfur-yellow perianth segments. The ovary and the tube bear areoles and glochids. The fruit is small, measuring just over 3/8 in. (1 cm.). It is deeply umbilicate, yellow, and often lightly scented. The species is quite variable in terms of the color of its spines, which may be gray, while the flowers may be a pale yellow and occasionally have a pinkish center. Fruit on older plants may be red. There are also varieties with smaller, rounder pads.

Cultivation   The plant is propagated from the pads. Young ones detach themselves easily, fall to the ground and take root.

---

239 OPUNTIA TOMENTOSA Salm-Dyck
Tribe Opuntieae — subgenus Opuntia

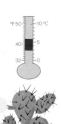

Place of Origin   Central Mexico.

Description   This arborescent plant may grow to 20 ft. (6 m.). The trunklike stem is smooth, spineless, and 4 to 12 in. (10 to 30 cm.) in diameter. The upper part ramifies, producing branches that become cylindrical and elongated and put forth many pads which are oblong and somewhat obovate, 4 to 8 in. (10 to 20 cm.) long, with a soft, smooth epidermis. When young they have low tubercles whose areoles bear yellow glochids. Spines are usually absent, but one or more short white ones may appear on older plants. Flowers are orange-red, with red outer perianth segments. The fruit is oval, red and smooth. Salm-Dyck described this species in 1822 on the basis of a cultivated plant; it has now become naturalized in parts of Central America and Australia. There are two much lower varieties found in the Mexican state of Sinaloa along the Pacific coast. *Rileyi* has white or gray spines, soft, smooth pads and white areoles bearing yellow glochids and one white spine curving downward. Yellow flowers are 2¾ in. (7 cm.) across. *Spranguei* has dark green pads that seem velvety because they are covered with soft white entangled hairs and yellow flowers spotted with red in the center.

Cultivation   Young plants do not tolerate cold. Propagation is by the pads.

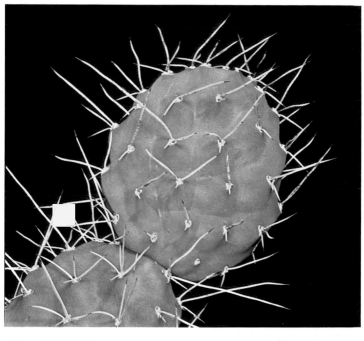

240 OPUNTIA TUNICATA (Lehmann) Link and Otto
Tribe Opuntieae — subgenus Cylindropuntia

Place of Origin The central Mexican plateau (where the plant has become a troublesome weed). It has been introduced and become naturalized in Ecuador, Peru and northern Chile.
Description Many *Opuntia* have specific names descriptive of their spines, but this species with the innocuous name *tunicata* has, perhaps, the most fearsome appearance. Lehmann named it *Cactus tunicatus* in 1827, and this therefore takes precedence over the more suitable *Opuntia furiosa* attributed to it ten years later by H. L. Wendland. The plant is a low, erect bush about 20 in. (50 cm.) high, ramifying from low down. The cylindrical shoots, up to 6 in. (15 cm.) long, are somewhat whorled. Some grow horizontally. They are covered with alternate diamond-shaped tubercles that have a large, white areole bearing yellowish glochids. The tubercles are completely covered by the 6 to 12 straight, stiff spines, 1½ to 2 in. (4 to 5 cm.) long, that grow from the areoles. The spines are reddish when young and pale yellow later, and are covered by a papery white sheath that comes away and catches in anything touching it. The yellow flowers are 1 in. (3 cm.) long and across. The fruit is tuberculate and spiny.
Cultivation The plant is easily propagated from the shoots, which come off readily and take root where they land. Cultivation presents no problems provided the plant is not injured.

241 OPUNTIA VERSCHAFFELTII Cels
Tribe Opuntieae — subgenus Cylindropuntia

Place of Origin In the eastern cordillera around La Paz, Bolivia. At least one variety grows in northern Argentina.
Description Cels described this species in 1898. It is one of the strangest and most interesting members of the genus. It consists of several stems that form a clump as much as 12 in. (30 cm.) across in its natural habitat. It is impossible to distinguish a main stem because all the stems spring from an underground base. In their natural habitat the stems are globular or oval; in cultivation they become cylindrical and as much as 8 in. (20 cm.) tall and 3/8 to 3/4 in. (1 to 2 cm.) in diameter. They are a palish green and have infrequent, indistinct tubercles that bear cylindrical leaves at the apex. The leaves persist for a short time before falling off, and in full sunlight turn reddish. There are also one to three weak, bristlelike, yellowish spines that grow from among tiny yellow glochids. In cultivation the spines often never appear. Flowers are exceptionally large for such a small plant, measuring 1½ in. (4 cm.) across. They are a fairly dark red, or sometimes orange, and last for several days. There are varieties with reddish-green stems, very persistent leaves, and longer, whitish, more flexible spines. Backeberg classified this plant as an *Austrocylindropuntia*.
Cultivation It should be kept in an unheated greenhouse in winter, and needs sun in summer. Propagation is by cuttings.

242　OPUNTIA VERSICOLOR Engelmann
Tribe Opuntieae — subgenus Cylindropuntia
Common name: Staghorn cholla

Place of Origin　Arizona and northern Mexico.
Description　This species was not classified until 1896, although C. G. Pringle had collected specimens of it as early as 1881. It is commonly found in the foothills of mountains, and only rarely on rocky plateaus. The plant is arborescent, reaching a height of 6½ to 13 ft. (2 to 4 m.), and its trunk and older branches become woody. Its numerous branches are about 8 in. (20 cm.) long and 3/4 to 1½ in. (2 to 4 cm.) in diameter. Their epidermis varies from dark green to purple. The fairly infrequent tubercles have gray or yellow areoles that bear reddish glochids, and 5 to 12 dark spines, up to 1 in. (2.5 cm.) long, enclosed in slender sheaths. The flowers are 1 to 2 in. (3 to 5 cm.) or more across, and vary greatly in color from plant to plant: they may be yellow, greenish, reddish or brown. The ovary is markedly tuberculate and has felted areoles that are covered with glochids and often also bear long, deciduous bristles. The fruit is 1½ in. (4 cm.) long and oval or pear-shaped, and persists on the plant for many months or even a year. Backeberg classifies this species as a *Cylindropuntia*.
Cultivation　In their natural habitat a group looks attractive because of the diversity of coloring, but they are too cumbersome to be cultivated by the ordinary grower. Small specimens need sun and much rest. Propagation by cuttings.

243　OPUNTIA VULGARIS Miller
Tribe Opuntieae — subgenus Opuntia

Place of Origin　Paraguay and the coast of Brazil, Uruguay and Argentina. Naturalized in India, South Africa and Australia, it's cultivated in the Mediterranean and the tropics.
Description　The specific name, established by Miller in 1768, has often been erroneously applied to *Opuntia humifusa*, and is largely disregarded in favor of *Opuntia monacantha*, used by Haworth in 1819. It is shrubby and arborescent, with a trunk 20 ft. (6 m.) high and about 6 in. (15 cm.) in diameter. It may or may not be spiny. In cultivation it does not grow so tall. Oval or oblong pads are 4 to 12 in. (10 to 30 cm.) long and 3 to 6 in. (8 to 15 cm.) across, and taper at their point of attachment. They are a bright, glossy green. The infrequent areoles are slightly woolly, bearing brown glochids and usually one reddish-brown spine 3/8 to 1½ in. (1 to 4 cm.) long, hence the plant's synonym, *Opuntia monacantha*, "having only one spine." If the trunk is spiny, however, each of its areoles may bear as many as ten spines. Flowers are up to 3½ in. (9 cm.) across, with sulfur-yellow to yellow-orange perianth segments. The fruit is pear-shaped, tapered at its base, umbilicate and up to 3 in. (7.5 cm.) long and has areoles capable of producing new plants; it is reddish-violet when completely ripe. There is a white or pink variegated form.
Cultivation　The plant is propagated from the pads.

244 OREOCEREUS CELSIANUS (Lemaire ex Salm-Dyck) Riccobon
Tribe Cacteae — subtribe Cereinae

Etymology The name comes from the Greek *oros*, mountain; its natural habitat is exclusively mountainous.

Place of Origin This species has an enormous range that covers the eastern slopes of the Andes in Peru, Bolivia, northern Argentina and northern Chile. It is very variable as a result.

Description For a long time the typical species, described as a *Pilocereus* by Lemaire in 1850, was believed to be the only member of the genus *Oreocereus*, established by Lemaire in 1909. The discovery of some new species led to a revision that classified at least six of them, including the well-known *Oreocereus trollii*, as varieties of *Oreocereus celsianus*. The typical form is just over 3 ft. (1 m.) tall. It has an erect stem 3 to 5 in. (8 to 12 cm.) in diameter, which, on adult plants, ramifies from the base. The 10 to 17 rounded ribs have swollen protuberances bearing large, white, oval areoles that are very woolly on young parts of the plants and have tufts of long, fine, white, silky hairs; they become almost glabrous on the plant's oldest parts. There are about nine conical, rigid, brownish-yellow, radial spines, 3/4 in. (2 cm.) long, and one to four reddish-brown thicker central spines up to 3 in. (8 cm.) long. Dark pink flowers are borne near the apex and have a hairy, bristly tube.

Cultivation Propagation is by seed or cuttings.

---

245 OREOCEREUS CELSIANUS (Lemaire ex Salm-Dyck) Riccobon
Variety **FOSSULATUS** (Labouret) Krainz
Tribe Cacteae — subtribe Cereinae

Place of Origin The department of Chuquisaca, Bolivia.

Description This plant was classified as a variety in 1885 by Labouret, but was raised to the rank of species by Backeberg, only to be demoted again to a variety by Krainz. It is still sometimes listed as *Oreocereus fossulatus*. It is shrublike, 6½ ft. (2 m.) tall, and has a thicker, tougher stem than the typical species. It ramifies sparsely, either from its base or from a little higher up, producing segments about 3 in. (8 cm.) in diameter. There are 11 to 14 rounded ribs, swollen around the areoles, above which are deep, wedge-shaped grooves. Areoles are large and much-felted when young and bear tufts of long, white hairs, particularly near the apex. There are about 16 white, very slender radial spines, while the one to four central spines are conical and stiff, up to 1½ in. (4 cm.) long, and yellowish, brown, or sometimes almost transparent with a dark base. Flowers, borne below the apex, are about 3 in. (8 cm.) long, and have a very hairy tube and purplish-violet perianth segments. The form *gracilior* has fewer, amber-colored spines, one of which is a single central spine.

Cultivation Very well-drained soil and strong sunlight are required. Propagation is either by cuttings or seed.

246 OREOCEREUS CELSIANUS (Lemaire) Riccobon
Variety HENDRIKSENIANUS (Backeberg) Krainz
Tribe Cacteae — subtribe Cereinae

Place of Origin   The Peruvian Andes.

Description   This plant tillers from its base to form fairly large clumps of stems up to 3¼ ft. (1 m.) in height and nearly 4 in. (10 cm.) in diameter. Each stem often has about ten ribs, 1 in. (2.5 cm.) wide, with flat, transverse depressions between the areoles. The latter are large, oval, set about 3/4 in. (2 cm.) apart, covered with yellow felt that turns gray later; they bear tufts of long, silky, white hair that almost completely covers the whole of the epidermis. There are eight or nine radial spines, 3/8 in. (1 cm.) long, and one to four central spines as much as 2 in. (5 cm.) long. All the spines are yellow and slender. Flowers are borne below the apex and have a long, cylindrical tube and crimson, irregular perianth segments. The fruit is spherical and yellowish-green. Until recently the plant was called *Oreocereus ritteri*, and it is still often referred to by this name.

Cultivation   This species needs cool but not cold surroundings, a strict rest period in winter, and an airy, sunny position in summer. It should be grown in slightly chalky soil. Growth is rapid. The plant tillers when it is only 16 in. (40 cm.) high. Propagation is by the basal shoots.

---

247 OREOCEREUS DOELZIANUS (Backeberg) Borg
Tribe Cacteae — subtribe Cereinae

Place of Origin   The department of Ayacucho, central Peru, on the western cordillera.

Description   The stem ramifies from the base, forming large clumps about 3¼ ft. (1 m.) tall and 3 in. (8 cm.) in diameter. When the stems flower, they swell out around the apex, which may reach twice the diameter of the base. With age, the stems may become more or less curved. There are 9 to 11 blunt ribs that protrude less than 3/8 in. (1 cm.) and are slightly prominent where the areoles are borne. The latter are circular, grayish-white and felted, separated by slight depressions. Initially, the 20 spines are all similar; they are needle-shaped, sharp, and up to 1 in. (3 cm.) long. Four central spines later become clearly visible; they are arranged in a cross, one pointing upward and another downward, and are thicker and 1½ in. (4 cm.) long. Spines vary from reddish-brown when young to a yellowish brown that eventually turns gray. In addition to spines, the apical areoles bear soft, silky hairs and thick, grayish wool, from among which flowerbuds emerge, forming a 2 in. (5 cm.) cephalium. Flowers are almost tubular, about 4 in. (10 cm.) long and 1 in. (3 cm.) across, with a scaly, hairy tube and sometimes somewhat irregular perianth segments. The outer ones are dark red; the inner ones, crimson.

Cultivation   Propagation is generally by cuttings.

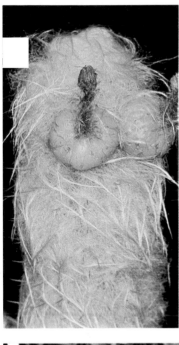

248 OROYA NEOPERUVIANA Backeberg
Tribe Cacteae — subtribe Echinocactinae

Etymology Britton and Rose named this genus after the village of Oroya, in the department of Junin in central Peru, since it was there that the first species to be described was found.
Place of Origin The Andes northeast of Lima, central Peru.
Description This plant has a large, fairly dark green spherical stem, about 16 in. (40 cm.) high with a diameter of 8 in. (20 cm.), which tillers, producing basal shoots when adult. There may be 24 to 35 ribs on old plants, but there are fewer on young specimens. All the spines tend to be honey-colored with a brown base, although the shade of yellow may vary. There are 20 to 30 radial spines, 1/2 in. (1.5 cm.) long, needle-shaped, splayed out so they overlap. The one or two central spines are easily distinguishable from the radials, but there may be a few more on old plants, which makes it more difficult to tell them apart. The flowers are small, about 3/4 in. (2 cm.) long, but numerous, with crimson perianth segments that are often paler toward the tip. The variety *depressa*, hardly 4 in. (10 cm.) high, has reddish-brown spines, and *tenuispina* has longer, slender, pectinate spines and flowers that are usually cream-colored.
Cultivation Like all members of the genus, this species needs strong sun and well-drained, sandy, gravelly soil; it tends not to be very floriferous in cultivation. Propagation is by seed.

249 PACHYCEREUS PRINGLEI (Watson) Britton and Rose
Tribe Cacteae — subtribe Cereinae

Etymology The name comes from the Greek *pachys*, thick.
Place of Origin Mexico, in the states of Sonora and Nayarit as far as the coast, and in Baja California, where extensive groves of this species are to be found.
Description In nature this plant is more than 32 ft. (10 m.) high. The trunk grows to about 6½ ft. (2 m.) with a diameter of 24 in. (60 cm.) or more and eventually becomes spineless and woody. Dark green branches are borne on the apical part of the trunk, rise obliquely and are very thick. They have 11 to 15 prominent, rounded ribs. Areoles are large, particularly if they are flower-bearing, set close together, covered with brown felt, and joined by a narrow, felted strip. Spines are variable in number and length; it is difficult to distinguish the radials from the central spines. There tend to be more spines on young plants—usually about 20—than on old ones, and they often are absent on large or old plants. Spines are sharply pointed, white with a black tip, and 3/4 in. (2 cm.) long when young. Later they are as long as 5 in. (12 cm.) and become entirely black. When the plant is mature the floriferous part is usually spineless. The white flowers have a hairy, scaly tube.
Cultivation Propagation is by seed, since the shoots are too thick to use as cuttings. The plant does not tolerate cold.

250 PARODIA AUREISPINA Backeberg
Tribe Cacteae — subtribe Echinocactinae

Etymology   This genus was named in honor of the Argentinian botanist Lorenzo Raimundo Parodi (1895-1966).
Place of Origin   The province of Salta in northern Argentina.
Description   The plant has a spherical stem up to 2½ in. (6.5 cm.) in diameter, with 16 or so tuberculate ribs spirally arranged. Old plants may have even more than 16 ribs. There are about 40 white, slender, bristlelike radial spines, and six thicker central spines, about 1/2 in. (1.5 cm.) long. The four strongest are arranged in a cross, and the lowest is hooked (as occasionally are some of the others). Spines are golden. Flowers are about 1 in. (3 cm.) across, and have bright yellow perianth segments. The species has many varieties. *Australis* is very similar to *Parodia rubriflora*, except that the down on its areoles is white and the eight central spines are red (particularly the six lower ones) and do not fade with age. Its flowers are a violet-crimson rather than scarlet. The variety *elegans* is densely covered with white wool at the apex, has extremely slender spines, a few hairlike bristles, and a single, hooked, central spine. This variety may in fact be a hybrid, since propagation by seed gives variable results. The variety *vulgaris* is similar to the species, but is taller, has more ribs and more numerous, thicker, central spines, some of which have reddish tips.
Cultivation   Propagation is by seed or shoots.

251 PARODIA BILBAOENSIS Cárdenas
Tribe Cacteae — subtribe Echinocactinae

Place of Origin   Near Mollenvique, department of Potosí, Bolivia. The plant is found at an altitude of 7,200 ft. (2,200 m.), growing in cracks between rocks and sheltered by bushes.
Description   The specific name of this plant derives from the province of Bilbao where it was discovered. Its stem is a short cylinder, 1½ to 2 in. (4 to 5 cm.) high and 2 to 2¼ in. (5 to 6 cm.) in diameter. It has about 13 ribs, arranged in loose spirals, that protrude 1/4 in. (8 mm.), are nearly 1/2 in. (13 mm.) wide at the base, and are set 3/16 in. (5 mm.) apart. They are covered with gray felt. There are 18 to 20 white, very slender, needle-shaped radial spines, about 1/4 in. (6 to 8 mm.) long, either lying fairly close to the stem or pointing obliquely outward. There are four straight or very slightly curved central spines that point upward at first, outward later. They are swollen at the base and about 1/2 to 3/4 in. (1.2 to 2 cm.) long, and vary from white to brown. The flowers are borne near the center of the apex. They are 1 in. (2.5 cm.) long and have a short tube covered with small yellow scales. The scales are less than 3/16 in. (5 mm.) long and bear short, thick, white down and a few brown bristles. The perianth segments are golden.
Cultivation   The plant needs perfectly drained soil and a long winter rest period. Propagation is by seed.

252 PARODIA MAASSII (Heese) Berger
Tribe Cacteae — subtribe Echinocactinae

Place of Origin   Southern Bolivia and northern Argentina.
Description   Britton and Rose placed this species in the now defunct genus *Malacocarpus*. Its bright green stem is spherical or oblong, 6 in. (15 cm.) in diameter, and has an apical corona densely covered with white down. The 13 to 21 spirally arranged ribs consist of tubercles that are sharply raised and divided by transverse grooves on young parts of the plant; on older parts they become elongated and fused, and are almost absent at the base of the plant. The areoles are very large and woolly when young, covering the tip of the tubercles; with age they become smaller and glabrous. They each bear eight to ten radial spines that are 1/4 to 1/2 in. (5 mm. to 1 cm.) long and are yellow when young, becoming white later. They are splayed outward and somewhat curved. Four central spines are much larger, the longest measuring to 2¾ in. (3 to 7 cm.). Near the apex they are brownish-yellow and point upward, while on older parts they become pale yellow, point downward and are curved or hooked. The large flowers have a scaly, woolly tube and numerous reddish-orange or bronze perianth segments. There are several varieties, many of which have red or crimson flowers, and one has golden spines.
Cultivation   It grows best in semishade. Propagation by seed, but growth is slow. Grafted plants develop more rapidly.

253 PARODIA OBTUSA Ritter
Tribe Cacteae — subtribe Echinocactinae

Place of Origin   Near Cotagaita in southwestern Bolivia.
Description   The plant's stem is light green and about 30 in. (80 cm.) high with a diameter of 3 to 6¾ in. (8 to 17 cm.). It has 13 to 21 ribs that protrude 3/8 to 3/4 in. (1 to 2 cm.), with prominent tubercles. The conical tubercles are very elongated and fairly compressed when young, becoming more rounded and finally blunt, because the apex becomes truncated by the areoles, which are oval on new growth, up to 3/8 in. (1 cm.) long, white and felted. They later become rounded and lose most of their felt. There are six to nine radial spines that are fairly slender, radially arranged and often slightly curved inward, from 3/4 to 2¼ in. (2 to 6 cm.) long. The one to three central spines (only one on young areoles) are thicker, 1½ to 2¾ in. (4 to 7 cm.) long. Frequently at least one is hooked. All the spines are subulate and pale yellow; however, those on new growth are often light brown, later turning a brownish-yellow. Flowers are about 1½ in. (4 cm.) long, with a scaly tube bearing white wool and perianth segments 1/4 in. (5 mm.) across that vary from golden to sulfur-yellow. The species is relatively new, having been classified and introduced in 1964.
Cultivation   The plant thrives even in semishade. As with many Andean species, it should be sheltered from the midday sun during really hot summers. Propagation is by seed.

254 PARODIA PENICILLATA Fechs. and v.d. Steeg
Tribe Cacteae — subtribe Echinocactinae

Place of Origin   The province of Salta in northern Argentina. **Description**   This plant has a cylindrical stem, 5 in. (12 cm.) in diameter, that grows to a height of 28 in. (70 cm.). It has 17 tuberculate ribs, spirally arranged, bearing large, very woolly, yellowish areoles. There are about 40 slender, close-set radial spines splayed outward. Between the radials and the true central spines there are about eight intermediate spines, differentiated from the centrals mainly by their position. The 15 to 20 slender central spines are longer, reaching a length of 1 ½ to 2 in. (4 to 5 cm.), and some of them are slightly curved, pointing upward at first, then outward, and finally downward. All the spines vary from golden to yellowish white, and may be nearly transparent. They cover the stem almost entirely. The flowers are small, campanulate and red. The variety *fulviceps* is almost spherical and 2¼ in. (6 cm.) in diameter, and has 20 ribs arranged in tight spirals and reddish-brown central spines. The *nivosa* variety has a long, slender stem with a napiform base that is often pendant, about 40 white radial spines and ten thicker central ones that have a yellowish base. The flowers are 1 ½ in. (4 cm.) long and across and vary from orange to red. **Cultivation**   Propagation is by seed. But often when the varieties are propagated, the offspring do not resemble their parent plant.

255 PARODIA RUBRIFLORA Backeberg
Tribe Cacteae — subtribe Echinocactinae

Place of Origin   Northern Argentina.
Description   This species was described by Backeberg in 1963. Its light green stem is a flattened sphere, measuring nearly 2¾ in. (7 cm.) in diameter and only 1 in. (3 cm.) in height. It has about 19 spirally arranged, tuberculate ribs. Each tubercle protrudes 1/4 in. (5 mm.) and bears an areole that is at first gray, whitish and felted, then becomes brownish in the center or lower down. There are about 20 bristlelike, white radial spines, nearly 1/4 in. (5 to 6 mm.) long. The four central spines are arranged in a cross. They are longer, growing to more than 3/8 in. (1 cm.), thicker and conical, and one of them is hooked. When they first appear they are a dark reddish brown; then they turn lighter and sometimes have a reddish-yellow base and a reddish tip. This species is peculiar in that it may later produce three more spines above the four central spines. The lowest of these is hooked, while the upper ones point toward the apex. They are thicker than the radial spines but are white, sometimes with a reddish tip. These additional spines constitute the main difference between *Parodia rubriflora* and *Parodia sanguiniflora*, which is very similar, particularly when young. The flowers are 1/2 in. (1.5 cm.) long and 1 in. (3 cm.) across and are bright red with a faint golden sheen. **Cultivation**   Propagation is by seed.

256 PARODIA SANGUINIFLORA (Frič) Backeberg
Tribe Cacteae — subtribe Echinocactinae

Place of Origin The province of Salta in northern Argentina at altitudes of 3,300 to 6,500 ft. (1,000 to 2,000 m.).

Description This small plant has a solitary, light green globular stem that is depressed at first and spherical when adult, measuring 2 in. (5 cm.) or more in diameter. The tubercles are conical, clearly separated, and spirally arranged, bearing apical areoles that are very woolly and felted when young, becoming almost glabrous with age. There are 10 to 15 bristlelike, white or whitish radial spines less than 3/8 in. (1 cm.) long. The central spines are arranged in a cross and are brownish, stronger and longer than the radials, particularly the lowest, which is hooked and may reach 3/4 in. (2 cm.). The upper part of the stem may bear numerous blood-red flowers (hence the plant's specific name) up to 1 ½ in. (4 cm.) across. The seeds are brown and minute. The variety *violacea* has purplish-violet flowers and probably comes from farther north, possibly from Bolivia.

Cultivation Since this plant does not put out shoots, it can be propagated by seed only. Its growth is very slow, but all adult plants flower abundantly.

---

257 PELECYPHORA ASELLIFORMIS Ehrenberg
Tribe Cacteae — subtribe Cactinae

Etymology The name comes from the Greek *pelekys*, ax or hatchet, and *phoreo*, I carry, because its long, laterally compressed tubercles resemble the blade of a hatchet.

Place of Origin The state of San Luis Potosí, Mexico.

Description This species is a rarity every grower would like to have. Like other very rare plants, only old specimens tiller, and growth is very slow, so even when seed is available it takes a long time before the plantlets become distinctive. The root is thick and fleshy, and the grayish-green stem, spherical when young, becomes almost cylindrical, growing 4 in. (10 cm.) tall and 2 to 2¼ in. (5 to 6 cm.) in diameter. Tubercles protrude 1/4 in. (5 mm.), are arranged spirally and are long, flattened at the sides. They are covered with narrow, elliptical areoles, woolly at first, which bear many minute, blunt spines. These are pectinate at the side and joined at the base, leaving only the tip free. Flowers are about 1 in. (3 cm.) across and appear at the apex of the stem, surrounded by the down on the young areoles. Their outer segments are whitish; inner ones are a crimson-violet. This species shares the common name *peyotl* with the *Lophophora*. Since it is considered sacred, it also probably contains some hallucinogenic alkaloid.

Cultivation The plant requires strong sunlight, careful watering, and a strict rest period.

258 PERESKIA ACULEATA Miller
Tribe *Pereskieae*

Etymology   Linnaeus named this plant after the French naturalist Nicholas Fabre de Peiresc (1580–1637), spelling the name in accordance with its French pronunciation.

Place of Origin   The West Indies to northern Argentina.

Description   This widely cultivated species was the first member of the genus to be discovered. The genus is considered the forerunner of the Cactaceae: it is the only cactus that bears a close similarity to bushes with ordinary leaves. The plant is shrubby and sarmentose, has slender branches and grows 32 ft. (10 m.) tall. Its persistent leaves are lanceolate or oblong, with a noticeable principal vein and lateral secondary veins, and have a short petiole; they fall off when old, leaving the plant's woody stem bare. Areoles on the stem bear two or three slender, straight spines, while the areoles at the axil of the leaves are hairy and have short, curved spines growing in pairs. The fairly large scented flowers are borne in clusters 1 to 2 in. (2.5 to 4.5 cm.) across. They have white, pinkish, or pale yellow petals that open very wide. The yellow fruit, 3/4 in. (2 cm.) in diameter, is smooth when ripe and edible. The variety *godseffiana* is smaller. Its leaves are pink to start with, turning light green with a red underside later. It should be grown in a greenhouse or well-lighted indoor surroundings.

Cultivation   Propagation by cuttings, which should be taken in summer. Growth is rapid. It tolerates low temperatures.

---

259 PSEUDOMAMMILLARIA CAMPTOTRICHA
(Dams) Buxbaum
Tribe Cacteae — subtribe Cactinae

Etymology   The name (false *Mammillaria*) was recently proposed by Buxbaum because the plant's botanical characteristics are similar to but sufficiently different from *Mammillaria* to prevent it from being classified as such.

Place of Origin   The state of Querétaro in Mexico.

Description   In 1905 the plant was described by Dams as a *Mammillaria*, but E. Tiegel then transferred it to the genus *Dolicothele* because of its long tubercles. Buxbaum's name is recent. Its globular stem tillers profusely, forming large clusters. The fleshy joints are about 2¾ in. (7 cm.) in diameter, have conical, fairly slender tubercles up to 3/4 in. (2 cm.) long that are wide at the base and bear a few long bristles at the hairy axil. Small areoles bear four to eight slender radial spines 1 in. (3 cm.) long. These are curved or contorted, whitish when young but soon turning yellow. They cross and intersect each other, particularly at the apex and when the plant is young. There are no central spines. Small flowers appear at the base of the tubercles around the apex and are shorter than the tubercles themselves. The perianth segments are white, sometimes with a greenish median line, and are lightly scented.

Cultivation   Propagation is by seed or shoots.

260 PYRRHOCACTUS BULBOCALYX
(Werdermann) Backeberg
Tribe Cacteae — subtribe Echinocactinae

Etymology The generic name derives from the Greek word *pyrros*, meaning flame-colored, but the flowers are predominantly yellow rather than fiery-red. Berger, who established the genus, transferred many species to it from *Malacocarpus*. Many others have since been discovered.

Place of Origin Northern Argentina.

Description The plant's grayish-green stem is spherical and has about 12 rounded ribs that are swollen around the areoles, forming fleshy tubercles divided by transverse depressions. The large, oblong areoles are covered in whitish or light-colored felt. There are 7 to 11 thick radial spines, 3/4 in. (2 cm.) long. Those at the sides curve inward somewhat and those at the bottom outward. There are four thick central spines that are longer than the radials and curve upward. This is particularly true of those on the upper part of the stem, which point toward the apex. All the spines are a light pinkish or reddish color, while their tip or upper part is brown. The flowers have a short tube that is thickly covered with scales and felt. They are borne around the apex and are pitcher-shaped, with yellow, pointed segments; the outer segments have a red dorsal stripe.

Cultivation Propagation is by seed. The plant thrives in strong sunlight.

261 RATHBUNIA ALAMOSENSIS (Coulter)
Britton and Rose
Tribe Cacteae — subtribe Cereinae

Etymology This genus was named in memory of the naturalist Richard Rathbun, specialist in marine invertebrates.

Place of Origin All the species of this genus come from the west coast of Mexico. This one was discovered on the coast near Alamos, in the state of Sonora.

Description The stem of this shrublike plant is 6½ to 10 ft. (2 to 3 m.) high and ramified. It puts out long fleshy shoots, 1½ to 3 in. (4 to 8 cm.) in diameter, that are initially erect but later become curved or bent down to the ground, where they root and produce new shoots. The five to eight blunt ribs have rounded, irregular protuberances divided by deep depressions. White, round areoles appear on the upper part of these protuberances. They bear 11 to 18 straight, whitish radial spines which point outward, and one to four central spines which are whitish, stiff, and much thicker than the radials. The lowest is longer than the others, reaching 1 to 1½ in. (2.5 to 3.5 cm.). Flowers are from 1½ to 4 in. (4 to 10 cm.) long and have a long, almost cylindrical narrow tube. At the opening the short, scarlet, evaginated perianth segments open obliquely.

Cultivation Of vigorous and rapid growth, this plant does not tolerate cold, so it needs shelter in winter. Young plants may be pot-grown. Propagation is by cuttings or shoots.

262 REBUTIA HAAGEI Frič and Schelle
Tribe Cacteae — subtribe Echinocereinae

Etymology   Karl Moritz Schumann named this genus in memory of P. Rebut, a French nurseryman who specialized in cacti.
Place of Origin   The province of Jujuy in northern Argentina at about 13,000 ft. (4,500 m.), near the Bolivian border.
Description   This small plant has undergone several name changes since it was discovered a few decades ago. After being given its present name (now recognized as correct), it was transferred by Backeberg to the genus *Mediolobivia;* he later changed its specific name to *pygmaea.* It is also widely known as *Rebutia haageana,* and may be referred to by any of these names. The plant is low, globular, and slightly cylindrical. It tillers profusely, producing numerous basal shoots. It has a long taproot, and the dark green stem may be glaucous or bronzed, depending on the exposure to sunlight. The tubercles are raised, forming about ten ribs set quite far apart and spirally arranged. There are 4 to 12 spines that are all radial, pectinate, rigid, 1 to 2¾ in. (3 to 7 cm.) long. They are very similar to bristles. They point sideways on each side of the tubercles, and those at the apex are arranged in a dense mass. Flowers are borne about halfway down the stem at the base. The tube is slender and the large petals are a pale or salmon pink; but the color is variable, and the petals are occasionally striped.
Cultivation   Propagation is from basal shoots.

---

263 REBUTIA MINUSCULA Schumann
Forma **KNUTHIANA** (Backeberg) Buining and Donald
Tribe Cacteae — subtribe Echinocereinae

Place of Origin   Northern Argentina. The species comes from the province of Tucuman, the form from the province of Salta.
Description   Weber described this species in 1896 as *Echinopsis minuscula;* in 1895 Schumann had taken it as the typical species of his new genus. The depressed-globular stem is only about 3/4 in. (2 cm.) high and 2 in. (5 cm.) in diameter, but the plant soon forms a clump because it produces numerous basal shoots. Its low, round, or slightly angular tubercles are arranged in 16 to 20 spirals. Whitish spines grow in tufts of 25 to 30 on the small, hairy areoles, and are only about 1/8 in. (2 to 3 mm.) long. Radials cannot be distinguished from central spines. Flowers are borne at the base and are 1½ in. (4 cm.) long, with a slender, funnel-shaped tube and many glossy red perianth segments blunt at the apex. It flowers profusely, and each flower lasts for several days. The form *knuthiana* is a paler green, with brown areoles. Spines are 1 in. (2.5 cm.) long and the flowers somewhat longer and dark crimson. Backeberg considered the species *violaciflora* to be only a variety, but it has not been reclassified as a form of *Rebutia minuscula.*
Cultivation   This plant does not tolerate severe winter cold, but it flowers very well in the spring air and sunshine if kept in a cold greenhouse or at least under shelter during its rest period.

264 REBUTIA PULVINOSA Ritter and Buining
Tribe Cacteae — subtribe Echinocereinae

Place of Origin Southern Bolivia.
Description This recently introduced species was described in 1963. Backeberg placed it in his genus *Aylostera*, which is no longer accepted, but it may still be referred to by this name. The plant is tiny, but it tillers profusely, forming dense cushions. The stems are spherical at first, later becoming somewhat elongated, with a diameter of only 1 in. (3 cm.). The ribs are separated into tubercles set far apart. These bear white, felted, oval areoles about 1/4 in. (5 mm.) long. There are 15 to 22 minuscule radial spines, scarcely 1/8 in. (3 mm.) long, and six thicker central spines that are brownish or sometimes very light-colored. Flowers are borne on lateral areoles and open above the mass of shoots. They are about 3/4 in. (2 cm.) long and 1/2 in. (1.5 cm.) across with a slender tube bearing white bristles, and a double row of yellowish-orange perianth segments. The small fruit is a reddish green and its seeds are tiny.
Cultivation This species is not commercially widespread. It may be propagated very easily from its numerous shoots and needs strong sunlight. It is sometimes grafted, although it is able to grow perfectly well on its own roots if the soil is porous and it has a definite rest period.

---

265 RHIPSALIDOPSIS ROSEA (Largerh.) Britton and Rose
Tribe Cacteae — subtribe Rhipsalidinae

Etymology The name comes from *Rhipsalis* and the Greek *opsis*, appearance: the two genera resemble each other.
Place of Origin The state of Paraná in southern Brazil.
Description This small, semi-erect or pendant epiphyte shows a marked dimorphism in growth. Its principal stems are usually erect, nearly circular or with four or five obtuse angles, and are reddish or pale green when young and dark green later. On the other hand, its fairly numerous terminal segments consist almost exclusively of flat sections about 1½ in. (4 cm.) long which only occasionally have three or four angles. The segments have slightly scalloped edges with small areoles that bear slender, bristly hairs, and one large apical areole that produces new growth and pink flowers. No areole bears flowers more than once, but as many as three flowers may appear simultaneously from one young areole. It is therefore very important that the plant should put forth new growth regularly. The scented flowers are about 1½ in. (4 cm.) across and have a short tube and pale pink perianth segments.
Cultivation It should be given only a semirest period, with reduced watering but frequent spraying. It can be grafted, but it is able to live well on its own roots if placed in the shade and given adequate warmth in winter. Propagation is by cuttings.

266 RHIPSALIS CAPILLIFORMIS Weber
Tribe Cacteae — subtribe Rhipsalidinae

Etymology The name comes from the Greek *rhips*, reed, because of its slender, flexible, often intertwined stems.

Place of Origin Eastern Brazil, but it has not been found growing wild.

Description This epiphytic plant forms dense, pendulous clusters of many slender stems, hence its specific name. The main stem is cylindrical and elongated. Subsidiary stems may be successively arranged, 4 to 6 in. (10 to 15 cm.) long, with a diameter of 1/10 in. (2 to 3 mm.), or they may be whorled, each verticil consisting of up to seven shorter, slenderer, sometimes slightly angular stems. All stems are bright green, bearing tiny areoles that, under the best conditions, will also produce many aerial roots through which the plant absorbs moisture from the atmosphere. This is necessary: true roots are minimal. Small flowers, less than 3/8 in. (1 cm.) across, appear readily, generally toward the tip of the stems. Outer perianth segments are bright yellow; inner ones are white. Sometimes there are only 5 white, stellate segments. The berries that follow the flowers of a thriving plant are round, white, 1/2 in. (5 mm.) in diameter, and very persistent.

Cultivation Like all epiphytes, a small flowerpot is better to keep its roots from suffocating. It needs a humid atmosphere and well-drained soil. Propagation is by stem cuttings.

---

267 RHIPSALIS MESEMBRYANTHEMOIDES
Haworth
Tribe Cacteae — subtribe Rhipsalidinae

Place of Origin The state of Rio de Janeiro, Brazil.

Description This attractive, unmistakable epiphyte, named by Haworth in 1821, seems to have been commonly cultivated as early as the beginning of the nineteenth century. It is a small shrub whose slender, erect trunk lignifies and grows to a maximum of 16 in. (40 cm.). It produces many pendulous branches that are cylindrical like the trunk, have a pale green, silky epidermis and are 4 to 8 in. (10 to 20 cm.) long. Branches bear many aerial roots, as well as many small secondary shoots 1/4 to 1/2 in. (5 mm. to 1 cm.) long and about 1/8 in. (2 to 4 mm.) in diameter. These grow along the length of the principal branches and are arranged spirally. This dimorphism gives rise to the plant's specific name, since the overall effect is reminiscent of the creeping stems and fleshy leaves of some members of the old genus *Mesembryanthemum*. Longer branches bear hardy, felted, infrequent areoles with one or two short, silky bristles. Areoles on the shoots are more thickly felted and bear three or four bristles. Small white or pinkish 3/8 in. (1 cm.) flowers grow laterally from the shoots or directly from their axils. Berries are generally white.

Cultivation It needs much light but no direct sun. It needs a brief semirest after flowering. Propagation by shoot cuttings.

268 RHIPSALIS MICRANTHA (Humboldt, Bonpland and Kunth) de Candolle
Tribe Cacteae — subtribe Rhipsalidinae

Place of Origin   Southern Ecuador and northern Peru.
Description   Humboldt, Bonpland and Kunth first described this species in 1823. It is an epiphyte that normally hangs in irregular, fairly long clusters from the forks of branches or the irregularities of tree trunks, where small amounts of humus collect. The principal stem is about 1/4 in. (6 mm.) in diameter, with four, or sometimes five, obtuse angles. It produces shoots that are never whorled. These are single or appear in twos or threes at the most. They are light green or yellowish, triangular, sometimes flattened, 1/4 to 1/3 in. (5 to 8 mm.) across, with slightly scalloped edges. Small areoles are somewhat woolly, bearing one small deciduous scale and one to four slender bristles. Secondary shoots usually have two angles or very rarely three. The lateral flowers are white, about 1/4 in. (7 mm.) long, and sometimes have a small scale and one or two spinescent bristles. The fruit is spherical or slightly elliptical, glabrous, white or reddish, and up to 2/5 in. (1 cm.) long. The withered perianth persists at its apex.
Cultivation   It can be grown in a shallow, wide, very small flowerpot. Perfectly drained soil, shade, humid atmosphere, frequent spraying are essential. Propagation by cuttings: these should be laid flat and pressed lightly into damp peat.

269 RHIPSALIS PACHYPTERA Pfeiffer
Tribe Cacteae — subtribe Rhipsalidinae

Place of Origin   The states of Rio de Janeiro, Minas Gerais, Santa Catharina and São Paulo in southern Brazil.
Description   Like many members of the *Rhipsalis* with joints similar to leaves, this species closely resembles *Epiphyllum* and related genera, although it differs in terms of all the botanical characteristics of the genus. The species has been known since 1788, when Wildenow described it as *Cereus alatus*. It subsequently changed names several times before and after Pfeiffer classified it under its present name. The plant is an epiphytic shrub that grows on tree trunks in forests near the coast to altitudes of 3,200 ft. (1,000 m.). It is erect at first and has an almost ligneous stem that later becomes pendant, sometimes growing to a length of 3¼ ft. (1 m.). Its primary branches are occasionally triangular, sometimes almost circular, but normally elliptical, 8 in. (20 cm.) long and 5 in. (12 cm.) across. The joints are dark green, but they often take on reddish-violet tints. This is particularly true of the large central rib. The winged parts are fleshy and unevenly scalloped, with scarcely felted areoles appearing in the depressions. The flowers, borne laterally from the areoles, are 1/2 in. (1.5 cm.) long, bright yellow and scented. The oval fruit is fairly light red.
Cultivation   It needs a humid atmosphere, winter warmth and a semirest period. Propagation by cuttings of the joints.

270 SCHLUMBERGERA RUSSELLIANA (Hooker)
Britton and Rose
Tribe Cacteae — subtribe Epiphyllinae

Etymology This genus was named after Frederick Schlumberger, collector of cacti, begonias and bromeliads.
Place of Origin The Organo mountains in Brazil.
Description This much ramified epiphytic shrub is similar to *Zygocactus truncatus* except its short, usually flat joints have crenate rather than dentate edges and their apex is truncated, not compressed, between the crenations on either side. Also, flowers are regular, with a long, funnel-shaped corolla tube, and their ovary and fruit are angular, not rounded. It may reach a length of 3¼ ft. (1 m.). Its principal stem is cylindrical, and its joints, which have a pronounced central vein, are 1½ in. (3.5 cm.) long and 3/4 in. (2 cm.) across. At the apex of the joints there is a long, narrow areole bearing a few scattered hairs that produces flowers with a funnel-shaped corolla and two rows of alternating segments. Lower ones are attached to the short tube; upper ones are long and arranged in a star pattern. They may vary from crimson to scarlet, but in cultivated forms they are generally a pinkish violet. Flowers bloom by day. The red fruit is oval, with four or five slightly winged corners, and persists on the plant for a long time.
Cultivation Propagation by cuttings from the joints. Since its root system is weak, it's often grafted onto other stock.

---

271 SOEHRENSIA OREOPEPON (Spegazzini) Backeberg
Tribe Cacteae — subtribe Echinocereinae

Etymology Backeberg named the genus after Johannes Soehrens, a Chilean botanist and taxonomist. The species name comes from the Greek *oros*, mountain, and *pepon*, melon.
Place of Origin Mendoza province in western Argentina.
Description All genus members live at a very high altitude. The plant has an olive-green stem that is thick and spherical or barrel-like and 12 in. (30 cm.) in diameter. There are 18 to 20 ribs on young specimens; old plants may have up to 30. They are 1 in. (2.5 cm.) wide, and depressed between the tuberculate protuberances, which bear at their apex gray areoles almost 3/8 in. (1 cm.) long. The youngest areoles have only a few spines; later there may be 12 to 20. One to five grow nearer the center and are 2 to 2¾ in. (5 to 7 cm.) long. The others, clearly radial, grow up to 1½ in. (3.5 cm.). All spines are slender and flexible, varying from yellowish to brownish red. Flowers are 3 in. (8 cm.) or more long and 1 in. (3 cm.) across. The tube is covered with greenish, tapering scales and perianth segments are yellow, although in some varieties they may be red. Spegazzini classified the species as a *Lobivia;* it may still be found under this name.
Cultivation The plant requires very porous soil and a strict winter rest period. Propagation is by seed.

272 STENOCEREUS GRISEUS (Haworth) Buxbaum
Tribe Cacteae — subtribe Cereinae

Etymology The name comes from the Greek *stenos*, slender, its stems being thinner than those of a true *Cereus*.

Place of Origin The northeastern coastal region of Venezuela and the adjacent islands of Curaçao, Aruba, Bonaire, Margarita, and Trinidad. In the state of Oaxaca in southern Mexico it has escaped from cultivated areas and grows wild. It is grown for its edible fruit in parts of tropical America.

Description In its natural habitat this plant is arborescent and up to 26 ft. (8 m.) high. It sometimes has a weak but definite trunk less than 16 in. (40 cm.) in diameter; more often it ramifies from the base. Old plants are smooth, but the upper part of their joints tends to be glaucous and has eight to ten blunt ribs protruding about 1 in. (3 cm.). Their slight protuberances bear oval areoles set 3/4 to 1 in. (2 to 3 cm.) apart. There are about ten needle-shaped, tough radial spines, 3/8 in. (1 cm.) long and gray or whitish in color, and one to three central spines up to 1½ in. (4 cm.) long. Flowers are 2¾ to 3½ in. (7 to 9 cm.) long. Outer perianth segments are pinkish, inner ones white. The spherical, spiny fruit is 2 in. (5 cm.) in diameter; spines fall off when the fruit ripens. It has red, edible pulp. This genus, established by Riccobono, includes species that once belonged to the genera *Lemaireocereus* (Britton and Rose) and *Ritterocereus* (Backeberg). These have been abolished but the plants may still be referred to by these synonyms.

Cultivation Does not tolerate cold. Propagation is by cuttings.

273 STENOCEREUS HYSTRIX (Haworth) Buxbaum
Tribe Cacteae — subtribe Cereinae

Place of Origin The most arid areas of the islands of Cuba, Jamaica, Haiti and Puerto Rico.

Description The plant has a short, more or less distinct trunk often 12 in. (30 cm.) in diameter and up to 47 ft. (12 m.) high. Its 10 to 50 erect branches have a diameter of 2¾ to 4 in. (7 to 10 cm.). There are 9 to 12 ribs whose slight protuberances are separated by wedge-shaped incisions. White or grayish felted areoles are borne on the upper part of the protuberances but not at the apex. New growth is more or less glaucous and covered with bloom and bears larger, hairier areoles. There are about ten radial spines and one to three central spines. One of the latter is longer than the others, measuring about 1½ in. (4 cm.). All the spines are gray with a brown tip. The flowers are 3 to 3½ in. (8 to 9 cm.) long. They have an obconical tube, about 2 in. (5 cm.) long and 1¼ in. (3 cm.) across at the opening, which bears a few large reddish or dark green scales. The perianth segments are white, opening wide when the plant is in full flower and sometimes almost evaginated. The fruit is oval, scarlet, 2 to 2¼ in. (5 to 6 cm.) long, bearing tufts of deciduous spines. When ripe it splits, exposing the dark red pulp.

Cultivation This seldom-cultivated species is pretty when young because of the color of its joints, but it does not tolerate cold and does not flower easily. Propagation is by cuttings.

274 STENOCEREUS MARGINATUS (de Candolle)
Buxbaum
Tribe Cacteae — subtribe Cereinae
Common name: Organ cactus

Place of Origin The states of Hidalgo, Querétaro and Guanajuato in Mexico, but the plant has become naturalized throughout the country.

Description This plant, classified in 1909 by Britton and Rose as *Pachycereus* (i.e., fat *Cereus*), is ironically known today as *Stenocereus* (i.e., thin *Cereus*). In the intervening years it was also called *Lemaireocereus*, a name that is still commonly in use. In its natural habitat the trunk of this species bears erect branches and measures 23 ft. (7 m.) in height. In cultivation it ramifies from the base, producing stems that are several meters high but fairly slender, measuring 6 in. (15 cm.) in diameter. The plant has five or six sharp ribs that, in time, become rounded; they bear areoles that are covered with brown or grayish felt and form a continuous line. The few dark-colored spines are borne laterally and have a large, scaly tube bearing woolly tufts, and short, evaginated, white perianth segments.

Cultivation In Mexico this plant is used for hedging; it is known as organ cactus because its stems are graduated in length. It requires heat and sunlight. It is not suitable for pot cultivation. Propagation is by cuttings.

275 STENOCEREUS PRUINOSUS (Otto) Buxbaum
Tribe Cacteae — subtribe Cereinae

Place of Origin Central and southern Mexico.

Description This columnar, almost treelike species has a principal stem that becomes a well-defined, ramified trunk and in its natural habitat may reach a height of 23 ft. (7 m.). Stems grow both from the base of the plant and laterally from the trunk. Their new growth is bluish-green and covered with white bloom. They have five or six ribs separated at first by sharp, deep grooves that become flatter later. The felted brown or white areoles are set about 1½ in. (4 cm.) apart. They bear five to nine radial spines that are reddish-brown when young, turning gray later, and one thicker, central spine, 1 in. (3 cm.) long. The floriferous areoles bear thick brown down. The funnel-shaped flowers bloom at night, but stay partially open the following day. They are 2¼ to 3½ in. (6 to 9 cm.) long, and have a scaly tube and white segments shaded witih pink. The oval fruit has felted, spiny pads, but the spines fall off when the fruit is ripe.

Cultivation The plant is difficult to identify when young and may easily be mistaken for a *Cereus*, which is perhaps why, for more than half a century, it was attributed to that genus. Propagation is by cuttings from the stems.

276 STENOCEREUS THURBERI (Engelmann) Buxbaum
Tribe Cacteae — subtribe Cereinae

Place of Origin From southern Arizona to the western part of Sonora, Mexico, and on both coasts of Baja California.

Description It is better known under its old name *Lemaireocereus thurberi,* now a synonym. In its natural habitat it has a columnar stem that reaches 23 ft. (7 m.) but does not become a well-defined trunk because it ramifies above the base, putting forth 5 to 20 branches 6 to 8 in. (15 to 20 cm.) in diameter that curve upward and ramify in their turn. Each branch has 12 to 17 not very prominent ribs sharper on new growth and more rounded on the old. Areoles, set close together, are brown and sometimes waxy. They each bear nine or ten radial spines, 3/8 in. (1 cm.) long, which are straight and radially arranged, and one to three longer central spines, the lowest sometimes 2 in. (5 cm.) long. All spines are brown or blackish on new growth, gray later. Diurnal flowers are borne laterally near the apex of the stems and are 2¼ to 2¾ in. (6 to 7 cm.) long. The scaly tube gradually gives way to large, overlapping, reddish outerperianth segments; reddish-violet inner segments open very wide and are sometimes evaginated. The variety *littoralis,* from Baja California, is only 35 in. (90 cm.) high and has slender branches and pink flowers.

Cultivation Propagation is by cuttings.

277 STENOCEREUS WEBERI (Coulter) Buxbaum
Tribe Cacteae — subtribe Cereinae

Place of Origin The states of Puebla and Oaxaca, Mexico.

Description In its natural habitat this arborescent plant grows 32 ft. (10 m.). Its trunk is just over 3¼ ft. (1 m.). Its many upward-pointing branches put forth straight, parallel stems, making it similar to a "candelabrum-shaped" succulent. Its stems are a bluish green and about 4 in. (10 cm.) in diameter. They have eight to ten blunt, rounded ribs bearing large, white, felted areoles set 1 to 2 in. (3 to 5 cm.) apart. There are 6 to 12 conical radial spines arranged in a star-pattern up to 3/4 in. (2 cm.) long, and yellowish-white when young, later reddish and eventually brown. There is one flattish central spine up to 4 in. (10 cm.) long. It points downward, except around the apex of the plant where it is erect, and is black with a red base, later gray with a black base, and eventually gray all over. Flowers are 3 to 4 in. (8 to 10 cm.) long, with a funnel-shaped tube bearing thin scales and long brown hairs. Inner perianth segments are white or cream-colored, oblong, and 3/4 in. (2 cm.) long. The fruit is oblong, 2¾ in. (7 cm.) or more long, with areoles bearing many spines which all fall off when the fruit is ripe. The fruit is eaten locally, and the plant is called *cardón.*

Cultivation Outside its natural climate the plant does not grow to its full size. Small pot-grown specimens may put forth joints that can be used for propagation.

278   STETSONIA CORYNE (Salm-Dyck) Britton and Rose
Tribe Cacteae — subtribe Cereinae

Etymology   Salm-Dyck placed the species in the *Cereus* genus in 1850. Britton and Rose removed it in 1920 and established *Stetsonia*, dedicated to Francis Lynde Stetson of New York.

Place of Origin   The arid areas of northwestern Argentina.

Description   This species is the only one of its genus. It is a large, candle-shaped, arborescent plant up to 26 ft. (8 m.) high. The thick, fairly short trunk is about 16 in. (40 cm.) in diameter and puts out a wide corona of erect branches, often more than 24 in. (60 cm.) long, which in turn produce secondary branches. Initially the branches are brilliant bluish green, turning grayish green later. They have eight or nine rounded ribs that protrude 1/2 in. (1.5 cm.) and have shallow grooves above the oval, felted areoles that later become glabrous. There are seven to nine 1 in. (3 cm.) long spines which are thicker at their base and are splayed out, and one more central spine that is straight, thicker, and 2 in. (5 cm.) or more long. All spines are yellowish-brown, soon becoming white with a dark tip. Flowers, 6 in. (15 cm.) long, are borne laterally from the area near the apex and bloom at night. They have a long tube, curving upward, which bears membranous scales. Outer perianth segments are green, inner ones white.

Cultivation   Seldom cultivated. Branch cuttings may flower.

---

279   STROMBOCACTUS DISCIFORMIS (de Candolle) Britton and Rose
Tribe Cacteae — subtribe Echinocactinae

Etymology   The name comes from the Greek *strombos*, meaning spinning top, or a conical, spiral object, such as a fir cone. The specific name means disk-shaped, which is apt because the plant tends to grow flattened against the ground.

Place of Origin   The state of Hidalgo in Mexico, where the plant grows from cracks in rugged clay or slate rocks.

Description   The genus consists of this one very rare species; all others previously attributed to it have been transferred to the genus *Toumeya*. The plant becomes a flattened sphere a few centimeters high only occasionally — mainly when cultivated. It is grayish-green or gray, rarely more than 3 in. (8 cm.) in diameter. It consists of flat, rhomboid tubercles, set close together, divided by deep, narrow grooves and arranged in spirals. These are the ribs. Adults may have 12 to 18 of them. Tubercles, which are about 1/2 in. (1 to 1.5 cm.) across, are somewhat irregular and tend to have a corrugated surface. The center of their flat upper part is slightly raised and bears a felted white areole. Areoles have four or five bristlelike spines on the new growth, but are glabrous and spineless on the older part of the plant. Flowers are white.

Cultivation   The plant requires sunlight, and does not tolerate cold. Propagation is by seed. Growth is slow.

280 SULCOREBUTIA ARENACEA (Cárdenas) Ritter
Tribe Cacteae — subtribe Echinocereinae

Etymology This genus was created by Backeberg to accommodate species similar to *Rebutia* but differing in various botanical characters. It was so called because of the depressions above the plant's long slender areoles.

Place of Origin The department of Cochabamba in Bolivia.

Description This small plant is sometimes solitary, but more often tillers to form cushions of stems 1 ½ in. (3.5 cm.) high and 2 in. (5 cm.) in diameter. The stems are completely covered by tubercles arranged in about 30 spirals, each bearing an elliptical, cream-felted areole with six or seven pairs of very short radial spines pointing sideways or outward, and one spine pointing upward, about 1/4 in. (5 mm.) long. All the spines are white, giving the plant an appearance of having been sprinkled with sand. The flowers are a yellowish orange and are 1 in. (3 cm.) long and across.

Cultivation This species, discovered around 1960, has only recently been introduced and is still difficult to find on the market. But it may be easily propagated from basal shoots. Like all plants from a similar habitat, it does not tolerate excessive heat in summer, and it requires a strict rest period. Since it does not have the large taproot characteristic of its genus, it should be grown in a wide, shallow pot.

---

281 SULCOREBUTIA RAUSCHII Frank
Tribe Cacteae — subtribe Echinocereinae

Place of Origin The department of Chuquisaca, Bolivia, at an altitude of 8,800 ft. (2,700 m.).

Description The specific name of this plant commemorates the Viennese plant hunter W. Rausch. A delightful plant of recent introduction, it deserves to be more widely cultivated. It tillers abundantly, producing stems about 3/4 in. (2 cm.) high and 1 in. (3 cm.) or slightly more in diameter. They vary from very dark green to violet. There are 16 ribs on an adult plant, spirally arranged and converging on the plant's concave apex. The tubercles are flat and almost 1/4 in. (5 mm.) long when fully developed; they bear long, slender, white areoles that are slightly felted. There may be up to 11 spines, all of which are radials. They are black, about 1/16 in. (1 to 2 mm.) long, point downward, and are flattened or bent back against the epidermis in a sort of herringbone pattern. The outer perianth segments of the flower are yellowish-green and pink toward the tip, while the spatulate inner segments are pinkish-violet with a white base.

Cultivation The plant needs a pot large enough to accommodate its taproot, very porous, gravelly soil and a strict winter rest period. It is advisable to surround its neck with coarse gravel or bits of stone to keep water from stagnating around it. Propagation is by shoots.

282 SULCOREBUTIA STEINBACHII (Werdermann)
Backeberg
Tribe Cacteae — subtribe Echinocereinae

Place of Origin The department of Cochabamba, Bolivia.

Description This species has a taproot and puts out a great many small green stems that are spherical with a slightly concave apex. These form large clusters. Each stem has about 13 somewhat indistinct ribs consisting of long, rhomboid tubercles arranged in irregular lines. On the upper part of each tubercle is a very elongated areole covered by white felt. Young cultivated plants often lack spines at first, but adult specimens usually bear six to eight blackish radial spines 1 in. (2.5 cm.) long, and one to three central spines up to 3/4 in. (2 cm.) long. The latter are dark at first, turning gray or whitish later. The scarlet flowers are 1½ in. (3.5 cm.) long. The species has many varieties. *Gracilior* has slenderer stems and fairly short, light-colored spines, all of which are almost always radial. *Rosiflora* and *violaciflora* have pinkish-crimson and reddish-purple flowers respectively, and were not described until 1964.

Cultivation Like similar plants, this species requires very porous soil, and no moisture must collect around the neck. The flowerpot should be large enough to accommodate the taproot, and since the plant is very easily scorched, it needs partial shade in summer. It is propagated from the shoots.

283 THELOCACTUS BICOLOR (Galeotti ex Pfeiffer)
Britton and Rose
Variety **TRICOLOR** Schumann
Tribe Cacteae — subtribe Cactinae

Etymology The name comes from the Greek *thele*, nipple: tubercles of adult plants fuse at the base, forming ribs, while their apex is raised. Britton and Rose formed the genus in 1922. Its species previously belonged to *Echinocactus*.

Place of Origin The species comes from southern Texas and central Mexico, and the variety from northeast Mexico.

Description There are several local varieties of this plant. The typical species is almost always solitary, with a globular, oval or cylindrical stem up to 8 in. (20 cm.) high and 4 in. (10 cm.) in diameter. The eight ribs (13 on old specimens) are oblique, divided transversally into tubercles 1/2 in. (1.5 cm.) across. Areoles, white and woolly when young, bear 9 to 18 slender radial spines up to 1 in. (3 cm.) long. These radiate in all directions and tend to be curved. Four central spines are 1 to 2 in. (3 to 5 cm.) long, and the lowest is thicker, longer and curved downward. All spines are bright yellow or red, often with a red base and an amber-yellow tip. Flowers, 2 to 2½ in. (5 to 6 cm.) long and across, have a scaly tube and pinkish-violet segments. The variety *tricolor* is more oblong, with thicker, brighter red spines that overlap even more densely.

Cultivation Attractive and easy to grow, propagation is by seed.

284 THELOCACTUS CONOTHELOS (Regel and Klein) Knuth
Tribe Cacteae — subtribe Cactinae

Place of Origin   Tamaulipas in northeastern Mexico. It was discovered near Jaumave by W. Karwinsky.

Description   The species was described as an *Echinocactus* in 1860 by Regel and Klein on the basis of specimens collected by Karwinsky. Quite recently, when precise information about its flowers became available, it was transferred to the genus *Thelocactus*. The plant's grayish-green stem is roughly oval, reaching up to 4 in. (10 cm.) tall and nearly 3 in. (7.5 cm.) in diameter. Its 12 to 18 ribs are spirally arranged and consist of very prominent conical tubercles (hence the plant's name), about 3/4 in. (2 cm.) long. Areoles are oblique, white and downy. There are 14 to 16 white radial spines that sometimes have a dark base, are close-set, somewhat curved, and nearly 3/4 in. (2 cm.) long. Two to four light-colored central spines are unequal, thicker, up to 1½ in. (3.5 cm.) long, sometimes curved but more often erect. Purplish violet flowers have a scaly tube and are about 1½ in. (3.5 cm.) across. The fruit, covered with tiny scales, is 3/8 in. (1 cm.) long; it is greenish at its base and reddish-violet on its upper part.

Cultivation   This plant grows on very sandy terrain and therefore needs an extremely porous substratum and excellent drainage. Propagation is by seed.

285 THELOCACTUS EHRENBERGII (Pfeiffer) Knuth
Tribe Cacteae — subtribe Cactinae

Place of Origin   Near Ixmiquilpán in the state of Hidalgo, central Mexico.

Description   Spherical at first, later oblong, the plant puts forth many basal shoots, forming clumps. Each stem may reach a height of 5 in. (12 cm.) and a diameter of about 2¾ in. (7 cm.). It is light green at first, becoming grayish-green later, and has many white wool and yellow spines at its apex. There are 8 to 13 spirally arranged ribs consisting of slanting, conical tubercles that protrude 3/8 in. (1 cm.). Areoles are elongated and covered with yellowish wool when young. They bear six slender, yellowish radial spines, pointing outward. The uppermost spine is the longest: about 3/4 in. (2 cm.). There may be no central spines or just one that is straight, sharp, brownish-yellow, and also 3/4 in. (2 cm.) long. All spines gradually turn reddish as new spines develop on young parts of the plant; eventually they fall off, leaving the plant's base spineless. Funnel-shaped flowers are 1½ in. (4 cm.) across. Outer segments are pale pink with a darker median stripe; inner segments are lanceolate, pale pink, or white. This species is very similar to *Thelocactus leucacanthus.*

Cultivation   Easy to cultivate, but growth is slow. It needs a large flowerpot. Propagation from basal shoots.

286 THELOCACTUS LEUCACANTHUS (Zuccarini) Britton and Rose
Tribe Cacteae — subtribe Cactinae

Place of Origin Near Zimpán and Ixmiquilpán in the state of Hidalgo in central Mexico.

Description In 1937 Zuccarini described this plant as an *Echinocactus*. Its stem is solitary initially, but tillers later, producing basal and lateral branches forming cushionlike clumps. The oval-elongated stem, up to 6 in. (15 cm.) high, has 8 to 13 often spirally arranged ribs that consist of large, conspicuous, blunt tubercles 3/8 in. (1 cm.) high, divided by a groove. Areoles are round and woolly and bear 7 to 20 radial spines, either spread wide or curved backward, of irregular length, the longest 1 ½ in. (4 cm.). They are pale yellow at first, whitish later, and may develop transverse rings. Central spines may be absent, but usually there is one that is blackish at first and gray later, thickish, and up to 2 in. (5 cm.) long. Flowers, borne at the center of the plant, are 2 in. (5 cm.) across. They have a tube bearing overlapping scales and many yellow perianth segments. The variety *schmollii* has densely set ½ in. (1.5 cm.) radial spines and purplish-violet flowers.

Cultivation Like all members of the genus, the plant has a thick root that requires a large flowerpot. This attractive species does not need to be grafted. Its growth is slow, however, and it is advisable to propagate it by cuttings rather than seed.

---

287 THELOCACTUS LOPHOTHELE (Salm-Dyck) Britton and Rose
Tribe Cacteae — subtribe Cactinae

Place of Origin The state of Chihuahua in Mexico.

Description The plant's stem is initially spherical, but with time it elongates to 10 in. (25 cm.). Adult plants are shrubby, producing basal shoots. There are 15 to 20 spiral ribs divided into irregular tubercles. The latter are furrowed by several depressions and are gnarled at their truncated apex, which bears white or pale yellow oval areoles. There are three to five thick, stiff, radial spines 3/8 to 1 in. (1 to 3 cm.) long, which are a darkish brown and bulbous at their reddish base. There are no central spines, but one that is a little longer than the radials may occasionally appear. The flowers, which are borne at the apex, are 1 ½ to 2 ¼ in. (4 to 6 cm.) long and 2 in. (5 cm.) across when they are fully open. The perianth segments are pointed, narrow, and dentate, varying from cream to light yellow to peach, while the outermost segments are often greenish with a red median line. It was described by Salm-Dyck as an *Echinocactus* in 1850 and was transferred to its present genus by Britton and Rose in 1922. It is now hard to find.

Cultivation This is one of the few species of the genus that prefers semishade to full sunshine. It requires a soil enriched with well-rotted leaf mold, and scant watering. Where possible, it is propagated from basal shoots.

288 THELOCACTUS NIDULANS (Quehl) Britton and Rose
Tribe Cacteae — subtribe Cactinae

Place of Origin   Mexico, but the precise location is unknown. The species was described from cultivated specimens.

Description   The plant is almost semiglobular, reaching a height of 4 in. (10 cm.) and a diameter of up to 8 in. (20 cm.). Its stem is a bluish green when young but later becomes grayish-green. Its slightly flattened apex is covered with thick white wool. There are about 20 ribs, spirally arranged and completely separated into conical tubercles that protrude 3/4 in. (2 cm.). They bear elliptical slanting areoles, about 3/8 in. (1 cm.) long, felted at first and glabrous later. Spines all look virtually the same; only when the plant is young can the radials be distinguished from the centrals. There are 15 spines altogether. The eight that are borne in the lower part of the areole are caducous and 3/8 in. (1 cm.) long; the others persist a little longer. The three on the upper part are 3/4 in. (2 cm.) long, and the four in the center are up to 2¼ in. (6 cm.) long. All are the color of dark horn, and sometimes striped. On the older part of the plant there are only four to six persistent spines. These are thicker and pale gray, and often divide into frayed fibers. The light yellow or off-white flowers are 1½ in. (4 cm.) long.

Cultivation   Rarely cultivated, it is of slow growth. It thrives in sun and does not tolerate cold. Propagation by seed.

---

289 TRICHOCEREUS CHILENSIS (Colla) Britton and Rose
Tribe Cacteae — subtribe Cereinae

Etymology   The name comes from the Greek *thrix* or *thricos*, meaning hair: flowering areoles of this plant are very hairy.

Place of Origin   Chile, from the northern province of Atacama south about 400 miles (600 km.) to Curicó.

Description   The stem is columnar, ramifying from the base. Its many thick branches grow at an angle to the stem but are soon erect, reaching 10 ft. (3 m.). There are 16 to 17 low, wide ribs with large tubercles divided by transverse grooves. Areoles, large, rounded, and covered by white wool, are borne on the upper part of the tubercles; on the older parts, where tubercles are more pronounced, they appear to be sunk in the depressions between them. The 8 to 12 1½ in. (4 cm.) thick radial spines, point outward. The single central spine is stronger and usually 1½ to 2¾ in. (4 to 7 cm.) long, occasionally up to 4¾ in. (12 cm.). All spines are amber-yellow at first, later gray. They almost always have a dark tip. Since the species is very variable, however, they may initially be dark, varying from blackish to brown. Flowers are 5½ in. (14 cm.) long, with outer perianth segments that are white shaded with red or brown, and white inner segments. Many varieties attributed to this species are probably only local forms.

Cultivation   Propagation by cuttings. It can't stand cold.

290 TRICHOCEREUS CRASSICAULIS (Backe-berg) Backeberg
Tribe Cacteae — subtribe Cereinae

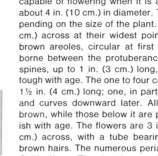

Place of Origin The province of Catamarca in northern Argentina.

Description The plant's stem is spherical at first, later elongating to a height of 6½ in. (16 cm.). It is sometimes slightly tapered toward the apex, and ramifies from the base. It becomes capable of flowering when it is about 6 in. (15 cm.) high and about 4 in. (10 cm.) in diameter. There may be 9 to 14 ribs, depending on the size of the plant. They are rounded, 3/4 in. (2 cm.) across at their widest point, and tuberculate. The light brown areoles, circular at first and shield-shaped later, are borne between the protuberances. There are 7 to 12 radial spines, up to 1 in. (3 cm.) long, that become quite thick and tough with age. The one to four conical central spines are up to 1½ in. (4 cm.) long; one, in particular, points outward initially and curves downward later. All the spines at the apex are brown, while those below it are pale yellow, becoming brownish with age. The flowers are 3 in. (8 cm.) long and 3½ in. (9 cm.) across, with a tube bearing pointed green scales and brown hairs. The numerous perianth segments are bright red.

Cultivation The plant is very vigorous, but needs to be sheltered from cold in the winter. Propagation is by basal shoots.

291 TRICHOCEREUS GRANDIFLORUS (Britton and Rose) Krainz
Tribe Cacteae — subtribe Cereinae

Place of Origin The Sierra Anconquija in northwestern Argentina between Andalgalá and Concepción, on the border dividing the province of Catamarca from that of Tucumán.

Description This species is still often referred to as a *Lobivia*, according to Britton and Rose's classification. It has a short, columnar stem, reaching a maximum of 14 in. (35 cm.) and a diameter of 2¼ in. (6 cm.); it is dark green, and ramifies from the base. There are about 14 ribs that bear areoles, yellow on new growth, in depressions along their edge, at intervals of 3/8 in. (1 cm.). There are eight or nine slender radial spines, sometimes as many as 12, that are yellowish-white with a brown tip. Normally there is only one central spine, which is thicker, 3/8 in. (1 cm.) long, and the same color, but old plants may produce four feebler, thinner ones. The flowers are borne laterally on the upper part of the stem. The buds are covered with gray wool, and the flowers measure about 3 in. (8 cm.) long. The tube is covered with slender scales that are rather hairy at their base, and the pointed perianth segments are bright red or vivid pink, although the shade may vary.

Cultivation It grows at an altitude of nearly 6,500 ft. (2,000 m.), so it tolerates cold if sheltered. In hot climates shade is advisable. Propagation by seed or shoots from old plants.

292 TRICHOCEREUS PASACANA (Weber) Britton and Rose
Tribe Cacteae — subtribe Cereinae

Place of Origin   These large plants are characteristic of the landscape in the mountains of northern Argentina and southern Bolivia. They generally grow on crags and rocky slopes, and their trunks are used locally to build cattle-pens or huts.
Description   The plant has a columnar stem 12 in. (30 cm.) in diameter and up to 32 ft. (10 m.) high. This is initially solitary, but it puts forth basal branches as an adult, when it becomes woody and inermous on its lower part. There are about 20 ribs, increasing to 38 or more later. They protrude 3/4 in. (2 cm.) and bear brown, close-set areoles that touch one another. The many spines are variable; it is difficult to distinguish radial from central spines. On old plants they may be 1½ to 5½ in. (4 to 14 cm.) long, and are rigid and pointed, varying from yellow to dark brown. On the upper part of the stem, and especially on the flower-bearing areoles, they are long and flexible, bristle-like, light-colored — often white. White nocturnal flowers are borne laterally on the upper part of the stem. They are 5 in. (12 cm.) long, their tube covered with long blackish hairs. The greenish fruit, about 1 in. (3 cm.), is spherical or oval; its local name is *pasacana*, and it is considered edible.
Cultivation   Although it may be cultivated outdoors in mild climates, it is too large to be pot-grown. Propagation is by seed.

293 TRICHOCEREUS PURPUREOPILOSUS
(Weingart) Backeberg
Tribe Cacteae — subtribe Cereinae

Place of Origin   The Sierra de Córdoba in the province of the same name in central Argentina.
Description   This species has a stem that reaches 3¼ ft. (1 m.) and is a dark glossy green. It has about 12 low, blunt ribs, and forms clumps of basal branches that are semiprostrate at first, becoming ascendant later. They are more than 12 in. (30 cm.) long and about 2¾ in. (7 cm.) in diameter. Whitish areoles, set less than 3/8 in. (1 cm.) apart, bear 15 to 20 radial spines that are straight, slender, pale yellow, and 1/4 in. (5 mm.) long. They also bear four central spines, arranged in a cross, which are slightly longer, and almost transparent or ivory-colored. All spines have an enlarged, red base. Flowers, which are 8 in. (20 cm.) long, bloom at night. The tube is covered with scales and brownish-violet hairs, and the outer perianth segments are greenish-violet, while the inner ones are pinkish-white. The species was described by Wilhelm Weingart, a German plant collector, as a *Cereus* around 1925.
Cultivation   In order to bring out the beautiful color of the spines, this plant needs strong sunlight. Winter temperatures must not fall too low. It should be grown in soil enriched by a large proportion of manure or well-rotted leaf mold. Propagation is by cuttings from basal shoots.

294 TRICHOCEREUS SMRZIANUS (Backeberg)
Backeberg
Tribe Cacteae — subtribe Cereinae

Place of Origin The mountains of northern Argentina. The plant grows in ravines rather than high up in the mountains.
Description This species was discovered several decades ago but has only recently been included in this genus. Initially it has a spherical stem that later becomes cylindrical, 6½ in. (16 cm.) or more high, swelling out to form a stumpy column. Young plants are very variable and in some cases may even develop prostrate stems that only later become ascendant. There are about 15 ribs up to 1 in. (3 cm.) wide on adult plants. They bear woolly areoles set fairly close together and very variable, irregular spines, which are sharp, stiff, radially arranged, and usually point downward. They change from whitish to brownish-yellow, and are more numerous and slender when young. Initially there are about 14 spines, but the number is gradually reduced to seven as the spines become thicker. The flowers are 5 in. (12 cm.) long and across, and have numerous perianth segments. In time the plant puts forth basal shoots, but its growth is slow, and it flowers only very rarely.
Cultivation Like all plants of fairly recent introduction, this species is hard to find. It is propagated from basal shoots, if available. Reproduction by seed is particularly slow.

---

295 TRICHOCEREUS STRIGOSUS (Salm-Dyck)
Britton and Rose
Tribe Cacteae — subtribe Cereinae

Place of Origin The Andean provinces of Mendoza and San Juan in western Argentina. The plant is very common in the valleys of the Andean foothills to the west of Mendoza.
Description In 1834 Salm-Dyck described this species as a member of the genus *Cereus*. It is very bushy, forming large colonies more than 3¼ ft. (1 m.) across. The stems do not ramify. They are prostrate at first and erect later, reaching a height of 24 in. (60 cm.) with a diameter of only 2¼ in. (6 cm.). There are very flat ribs with 12 to 18 round, large, very close-set areoles. New areoles are white and very hairy, but in time they shed their hair and turn grayish. There are about 20 spines; it is difficult to categorize them as radial or central, but the central ones are generally considered to be the four thickest, up to 2 in. (5 cm.) long, the longest of which points downward. The other spines are much thinner and only 1/2 in. (1.5 cm.) long. They may vary from white, yellow or pink to blackish, and there are a few specimens whose spines turn almost orange if they have the right amount of light. The flowers are up to 8 in. (20 cm.) long, they are nocturnal and sometimes scented. Their tube bears brownish hairs and white or pink petals.
Cultivation The plant grows slowly, but it tillers even when young. It is propagated from basal shoots.

296 TRICHOCEREUS TEPHRACANTHUS

(Labouret) Britton and Rose
Tribe Cacteae — subtribe Cereinae

Place of Origin   Bolivia, in the department of Cochabamba.
Description   This species was first included among the *Cereus* by Labouret and for a short time was called *Roseocereus* by Backeberg. This monotypical genus is no longer accepted, but the plant is sometimes still listed under the name. It is shrubby, with an erect stem that ramifies from the base to a limited extent. The stem and the branches, measuring about 2¼ in. (6 cm.) in diameter, usually have 8 ribs, which are rounded and tuberculate below the areoles, particularly on old branches; the tubercles are hardly noticeable on younger branches. The areoles are large, white, felted and shield-shaped. their four to seven radial spines are white, thick and stiff, are 3/8 in. (1 cm.) long and often have a brown tip. The one central spine is much thicker, almost twice as long and brown at first, soon becoming ash-gray with a more or less dark tip. The flowers are borne on the upper part of the stem and the branches. They are 7 to 8¾ in. (18 to 22 cm.) long, and their tube is covered with large scales bearing twisted, very curly hairs at the axil. The elongated base of the scales give the tube a fluted appearance. The perianth segments are white, and the flowers bloom at night.
Cultivation   It grows slowly. Propagation by cuttings.

---

297 UEBELMANNIA MENINENSIS Buining

Tribe Cacteae — subtribe Echinocactinae

Place of Origin   The state of Minas Gerais in Brazil. The plant often grows at very high altitudes, in cracks between rocks or on the rocks themselves, usually where there is a very high degree of atmospheric moisture, which compensates for the fact the soil is perfectly drained. In its natural habitat the plant frequently grows among lichens, which may even cover it.
Description   This genus, which is hardly ever cultivated except in very specialized collections, was created in 1973 by the Dutch botanist Albert Buining to include some species discovered a few years earlier, and the two he discovered himself. He found *Uebelmannia meninensis* growing among quartz rocks near a place named Pedra Menina. The plant's stem is globular when young, later becoming elongated and cylindrical. It is green or reddish-green, nearly 20 in. (50 cm.) high and 4 in. (10 cm.) in diameter. When fully mature it has up to 40 markedly tuberculate ribs, but initially it has considerably fewer. The tubercles protrude about 1/3 in. (8 mm.), are separated by transverse grooves and have apical areoles. There are two or three spines, pointing downward except for the upper one, which is shorter. The flowers are light yellow.
Cultivation   Almost all these plants are imported and become established with difficulty. They require warmth and a humid atmosphere. Propagation is by seed.

298 WEBERBAUEROCEREUS WINTERIANUS

Ritter

Tribe Cacteae — subtribe Cereinae

Etymology This plant was named after the German botanist Weberbauer, who studied the flora of the Peruvian Andes.

Place of Origin La Libertad department, northwestern Peru.

Description This plant reaches 19½ ft. (6 m.). The trunk is 6½ ft. (2 m.) high and the series of ramifying branches consists of parallel, ascendant stems 2 to 3 in. (5 to 8 cm.) in diameter. On the adult part there are 22 to 27 barely tuberculate ribs that protrude 1/4 in. (5 mm.). Young plants have 12 to 14 ribs. Areoles are brown and almost 1/4 in. (5 mm.) long. They each bear 20 to 30 slender, close-set radial spines. Lower ones are thinner and more numerous, reaching 1/2 in. (1.5 cm.); upper ones are few, thicker, and shorter. The 12 to 15 central spines are thicker than the radials and more than 1/2 in. (1.5 cm.) long. All spines are golden but become lighter on old plants. On the flower-bearing part of the plant areoles have 30 to 40 slender, golden, bristlelike spines up to 2¾ in. (7 cm.) long. The upper part of the areole, which bears the flowers, is wide and felted. Flowers are nearly 3 in. (7.5 cm.) long, with a tube bearing blackish hairs. Outer perianth segments are pink, and the inner ones very pale pink. The variety *australis* has thicker branches, more numerous ribs, broader areoles and thinner spines. The species was described in 1962.

Cultivation Propagation is by cuttings.

---

299 WEBEROCEREUS BIOLLEYI (Weber) Britton and Rose

Tribe Cacteae — subtribe Hylocereinae

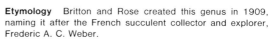

Etymology Britton and Rose created this genus in 1909, naming it after the French succulent collector and explorer, Frederic A. C. Weber.

Place of Origin Costa Rica and Panama.

Description This very slender plant was described in 1902 by Weber, who classified it as a *Rhipsalis*. It is an epiphyte with slender, supple stems that usually hang from the branches of trees but that sometimes take root through the aerial roots they develop. The principal stem is long, cylindrical or somewhat irregularly angular, smooth, and only about 1/4 in. (4 to 6 mm.) in diameter. The small areoles, set far apart, are usually inermous, but occasionally have one to three small yellow spines. The joints are often flat; when young they sometimes have three raised wings and the areoles bear slight traces of whitish felt; in time the joints become smooth, or have barely perceptible angular ribs. The flowers are nocturnal, 1 to 2 in. (3 to 5 cm.) long, with a scaly tube and a few bristles. The outer perianth segments are dark pink, while the inner ones are paler, but the color varies. Some specimens have crimson flowers.

Cultivation Like all epiphytes, this plant requires a shady position, a humid atmosphere and humusy, porous soil. It does not tolerate cold. Propagation is by cuttings.

300 WILCOXIA VIPERINA (Weber) Britton and Rose
Tribe Cacteae — subtribe Cereinae

Etymology Britton and Rose created this genus in 1909, naming it after General Timothy E. Wilcox, of the United States Army, who was a keen plant collector.

Place of Origin Between Tehuacán and Zapotitlán, in the southeastern part of the state of Puebla, south-central Mexico.

Description This plant, which ramifies to form a semicreeping shrub, has thick roots forming tubers that act as an underground storage system. The branches may reach a length of 6½ ft. (2 m.). The lower branches are woody, with a diameter of 3/4 in. (2 cm.), while the younger ones are olive- or grayish-green, and velvety due to dense pubescence. The branches have eight to ten ribs that are so flat that they are hardly distinguishable. They bear slightly felted areoles. The eight or nine very close-set radial spines are black, slender, about 1/6 in. (3 to 5 mm.) long, and point sideways. There are three or four blackish central spines at the most. These are very short, conical, wide at the base and usually point downward. All the spines fall off in old age, leaving the stems inermous. The flowers are 2¼ in. (6 cm.) long and are borne around the apical part of the shoots. The tube is covered with a grayish down and slender, bristlelike spines. The perianth segments are red.

Cultivation The plant needs very sandy soil and strong sunlight. Propagation is by cuttings.

---

301 ZYGOCACTUS TRUNCATUS (Haworth) Schumann
Tribe Cacteae — subtribe Epiphyllinae
Common name: Christmas cactus

Etymology This plant was named *Epiphyllum truncatum* by Haworth in 1812, and is still sometimes referred to by this name. In 1810, Schumann created the genus *Zygocactus*, taking the name from the Greek *zygos*, yoke: joints are connected at the tip. *Zygocactus* was the official name until recently, when the species was transferred to the genus *Schlumbergera* and the main species of the latter was transferred to the *Rhipsalidopsis* as *Rhipsalidopsis gaertneri* (Easter cactus). We retained the synonym, which is better known.

Place of Origin The Rio de Janeiro mountains in Brazil.

Description This well-known shrub is often crossed with similar genera and has many varieties. It is an epiphyte up to 12 in. (30 cm.) long, composed of a series of short branches that are dentate along the edges and have two curved teeth at their truncated apex. This bears the felted, flower-bearing areoles and produces new branches. Flowers have a curved tube and several rows of segments. They are irregular, with an oblique edge and may be pink, red or purple. They bloom in winter.

Cultivation Only new branches bear flowers at their apex. It requires peaty soil, shade, and a semirest after flowering. Propagation is by cuttings or grafting.

INDEX OF PRINCIPAL AUTHORS

Edward Johnston Alexander. 1901– . U.S. botanist, specialist in Cactaceae.

Curt Backeberg. 1894–1964. German cactus specialist who traveled widely in Central and South America. Principal works: *Die Cactaceae*, 1958-1962; *Kakteenlexicon*, 1966; with F. M. Knuth, *Kaktus-ABC*, 1935.

Domingo Bello y Espinosa. 1817–1884. Spanish naturalist who lived in Puerto Rico and studied its flora.

Lyman D. Benson. 1909– . U.S. botanist; director of the Herbarium of Pomona College; specialist in Cactaceae. Wrote *The Cacti of Arizona*, 1969; *The Native Cacti of California*, 1969; *Cacti of the United States and Canada*, 1982.

Alwin Berger. 1871–1931. German specialist in succulents; curator of the Hanbury Gardens at La Mortola from 1915 to 1926. Wrote *A Systematic Revision of the Genus Cereus*, 1905; *Kakteen*, 1929.

Jacob Bigelow. 1787–1879. U.S. doctor and botanist; professor at Boston University. With George Engelmann wrote *Description of Cactaceae*, 1856.

Frederick Boedecker. 1867–1937. German scholar who wrote *Ein Mammillarien-Vergleichsschlussel*, 1933.

Aimé Bonpland (actually Aimé Jacques A. Goujaud). 1773–1858. Director of gardens at Malmaison; he became a professor at Buenos Aires in 1818. Wrote about New World plants with Humboldt and Kunth.

John Borg. 1873–1945. Wrote *Cacti*, 1937.

Katherine Brandegee. California botanist. She and her husband, Townsend S. Brandegee, gave their large herbarium and library to the University of California.

Helia Bravo-Hollis. 1903– . Mexican botanist specializing in *Cactaceae*.

Nathaniel Lord Britton. 1859–1934. Director of New York Botanical Garden. With J. N. Rose wrote *The Cactaceae*, 4 vols., 1919-1923.

Albert F. H. Buining. 1901–1976. Dutch botanist and specialist in succulents.

Franz Buxbaum. 1900–1979. Austrian botanist. Wrote *Morphology of Cacti*, 1951-55; *Kakteenpflege biologisch richtig*, 1959; and many important botanical papers on cacti.

Alberto Castellanos. 1896–1968. Argentinian botanist specializing in South American cacti. Wrote *Los Generos de las Cactaceas Argentinas,* 1938.

Augustin Pyrame de Candolle. 1778–1841. Swiss professor of botany. Published *Plantarum Succulentarum Historia,* 1798; *Revue des Cactées,* 1829.

August Louis Cels. French botanist.

John Merle Coulter. 1851–1928. University of Chicago. Founder of *Botanical Gazette.* Wrote *Preliminary Revision of the North American Opuntia,* 1896.

Robert T. Craig. California dentist; specialist in cacti. Published *The Mammillaria Handbook,* 1945.

Johann Jacob Dillenius, 1687–1746. Professor of botany at Oxford.

George Engelmann. 1809–1884. U.S. botanist of German origin. Author from 1848 to 1876 of five books about the Cactaceae.

Alberto V. Frič. 1882–1944. Czechoslovakian scholar who traveled in Mexico. With K. G. Kreuzinger, wrote *Verzeichnis Amerikanischer und Anderer Sukkulenten mit Revision der Systematik der Kakteen,* 1935.

Joseph Gaertner. 1732–1791. German doctor and botanist who classified and named a large number of plants.

Heinrich Rudolph August Grisebach. 1814–1879. German botanist. Wrote *Flora of the British West Indian Islands,* 1859-64; *Catalogus Plantarum Cubensium,* 1866.

Robert L. Gürke. 1854–1911. German cactus specialist. With K. M. Schumann, wrote *Blühende Kakteen* from 1900 to 1921.

Frederick A. Haage. 1858–1930. Wrote *Kacteen in Heim,* 1928.

Adrian Hardy Haworth. 1772–1833. Published *Synopsis Plantarum Succulentarum,* 1812; *Supplementum et Revisiones Plantarum,* 1819. His works were republished in facsimile in 1965 as *The Complete Works on Succulent Plants 1794–1831.*

Friedrich Alexander von Humboldt. 1796–1859. Greatest of the German naturalists. Traveled in Central and South America. Wrote his 30-volume *Voyage aux régions équinoxiales du Nouveau Continent fait en 1799–1804,* between 1805 and 1837. With Bonpland and Kunth, edited *Nova Genera et Species Plantarum,* 1815–1825.

Hermann Gustav Karsten. 1817–1908. German professor of botany. He traveled in South America and wrote *Florae Columbiae,* 1857–69.

Frederic M. Knuth von Knuthemborg. 1904– . Danish botanist who, with Curt Backeberg, wrote *Kactus-ABC,* 1935.

Hans Krainz. Cactus specialist who wrote *Die Kakteen,* 1956-75 (unfinished).

Carl Sigismund Kunth. 1788–1850. Author of numerous botanical works. With Bonpland and Humboldt, edited *Nova Genera et Species Plantarum,* 1815–1825.

J. Labouret. French cactus expert who wroye *Monographie de la Famille des Cactées,* 1853.

George Lawrence. An English gardener at Hendon Vicarage, Middlesex, who was an expert on cacti and wrote an account of his employer's cactus collection in 1841.

F. C. Lehmann. German plant collector in South America.

Charles Lemaire. 1801–1871. Belgian botanist. Wrote *Iconographie Descriptive des Cactées,* 1841; *Les Caotées,* 1868.

Heinrich Friedrich Link. 1767–1851. German director of the Berlin Botanical Gardens.

Carl von Linné (Carolus Linnaeus). 1707–1778. Swedish naturalist. Wrote *Systema Naturae,* 1735; *Genera Plantarum,* 1737; *Classes Plantarum,* 1738; *Philosophia Botanica,* 1751; and *Species Plantarum,* 1753.

William Taylor Marshall. 1886–1957. U.S. botanist. With T. M. Bock, wrote *The Cactaceae,* 1941. Published *Arizona's Cactuses,* 1950.

Carl Friedrich Philipp von Martius. 1794–1868. German director of the Munich Botanical Gardens. Founder and first editor of *Flora Brasiliensis.*

Phillip Miller. 1691–1771. Englishman best known for his *Gardeners' Dictionary,* 1st ed. 1731.

M. Monville. Eighteenth-century French plant collector and cactus expert.

Charles Russell Orcutt. 1864–1929. U.S. botanist specializing in Californian and Mexican cacti. Wrote *American Plants,* 1901-12; *Cactography,* 1926.

Friedrich Otto. 1782–1856. German botanist and horticultur-alist. With L. G. K. Pfeiffer, wrote *Abbildung und Beschrei-bung Blühender Cacteen,* 1843.

Ernest J. Palmer. 1875–1962. U.S. botanist of English origin.

Ludwig G. K. Pfeiffer. 1805–1877. German botanist. Besides numerous general works on botany, he wrote *Enumeratio Diagnostica Cactearum Hucusque Cognitarum,* 1837.

Rudolph Amandus Philippi. 1808–1904. German-Chilean bot-anist who specialized in the flora of the Antofagasta and Ata-cama regions of Chile.

Heinrich Poselger. Nineteenth-century German doctor of medi-cine and cactus specialist.

Joseph A. Purpus. 1860–1932. German botanist. His brother C. A. Purpus traveled throughout the United States and Mexico collecting many new plants, which Joseph de-scribed.

Leopold Quehl. 1849–1923. German cactus specialist who established an important collection at Halle.

Constantino Samuel Rafinesque-Schmaltz (also known as Peter Hamilton Rafinesque). 1784–1842. U. S. naturalist of Italian descent. Professor at Transylvania University, Ken-tucky. Wrote *New Flora and Botany of North America,* 1836-38.

Vincenzo Riccobono. 1861–1943. Director of the botanical gardens at Palermo and cactus specialist.

Friedrich Ritter. 1898–1983. German traveler and cactus spe-cialist. Between 1927 and 1959 he discovered and de-scribed several new genera.

Joseph N. Rose. 1862–1928. Assistant curator of the National Herbarium, Smithsonian Institution. With N. L. Britton, wrote *The Cactaceae,* 4 vols., 1919–1923.

Theodor Rumpler. 1817–1891. Editor of Carl Forster's *Hand-buch der Cacteenkunde,* 2nd ed. 1885-96.

Joseph M. F. Fürst zu Salm-Reifferscheidt-Dyck. 1773–1861. German botanist who owned one of the most comprehensive collections of succulent plants of his time at Düsseldorf. He described them in various monographs, one of which was *Cacteae en Horto Dickensi Cultae,* 1841, 1845, 1850.

Frederick Scheer. 1792–1868. English botanist of German origin. Wrote *Kew and Its Gardens,* 1840.

Michael Joseph Scheidweiler. 1799–1861. Professor of botany and horticulture at the Horticultural Institute of Ghent, Belgium.

Christian J. W. Schiede. 1798–1836. German traveler and botanist who introduced many Mexican plants into Europe.

Karl Moritz Schumann. 1851–1904. German curator of the Botanical Museum in Berlin. Wrote *Gesamtbeschreibung der Kakteen*, 1897-99; *Blühende Kakteen*, 1900-03.

Ernest W. Shurley. 1888–1963. English student of cacti and specialist in *Mammillaria*.

Carlos Spegazzini. 1858–1926. Italian-Argentinian botanist who settled in Argentina in 1879. Wrote *Flora de la Provincia de Buenos Aires*, 1905.

Friedrich J. Vaupel. 1876–1927. German botanist. Curator at the Berlin Botanical Museum. Wrote *Die Kakteen*, 1925.

O. Voll. Died 1959. German-Brazilian director of the Botanical Gardens in Rio de Janeiro.

Sereno Watson. 1826–1892. Harvard University. With W. H. Brewer, wrote *Botany of California*, 2 vols., 1876-80.

Frederic A. C. Weber. 1830–1903. German succulent specialist who took part in a French scientific expedition to Mexico, 1865-66.

Erich Werdermann. 1892–1959. German botanist who was director of the Berlin Botanical Gardens. He published *Blühende Kakteen und andere sukkulente Pflanzen*, 1930; *Brasilien und seine Säulenkakteen*, 1933; and, with Curt Backeberg, *Neue Kakteen*, 1931, and other works.

Joseph Gerhard Zuccarini. 1797–1848. German botanist and taxonomist.

GLOSSARY

Acicular   needle-shaped, slender and pointed.
Alate   winged.
Alternate   set apart and opposite on a stem or branch.
Anther   the part of the stamens which contains pollen.
Apex   tip or terminal part of an organ.
Aphyllous   leafless.
Apical   pertaining to the apex of any part of a plant.
Arborescent   treelike in size and form.
Areole   generally, an interstice in an organ; specifically regarding the Cactaceae, a small external portion that produces felt, spines and new growth.
Armed   bearing defensive or protective organs, such as spines or bristles.
Articulate   subdivided into segments or joints.
Attenuated   tapered at one end.
Axil   angle between secondary growing parts and the supporting stem or branch.
Basal   of the base or lower part of a structure.
Basal shoot   a branch that grows underground from the root, rhizome or neck of the plant and takes root, producing an independent offshoot.
Beak   a slightly rounded prominence beneath a sunken areole and above a transverse groove.
Berry   fleshy, usually indehiscent fruit whose pulp contains one or more seeds.
Bract   modified leaf assuming various forms, color and consistencies that may be borne at the base of leaves or flowers.
Bud   small protuberances containing rudimentary leaves, flowers or branches.
Caducous   of organs that fall off prematurely.
Calyx   outer perianth segments around flower bud that protect the flower's inner organs. Its components are known as sepals.
Carinate   curved with a fairly sharp ridge, as in the keel of a ship.
Cephalium   broadly speaking, the apical part of the globular or columnar cactus where spines and hairs are concentrated. It produces new growth. In a strictly technical sense, formations peculiar to some genera of Cactaceae, bearing anomalous clumps of wool, hairs and bristles in their flower-bearing area.
Chin   a beak.
Clavate   club-shaped, tapering at the bottom.
Corolla   usually colorful, internal floral leaves, developed to a greater or lesser degree. It attracts pollinating insects. Its components are known as petals.
Crenate   of the edge of a leaf or stem which has rounded indentations or scallops.
Cristate   of an organ with irregular indentations resembling the crest or comb of a bird; also applied to plant forms with anomalous growth due to the fasciation or the fusing of tissues, parts of which are generally crested.
Cuneate   wedge-shaped.
Deciduous   of limited duration; generally applied to plants

that lose their leaves in winter, but applicable to all organs that fall off for whatever reason.

Decumbent   hanging down or lying on the ground, with an ascendant apical part.

Dehiscent   a fruit which opens spontaneously to release its seeds.

Dioecious   of plants that bear male and female flowers on different individual specimens.

Ephemeral   lasting for a very short time—generally only for one day.

Epiphyte   plant which grows upon another without being parasitic.

Fasciation   abnormal growth in which a stem enlarges into a flat ribbon that resembles several stems fused together.

Flower   part of plant, consisting of reproductive organs and a protective envelope, that attracts pollinating insects.

Glabrous   lacking in hair, wool, or tomentum.

Glaucescence   white or pale blue color of stems and leaves resulting from a thin layer of wax (pruina) that serves as protection against adverse external conditions.

Glaucous   covered with a waxy bloom.

Glochid   little tufts of barbed bristles or hairs.

Hybrid   plant grown from the seed produced by cross-fertilization, whether natural or artificial, of different forms, species, or genera.

Indehiscent   of fruit that does not open to release its seed; these escape when the fruit is eaten or disintegrates because of wind action, etc.

Joint   generally, an internode; more specifically, transformed portions of a branch or stem, swollen or flattened to some extent and narrow at their point of insertion.

Latex   milky juice, varying in density and color, which issues from some plant tissues if they are damaged.

Leaf   appendage attached to a node on a stem or branch; its chief function is to effect photosynthesis, but in the great majority of cacti this is carried out by stems and branches.

Neck   point of junction of root with stem.

Node   the point where a bud, and therefore new growth, originates.

Pectinate   comb-shaped; in terms of cacti, it refers to radial spines, borne on both sides of the areoles, that are straight or slightly curved, flat and only slightly divaricate, like the teeth of a comb.

Perianth   petals and sepals, usually not distinguishable.

Petals   components of the corolla.

Pistil   female part of a flower.

Pollen   granules producing male gametes which form in the anthers.

Prostrate   lying flat on the ground.

Pubescent   covered with short, soft hairs; velvety.

Radial   set at the edge of a given area; for example, radial spines are borne on the edge of the areole.

Sepals   components of the calyx.

Stamens   male organs bearing the anthers, usually at the end of a filament.

Stigma   swollen terminal part of the pistil that receives pollen grain.

Suberization   process by which a tissue becomes waterproof and loses its herbaceous appearance, through the impregnation of cell walls with suberin.

Suberose   corklike.

Taproot   fleshy, large primary root that grows deep in the soil; it stores nutrients.

Tissue   complex of cells carrying out an identical function in an organ.

Tomentose   densely covered with short, usually soft, hairs.

Tubercle   raised portion or protuberance that may appear on any organ; its origin, shape, size and consistency are as variable as the functions it performs.

Tuberculate   bearing tubercles.

Umbilicate   having a rounded, conical depression similar to a navel.

Verticil   whorl of more than two leaves, flowers, hairs, etc., attached to the same node on the same stem.

Verticillate   of a number of branches or leaves borne in a whorl or circle from the same node.

Xerophyte (or xerophile)   plant typical of arid areas, or one that has adapted to survive in very dry regions.

BIBLIOGRAPHY

Backeberg, Curt. *Cactus lexicon*. Poole: Blandford Press, 1977.

Bailey, Liberty Hyde. *The Standard Cyclopedia of Horticulture*. 19th ed. 3 vols. New York: The Macmillan Co., 1961.

Barthlott, Wilhelm. *Cacti: Botanical Aspects, Descriptions & Cultivations*. State Mutual Books, 1979.

Benson, Lyman. *The Cacti of Arizona*. 3rd ed. University of Arizona Press, 1969.

Berger, Alwin. *Kakteen*. 1929.

Borg, John. *Cacti*. 4th ed. Poole: Blandford Press, 1976.

Britton, Nathaniel Lord, & Rose, John N. *The Cactaceae*. 2nd ed. 1937, reprinted in 2 vols., Dover Publication Inc., 1963.

Buxbaum, F. *Cactus culture*. London, 1958.

Carlson, R. *The flowering cactus*. McGraw-Hill Book Co.

Dawson, E. Yale. *The Cacti of California,* University of California Press, 1966.

Earle, W. Hubert. *Cacti of the Southwest*. Rancho Arroyo Book Distributor, revised 1980.

Encke-Buchheim-Seybold. *Zander, Handwörterbuch der Pflanzen-namen*. 12 ed. Stuttgart: Eugene Ulmer, 1980.

Engelmann, Georg. *Cactaceae of the Boundary*. 1859.

Gerste, A.S.J. *La médecine et la botanique des anciens mexicains*. Rome: Imprimerie Polyglotte Vaticaine, 1910.

Graf, Alfred Byrd. *Exotica III*. Rutherford, N.Y.: Roehrs Co., 1963.

Haage, Walther. *Das praktische Kakteenbuch in Farben*. 1978.

Index Kewensis and supplements (1893-).

Innes, Clive. *Cacti, from desert and jungle*. Journal of R.H.S., January, 1972.

Lamb, Edgar, & Brian. *Illustrated references on cacti and other succulents,* vols. I-V. Blandford Press.

Lamb, Edgar, & Brian. *Pocket Encyclopaedia of Cacti in colour*. Blandford Press, 1970.

Marshall, W. Taylor, & Bock, T.N. *Cactaceae*. Pasadena, 1941.

Martin, M.J., & Chapman, P.R. "Grafting cacti." *Gardener's Chronicle,* vol. 163, no. 16, 1968.

Schelle, Ernst. *Handbuch der Kakteenkultur*. Stuttgart: Eugene Ulmer, 1907.

Smith, A.W., & Stearn, W.T. *A gardener's dictionary of plant names*. London: Cassel, 1972.

Weberbauer, A. *El mundo vegetal de las Andes peruanas*. Lima, 1945.

Weniger, Del. *Cacti of the Southwest*. University of Texas Press; *Cacti of Texas and Neighboring States,* University of Texas Press, 1984.

Willis, J.C. *A dictionary of the flowering plants and ferns*. 7th ed. Cambridge University Press.

INDEX OF ENTRIES

Photographs:

All the photographs are by Giuseppe Mazza, with the exception of those on p. 11 (Enzo Arnone) and p. 25 (Bodleian Library, Oxford).

Drawings:

Marco Bertin, Verona: 18. Raffaello Segattini, Verona: 15, 20, 21, 35, 42, 44, 45.